ISLAM, SCIENCE & RENAISSANCE

THEIR IMPACT ON UNIVERSE & SOCIETY

DIVIDED IN TWO PARTS

PART ONE FOCUSES ON THE UNIVERSE AND ISLAMIC RENAISSANCE

PART TWO FOCUSES ON ISLAMIC SCIENCES AND THE SOCIETY

CO-AUTHORED BY

PROF.SYED AKHEEL AHMED, PH.D.
&
SYED SHARIEF KHUNDMIRI, M.A.,B.COM

Order this book online at www.trafford.com
or email orders@trafford.com

Most Trafford titles are also available at major online book retailers.

Printed in the United States of America.

ISBN: 978-1-4669-8785-2 (sc)
ISBN: 978-1-4669-8784-5 (e)

Trafford rev. 06/28/2013

 www.trafford.com

North America & international
toll-free: 1 888 232 4444 (USA & Canada)
fax: 812 355 4082

DEDICATED TO MY BELOVED PARENTS UNDER WHOSE STRICT GUIDANCE AND ADVICE I SOLENMLY AND FAITHFULLY VENTURED INTO THE STUDY OF ISLAM

PART ONE

TABLE OF CONTENTS

PART ONE

FOREWORD

The Qur'an invites us to see how all his creation, both animate and inanimate, worships God and obeys his laws.

Seest thou not that it is Allah whose praises all beings in the heaven and on earth do celebrate, and the birds (of the air) with wings outspread? Each one knows its own (mode of) prayer and praise. And Allah knows well all that they do. (Sura 24: verse 41)

Brother Syed Sharief Khundmiri and Professor Syed Akheel Ahmed have done Islamic literature a service by providing a multitude of reflections on all kinds of natural phenomena, from astronomy, the earth, human evolution, human reproduction to the Islamic Renaissance, thereby emergence of so many branches of modern-day science. Although there are several other books on this subject, what I like about this study is that the authors take you step by step to show that what we have learned in the last century or two was indeed documented fourteen centuries ago in the Holy Qur'an and thus establishing that it is transcendental and divine in origin.

The introductory chapter of this book gives an overview of the life of Prophet Muhammad (peace be upon him). It is a splendid introduction—carefully researched and comprehensive. It presents a balanced view of the man whose religion continues to have dramatic effect on the course of history. This is followed by an extensive and in-depth examination of the creation of the universe as outlined in the Qur'an and then with clarity and thoroughness showing that it is totally in keeping with modern scientific knowledge. One of the difficulties in addressing subjects like this is that the Qur'an does not provide a unified description of the creation. Instead of a continuous narration, there are passages scattered all over the holy book, which deal with certain aspects of the creation and provide information on the successive events marking its development with varying degrees in detail. This dispersal throughout the book of references to the same subject is not unique to the theme of the creation. Many important subjects are treated in this manner in the Qur'an such as earthly or celestial phenomena. To gain a clear idea of how these events are presented, the fragments scattered throughout a large number of verses have all to be brought together. Both authors have painstakingly assembled all the verses relevant to the subjects discussed in this book and have presented the material in a clear and coherent manner.

The confrontation between the texts of the scriptures and scientific data has always provided man with food for thought. In the next section, Brother Khundmiri tackles the question of creation versus evolution—a subject of much debate. Our current social and moral problems are largely a result of the humanistic philosophy, which has been spawned by evolutionary thinking. The so-called new morality we are presently witnessing is actually no morality, the inevitable result of the atheistic, evolutionary philosophy.

The solutions to man's massive social problems depend on a correct understanding of origins. If the evolutionary philosophy is correct, then life is without purpose. On the other hand, if we were created by Allah, our lives have meaning, direction, and purpose. Clearly, the proposition of origin is the foundation of all other convictions, actions, and beliefs. Thus, the question of origin is a vital issue that can be ignored only at great peril. Brother Khundmiri has convincingly debunked the Darwin's theory of evolution and at the same time showed that facts of science correlate much better with Qur'an creationism.

Furthermore, what initially strikes the reader of Holy Qur'an is the sheer abundance of subjects discussed. Brother Khundmiri cites several verses to illustrate a wide range of subject matter ranging from astronomy, oceanography, metallurgy, anatomy or obstetrics to archeology that are discussed in the Qur'an while emphasizing that the Qur'an is not a book that has object of explaining laws governing the universe but it has an absolutely basic religious objectives. And when comparison is made between scientific data and statement contained in the scripture, as the authors have done in this book, the only conclusion that can be drawn is that the Holy Qur'an does not contain a single proposition at variance with the most firmly established modern knowledge.

The purpose of this book is to promote Qur'anic teaching and to clarify misconceptions about Islam. Especially, in the aftermath of the tragic events of 9/11, the most popular image of Islam in the minds of many is that it is, to some extent, a religion of violence, fanaticism, and terrorism. This negative image of Islam among American and European public is essentially due to their ignorance and hypocrisy. At a time when Islam is frequently misunderstood and often maligned, this sensitive and insightful book comes as a ray of sunshine.

The book has dispelled many of these misconceptions and has provided ready access to several venerable verses that contain the essential worldview of the Qur'an as it relates to the meaning of life and possibility of justice—the two interconnected themes that are central to the Islamic thought.

Brother Khundmiri and Professor Akheel have cited more than two hundred verses in this book and have mediated seriously upon the relations between science and belief. They have presented the sparkling results of this mediation in a gracefully written, clear, and coherent exposition.

This book, which sheds new lights on previously neglected and/or less understood aspects of Qur'anic teachings, should have appeal for all young readers and adults who are interested in the relationship between science and Islam.

Dr. Syed Masood Hassan, PhD

PREFACE

The Holy Prophet Mohammad (pbuh) has advised, "Seek for science; even in China." And in yet another hadith directed "search for knowledge" as a strict duty for every Muslim, man and woman." In an age where scientific learning was obscure and which was coined as the Dark Period, the Prophet's instructions were wholly based on the revelations of the Holy Qur'an, which, while inviting mankind to cultivate and understand science, in itself contained many observations on natural phenomena and logistically included explanatory details, which are observed as compatible with modern scientific data as a whole.

Under these guidelines both authors of this book have studied the Qur'an keeping in view the compatibility of those verses that have direct impact on the threshold of the universe and mankind. Through the interpretation of the verses of the Qur'an, it is asserted in the book that the divine power alone governs the universe and the human life; and verily that power alone is the generating power, without which the ever changing cycle of the events would stop to exist. The authors have attempted to introduce those verses of the Holy Qur'an in their carefully crafted book that speaks most directly to every human being, regardless of religious confessions or cultural background. The purpose of this introduction is to clarify the cultural and historical matrix in which the Qur'an was revealed, whose central theme is manifested in the hymnic verses and the manner in which the Qur'an is studied and bye-hearted by the Islamic societies.

The main theme of the book is to promote the Qur'anic message to attract and inculcate those who do not have access to the Qur'an itself. The Arabic language is translated into legible English to introduce one of the most influential texts in human history in a manner that can be read and understood easily. These valuable and venerable verses of the Qur'an contain the essential worldview of the Qur'an concerning the meaning of life and the possibility of justice, the two interconnected themes that are the basics of the Islamic thought. The book deals with the selected few verses of the Qur'an starting from the early life of the Prophet to the last of the revelations, which encompass the components of the universal phenomena and the basics of the human life, culture, and civilization.

The authors have devised a theme to interpret certain Qur'anic verses whose exact meaning could not possibly have been grasped. This implies that a thorough linguistic knowledge is really needed to understand these verses of the Qur'an. Therefore, this book inculcates the highly diversified knowledge of science to the reader. In brief, the study such as the present one embraces many disciplines and provides not only general academic knowledge but specific as well. Thus, the authors have tried their best in discussing the variety of scientific knowledge essential to the understanding of certain verses of the Holy Qur'an.

In a significant chapter "Qur'an as a Guide," the author has tried to introduce the Qur'an, which describes that it is not the book for explaining laws governing the universe, but it has basic religious objectives. The description of divine commands principally incites man to reflect on the domain of creation of man on his own image and subjected whole of the universe under his vicegerents. They are accompanied by references to the facts accessible to human observation of laws as defined by the omnipotent who guides the organization of the universe both in the sciences of nature and as regards man.

In this context, if the reader of this book has the essential scientific knowledge, then he/she can easily grasp the subject matter of the book. The authors have tried their best to present only selected verses from the Qur'an that are to be studied for the purpose of scientific understanding, which may seem too short for some readers who have already studied them in detail. In this way the authors have singled out several verses that until now have not been granted the importance they deserve from a scientific point of view. Without prejudice to those readers, the authors, with an open mind and conscience, have attempted to give their own interpretations of some verses, which are mostly and aptly compatible to the present-day scientific data, which is the subject matter of the book.

The book provides elaborate data on science, keeping in view the compatibility to the verses that would benefit the reader as well as the research scholar who is in search of such verses that are compatible to the laws of the universe. In that sense, the authors feel their endeavor to have succeed in entirety.

Editorial Board

Geopolitical Academy, USA

ACKNOWLEDGMENT

BOOKS REFERRED IN COMPLETING THIS VALUABLE TREATISE:

1. The Holy Qur'an by A. Yousuf Ali
2. Tarjumanul Qur'an by Abul Kalam Azad
3. *Al Qur'annul Mubeen* by Syed Abid Khundmiri
4. *Dictionary of Islam* by Thomas Patrick Hughes
5. Encyclopedia Britannica Internet
6. *The Bible, the Qur'an, and Science* by Maurice Bucaille
7. *The Europa World Yearbook* (2007)
8. *The Basic Concepts of Chemistry* (Boston, USA)
9. *Anthropology* by Lewis John
10. *Anatomy of Man* (USA)
11. *Astronomy USA*
12. *The New Book of Popular Science* (Grolier Incorporated)
13. *Birth of Adam and Evolution Theory (Urdu)* by Shahabuddin Nadvi
14. *Qur'an and Plant Kingdom (Urdu)* by Shahabuddin Nadvi
15. *Asimov's Guide to Science* by Asimov, Isaac
16. *Relativity Theory* by Albert Einstein
17. *History of Science* by Dampier, W. C.
18. *The Encyclopedia of Ignorance* by Duncan, Ronald
19. *The Guide to Modern Thought* by C. E. M. Joad
20. *The Mysterious Universe* by Sir James Jeans
21. *Macmillan Dictionary of the History of Science* by University of Cambridge
22. *Qur'an and the Natural World (Urdu)* by Shahabuddin Nadvi
23. *A Global History of Man* by Allyn and Bacon
24. *Making of the Humanity* by Robert Briffault

25. *The Origin of Species* by Charles Darwin

26. *The Collapse of Evolution Theory* by Harun Yahiya

27. *How Wonderful Is Our Universe* by the author

28. *The Changing Map of the Muslim World* by the author

29. *The Timetables of History* by Richard Grun

30. Wikipedia Internet

I am grateful to Dr. Syed Masood Hassan, who, while reviewing and vetting, skillfully pointed me the categorization of relevant chapters, which helped me profusely in rearranging chapters of this book and for his valuable foreword to this book, which is appended above.

I am very much thankful to my grandchildren who helped me in compiling, computerizing, and proofreading the book and gave final touches, which brought the manuscript to its present shape.

CHAPTER I
Advent of Islam

INTRODUCTION

Islam, the Holy Prophet, and the Muslim World

A clarion call reverberated in a densely populated ancient city named Ur of the renowned Babylonia, adjacent to the western shores of the river Ferat (Euphrates),governed by Nimrod; and that was a call of the Prophet Ibrahim (Abraham).The call was completely in harmony with the Semitic tradition asking the people, "Bow your heads before the only God and do not associate any lifeless deity with him."

That call of the Prophet reverberated constantly asking the inhabitants to abhor polytheism and worship the only God, the Creator of the universe, who is all-powerful, omnipresent, and omniscient. His call just merged into the wilderness. He started destructing their deities. He was caught, charged, and brought before Nimrod, the ruler, for punishment. Nimrod questioned him as to why he had destroyed the deities. The Prophet countered, "Why should you worship such helpless deities who could not protect themselves?" Enraged with this arrogant reply, Nimrod ordered him to be thrown onto the burning fires. He bravely resigned to the will of God, seeking his mercy from this horrible chastisement of the fire. His prayer was granted. When he was thrown into the burning flames, the fire became cool. Fire did not hurt him, and he was safe and alive. Even this miracle did not change the mind of Nimrod, leave aside his subjects.

Prophet Ibrahim, the only monotheist among the multitude, became disgusted and decided to migrate toward the West in the year 1890 BC, some four thousand years ago, and first settled down in Canaan, near present Palestine, then settled down on the command of God on the scorching sands of the deep desert of the Arabian peninsula, along with his wife, Hajeran (Hager), and a newborn son Ismail. After a while, Abraham left them with a meager supply of foodstuff and water at that barren place. When his wife asked him why he was leaving them at such an in habitual and a barren place, he told her, "On commands of God." She became satisfied that when God's command was there, God alone could provide security and sustenance, and she kept quiet.

How long could the foodstuff and water suffice them? It was consumed very soon. They became hungry and thirsty. Particularly the baby started crying. Without food, how long could the mother provide milk to her son? The mother started running frantically in between Safa and Marwah, the two hillocks, in search of water for about seven times in a frustrating manner. But behold the miracle! The baby, being very much thirsty, started digging the grounds with his tiny heels, and suddenly a spring of water became visible. She rushed back to that spring and, fearing that the water should not absorb in the sands, started mumbling "Zam! Zam! [Stop! Stop!]" asking the water to stop. Miraculously it did stop. She made a small pool for containing the water by her hands and started quenching their thirst.

This wonderful miracle is enough to come to the fold of Islam since this venerable water is the result of thrusting the tiny heels of a baby of few months. It came gushing from the underground some four thousand years ago and still serving thousands of millions of people from its unknown source. According to a Japanese scientist, this water has the medicinal quality to heal many diseases, comparative to other sources of the water around the world.

Luckily, a Bedouin tribe was passing from that vicinity and saw birds flying at a certain spot, probably a water spot. They rushed to it and found that a lady and a minor son, the only inhabitants, were living at the water spot. They took permission from the lady and settled down there which became the source of their livelihood. That is how God protected them.

After a long time, Prophet Ibrahim again visited the place and found his family was thriving well. In a certain night, the Prophet saw a dream that he was slaughtering his own twelve-year-old son Ismail at a hillock. He became perturbed and very much shocked. However, he had to tell to his son about the dream. The brave son responded positively by saying that if the will of God was such, then, he should not hesitate to slaughter him. To hide the action of slaughtering the son from the mother's sight, Prophet Ibrahim took his son to a distant place, Mina, and started slaughtering his own son, blindfolded. God was just testing him whether Prophet Ibrahim would sacrifice his dearest son or not. When God saw the act of slaughtering, in obedience to his commands, he ordered angel Gabriel to place a lamb in place of Ismail. When the lamb was put in place of Ismail, Prophet Ibrahim, thinking that he had performed what God had intended for, took away his blindfold and found to his astonishment that actually a ram, instead of Ismail, was slaughtered by him. His son was standing before him alive. They offered their humble prayers to the Almighty God for saving the life and came back to the place of residence.

That became the tradition of *qurbani* (to sacrifice by slaughtering any animal in the name of Allah) by the Muslims during the Hajj period in commemoration of Prophet Abraham's slaughtering of the lamb.

Under the commands of Almighty God, they jointly put their might in construction of a four-walled shrine, and they named it the House of Allah, Kabatullah. On completion, they very submissively offered their humble worship and prayed the Lord of the Kabah:

> Our Lord raise a Prophet from our lineage to recite Thy Verses and teach
> Thy Book and the purpose underlying in it to purify the humanity. Indeed
> Thou Art Magnificent and Wise. (2:129)

Their prayer was granted by the Lord positively, and the foundations of the Muslim world were basically laid down on the Arabian soils some four thousand years ago.

This remote piece of sandy desert, in due course of time, became known to the world as the city of Makkah, where the first-ever-built House of Allah stands, attracting peoples of the various cultures and creeds of different parts and regions of the world and nations, who assemble to worship the Lord of the same house. Thus, Makkah, even before the advent of Islam, became a place of worship and pilgrimage.

History tells us that an Arabian chieftain Qussay, of the tribe Qureysh, conquered most of Arabian Peninsula in 400 BC and established his dominance. The Qureysh had many tribes in their fold; prominent among them were Banu Hashim, Banu Kalab, Banu Kanan, and Banu Quza. Banu Hashim were acclaimed as nobles; hence, they held the keys of the

Holy Shrine of Kaa'bah while others became administrators and civil workers of the city of Makkah.

Makkah lies on the crossroads of the north, south, east, and west. Hundreds of caravans used to bring their merchandise for going onward for trade with Constantinople, Madagascar, Egypt, Persia, the Far East Islands of Malaya, Indonesia, Philippines, China, and India. Thus, Makkah became not only a sacred place of pilgrimage but also a commercial center from centuries. The Qureysh, in order to maintain peace and harmony among the congregation, declared the city of Makkah the *hurm* where battle was strictly forbidden since the shrine was to them a sacred place of worship. The Arabs had inherited the ancient Semitic traditions and the teachings of the Prophet Adam, Noah, Abraham, Ismail, and their successors. They were monotheist at first; but as time passed on, deviation from the right path started, and polytheism became their religious practice. In the Kaa'bah itself, they installed three hundred and sixty idols to worship, one idol each a day by rotation. However, they had their belief in their inner conscience that among all these idols there is one, the supreme, the Creator of the universe; and they named him Ilah.

That was the environment when the Holy Prophet of Islam, Muhammad (pbuh), was born in the noble tribe of Banu Hashim, the key bearers of the Kaa'bah, in the year AD 571. From the very childhood, he had exemplary qualities and a distinct attitude for monotheism. In his younger age he was named Al Sadiq ("one who speaks truth") and Al Ameen ("the trustworthy"). Coming from the sacred lineage of the Prophet Ibrahim (Abraham), he inherited the same old Semitic tradition of monotheism. To him, the Kaa'bah was the House of God in true sense; but he could not digest the fact that in the same House of Allah, who is one and alone, how could 360 idols be worshipped by rotation each a day?

This was a challenge to his conscientious mind, and he just could not compromise with the way Qureysh were following. His conscience awakened. He disregarded and refused to follow this way of life. He was very sensitive and contemplative, always thinking about the nature of the universe and beliefs of his people. He was meditating always to understand about himself and the reason and purpose of creation of a gigantic natural phenomenon with a contemplative mind.

Disgusted and dejected with the uncompromising and unaccommodative milieu, he separated himself from the multitude and started going in seclusion to the Hira cave in the nearby mountain to meditate and concentrate his inner self. Days and nights he spent there alone in search of the truth. Suddenly, in the dead of the night, he witnessed a divine personality urging him to recite:

> Recite in the name of Allah, who created man with a clot of blood, and who taught man, the ignorant, with pen. (96:1)

At this unfamiliar experience, he started trembling and sweating, continuing to recite what was asked for in a subdued voice. When the encounter was over, he rushed toward his house and narrated this experience to his wife, Khadeja, who was a learned and wise lady, and luckily who had heard the legends of the Jews through her uncle Zarqa Bin Nufil of appearance of a messiah anytime soon.

She took him to her uncle who, after hearing the episode from him, consoled him and accepted his version and testified that the divine personality was that of the archangel Gabriel and that he had been chosen by Allah as his apostle to guide the humanity. On getting confidence, his wife was the first to accept Muhammad (pbuh) as the apostle of God, and then he informed his closest friend Abu Baker and his cousin Ali. Both believed in him and admitted him to be the prophet of Allah.

From that night onward (the night has been accepted by the Muslim Ummah to be the twenty-seventh night of the month of Ramadan, the Lailatul Qadr), revelations started pouring onto him either through archangel Gabriel or even directly till his death in AD 632. Thus, on receiving commands from the Lord of the universe, he started preaching to the Arabs asking them to worship the only God, Allah, and avoid polytheism of the pagan worshipers. The Qureysh refused to believe him to be the messenger of Allah since he was a man, one among them. Sensing the danger of losing the dominance over the city of Makkah and the commercial benefits attached to it, they harassed him, heckled him, and threatened even to kill him. Disheartened and disgusted with that hostile situation, and in accordance with the divine direction, he migrated to Yathrib toward north, some three hundred miles away from Makkah.

The inhabitants of this new city welcomed him and revered him as the true apostle of Allah. They handed over keys of the city to him and renamed it as Madinath-un-Nabi, the city of the Prophet.

The Qureysh did not tolerate that the same Muhammad (pbuh) whom they had tormented was being profoundly honored, and the city was offered to him for administration where he preached that new faith, which they had rejected to accept. They were planning to destroy Medinah and capture Muhammad (pbuh) alive to punish him. For that purpose, they brought a huge military of one thousand troops well equipped with ammunition. When the Prophet heard about attacking army of the Qureysh, he pragmatically planned to meet the aggressors at Badr, some eighty miles away from Medinah, along with 313 ill-equipped companions. Allah is great. He who chose Mohammed (pbuh) to be his last messenger—how could he allow the polytheists to become successful? The enemy utterly failed, Muhammad (Slm) defeated them and became successful. Finally, after a period of nine years or so, he conquered Makkah during his lifetime only, but behold his open heartedness toward his bitter enemies! He did not take any revenge against them, instead pardoned them and declared general amnesty to all—peace be to all—and he let all go free. His mission was successful in its entirety, and the inhabitants of the Arabian Peninsula accepted him as the true apostle of Allah and obeyed his commands. Thus, he established the first Islamic state in the Arabian Peninsula in AD 632.

What was his preaching? His preaching was nothing new. It was the same message as was taught by the prophets Ibrahim (Abraham), Musa (Moses), and Isa (Jesus). They were the same Semitic traditions of monotheism. This is a fact that all the three monotheist religions belong to the region of the Middle East alone: prophet Musa (Moses) from the Sinai Desert, prophet Isa (Jesus) from Jerusalem, and Prophet Muhammad (pbuh) from Makkah. All these prophets come from the sacred lineage of the prophet Ibrahim. They are all cousins as a matter of fact.

The Semitic beliefs were embedded in them. And it is a fact that the Muslims pray five times in their prayers for the betterment of the sons of the prophet Abraham (*Kamaa Baraktha alaa aale Ibrahim*)—the Jews, the Christians, and the Muslims—all sons of the prophet Abraham indeed. Allah is basically the same God of the Jews and of the Christians. It is acknowledged by them all to be true. Then why this Islam phobia?

Before the advent of Islam, the Arabs were monotheists. But human nature is wavering. As time passes on, history of the nations points out that differences and deviations in beliefs start always from the root. It happened within the Judaism, it occurred in the Christianity, and also the Arabs deviated from their Semitic traditions. And in such challenging circumstances, the will of Allah prevails. Disbelieving in the oneness of Allah and disobeying his commands were never tolerated by the Creator of this universe who has a perfect plan for mankind. He commands his creations to obey his orders and to worship him alone. Man is the finest of all his creations, bestowed with unique qualities to learn, understand, and speak. These qualities are the gifts from the Creator of the universe to human beings alone. Therefore, our submission to him is nothing but our gratitude and acceptance of his greatness. Messengers of Allah were sent by him in all regions of the world for guiding the human beings according to a chalked-out program of the Almighty. When he notices that certain people are not obeying his commands, he punishes them and sends his new messengers to admonish them.

It happened in Arabia too. At a time when humanity was in wilderness and worshipping lifeless deities out of ignorance, he sent his last messenger, stamping on him the seal of the prophethood, and revealed through him his final commands to the entire humanity in the shape of the Holy Qur'an.

What is Islam? Just submission to the Creator of the universe, all-powerful, beneficent, merciful, Lord of the Day of Judgment, omnipotent, omniscient, powerful to reward the believers and punish the disbelievers. Thus, the beauty of Islam lies in its simplicity. It is a pure, plain, and perfect religion, which teaches equality and fraternity among the human beings. There is no distinction between man and man, man and woman, white and black, red and brown; it inculcates brotherhood among the peoples; and it exterminates barriers of the caste, color, race, creed, regions, and nations.

Muhammad (pbuh) proclaimed himself as the servant of Allah, a human being, having no supernatural attributes, a common man of the same blood and flesh as his fellow beings. Allah chose him as his last messenger and prophet. Therefore, he preached his people the commands of Allah. He declared that all messengers of Allah must be revered as equal; all scriptures must be respected. The basic five tenets of Islam taught by Muhammad (pbuh) are the following:

1. Believing in oneness of Allah and Muhammad (pbuh) is his last prophet
2. Offering prayers (*salath*, *namaz*) five times every day
3. Giving alms, *zakath*, a tax to the needy
4. Observing fast during the month of Ramadan to control one's passion
5. Going to Makkah for pilgrimage (Hajj) at least once in his or her lifetime if affordable and having no monetary obligations

Furthermore, he directed people to do good things such as speak always truth; help the needy; behave properly with neighbors; assist orphans, widows, the poor; and promote goodwill in the society; and obey orders of the elders and of the authorities. On the other hand, he admonished and warned not to eat dead animals, blood, and pork and not to drink wine, as well as avoid lending money at high rates, gambling, telling lies, murdering human beings, committing adultery and wrongdoings, and backbiting. It is an established fact that the period before the advent of Islam was a dark period. The crucifixion of Jesus Christ and its consequences thereafter resulted in an utter chaos in the European and Asian nations of that time. Religious bigotry and the notion of political "might is right" created tumult and disaster in the world. Rome raged wars against the Byzantine Empire, and the Berber of northern Europe invaded and destroyed the south. Precious libraries that contained literary and scientific works of the philosophers and scientists of the past were ruthlessly burnt to ashes. Tribal wars, feudalism, gambling, drinking, usury, and burial of the newly born girls in Arabia became the laws of the land. Learning, scientific research, and scholarly writing were scarce commodities.

While so, the revelations started pouring onto the conscious mind of Muhammad (pbuh), and he was pronouncing them spontaneously in a well-toned form, in a well-attributed masterly worded sermons, that even the scholars around him were astonished to hear from the mouth of that Mohammad (pbuh) whom they knew as an unlettered man. The force of the properly worded sermons was so great and challenging that no poet dared to compose a similar verse like it.

The Jewish and Christian scholars have false notion about the Holy Qur'an—that it was either got dictated by some Arabic author or dictated by Mohammed (pbuh) himself. They are manipulating on the false allegations just to disregard and delete this holy book from the list of the holy scriptures, Torah, gospel, and Zaboor so that their people should avoid reading it. On the other hand, it is an admitted fact by the Western scholars and scientists that the Holy Qur'an is really God's revelations, spoken directly by God and preserved by Mohammad (pbuh) word to word. Just imagine, if the holy prophet had been the author of Qur'an, then, how could he have written in the AD seventh century about such universal facts that have been confirmed by the authorities of today as being the modern scientific knowledge of the previous two or three centuries only? The period in which Prophet Mohammad (pbuh) lived in Arabia had been historically proven to be a dark period, where every society of the world was stagnant. Then, how did Prophet Mohammad (pbuh) gain that scientific knowledge on certain natural phenomena of the universe that would happen fourteen centuries ahead of his time? And this also is a proven fact that the prophet was known as an *ummi* or an unlettered man! To elaborate our discussion, we just like to mention a single verse of the Holy Qur'an that informs about the ongoing space exploration nowadays. Read 55:33 of the Holy Qur'an:

> Ye assembly of Jin 0 Men, if you can penetrate into the regions of the heaven and earth, then penetrate, surely, you may not penetrate without the power. (55:33)

Obviously, this verse declares that it is not possible for man to penetrate the regions of heaven and earth without power. Here, power means the atomic power alone with the help of which man could defeat the earth's gravitational force and reach the far regions of the space. Certainly this power has empowered man to reach the moon, and every now and then rockets and space shuttles are being fired into the vast space traversing around the planets Mars, Venus, Jupiter, and many more.

The astrophysicists and the scientists of this century have verified these prophecies mentioned in the Qur'an and came to the conclusion, "Of course a verse of such prophecy does exist in the Qur'an, predicting how one day man would conquer space with the help of atomic power." Likewise, take the penetration of the regions of the earth. We are getting petrol and running our cars, we are getting gas and burning our stoves, and we are getting water from the underground. How many minerals are we utilizing from beneath the strata of the earth? All these ventures have rightly been prophesied in the Qur'an.

Apart from the prophecies about the modem endeavors, Qur'an has a universal appeal to humanity. It teaches the way of life, and most importantly it gives laws to the nations. Its doctrines are supreme in the sense that they encompass the whole of humanity of all times and for all regions and nations. It civilizes humanity and promotes culture. Fundamentally, it asks one to obey, worship, and fear the Creator of the universe alone. **Do good and avoid wrongdoings.** As a citizen, one is bound to adhere to the laws of the society and its norms. If anyone confronts those laws and norms, society has the right to punish him. In the same manner, the Creator of this gigantic universe has chalked out a plan of life for man, and the guidelines have been revealed through his messengers. Should man not obey Allah? If he obeys, it is good for him. If he does not, he will surely get punishment. This is what the Qur'an tells.

Sublime Attributes of the Prophet Mohammed (pbuh)

Prophet Mohammed (pbuh) was born in the deep desert of Arabian Peninsula full of scorching sands and dunes, a perfect desolate and in habitual remote piece of land, where polytheism, tribal wars, feudalism, barbarism, drinking, gambling, usury, and burial of the newly born female babies became the laws of the land and where might was right. In such an inhuman and barbaric atmosphere, the holy prophet inculcated among the staunch polytheists to bow before the only God who is the Creator of this vast universe and thus pioneered a new world order, shaping the life of those uncivilized barbarians who used to fight lengthy wars for petty family disputes. He taught them the moral values and human dignity, cultural behavior, and civility. He introduced a new civilization. He laid foundations of such a puritanical state the world never knew before and which flourished in a short spell of time, even during his lifetime, which in due course of time became the largest Muslim state in the world. Later, his preaching spread from Morocco to Indonesia and influenced the peoples living in almost three continents of the globe. Although he was an unlettered man, still his superb teachings changed the patterns of the life of the peoples to whom he was deputed by the Almighty Allah for their betterment and emancipation. It was not an ordinary job to convert the staunch polytheists of the Arabian soil to become utter monotheists during his lifetime only. It was the mesmerizing effect of his eloquent oratory that whenever he, with his graceful, exquisitely brilliant, and bright eyes, came to the podium with his melodious, lovely, sweet, and heart-touching voice, recited the verses of the holy Qur'an in a properly worded tone, it seemed as if not words but flowers were pouring out from his mouth, touching the inner conscience of the listeners, causing tears coming out spontaneously from the eyes of the masses. He preached self-control and discipline to the extent of praying on the battlefield in congregation while other warriors had the duty to protect the prayers from any eventuality. He strictly altered the strategy of the battlefield. He commanded to wage a war just for self-defense only, not to mutilate the dead bodies, not to kill a woman or an elderly person or even a child, not to destroy agriculture farms, gardens, and fruit groves. When he conquered Makkah, he never took revenge from those who humiliated, tortured, harassed, and even threatened to kill him; but he declared complete amnesty to all by pronouncing peace and freedom to each and every one living in Makkah. This is a lesson to the conquerors to pardon their enemies and to treat human beings as equals. He used to set free prisoners of war if their relatives stand surety for their good conduct and pay ransom for them. He declared all human beings are equal. There is no distinction between a man and a woman, a black and a white or brown, of the East or the West, of any region, any caste or creed or race. He presented himself as the servant of the Almighty God first and then as a messenger, coming from the same stock of the Arabian families, of the same flesh and blood that running among the Arabs, with no supernatural claim. Thus, he founded the universal brotherhood and preached the doctrine of equality among mankind and proclaimed social justice to all. These sublime principles he put into practice during his lifetime. They became the cornerstones of his international diplomacy and were strictly followed by his successors and many of them are incorporated in UN Charter.

Even before his priesthood, he was acclaimed by the Qureysh as the trustworthy and as the honest, Al-Ameen and Al-Sadique in Arabic. His superb qualities, his unquestionable honesty, his unblemished sincerity, and his absolute trustworthiness are such attributes that even his contemporaries, both friends and foes, acknowledged. Even the Jews who did not accept his new religion had accepted him as the impartial arbitrator in their personal disputes.

If remarkable characteristic consists in the purification of a nation, he is the one who had transformed, refined, and uplifted not only his followers but the entire mankind as he was declared by the Almighty that he was made the prophet an emblem of mercy for the entire mankind (Rah Matil-lil Alamain ["blessings to the mankind"]) and his followers became the torchbearers of a new civilization. If superiority lies in unifying the warring factions of a society, by the sublime principle of universal brotherhood, he is the one to whom this distinction goes. If greatness consists in promoting goodwill and justice in the society and reforming those steeped in degrading superstitions, barbarism, and immersed in absolute immorality, then this quality goes to him.

He was an unlettered man, never went to a school or an academy, but he had given the highest truths of eternal values to mankind; he could speak with such an eloquence and zeal, which could move men to tears. He had not attended any military academy to learn the art of waging wars, yet he had the superb ability to arrange his forces against unspeakable odds and gained victories through his moral force, which was his domain. He was not a philosopher, not even a scientist, but a great teacher who taught his followers to study nature and its laws, to understand them, to appreciate the glory of God, and to study the inner meanings of the 730 verses of the Qur'an inviting close observation of nature and the natural phenomena. This persuasion ignited the zeal to observe nature closely and thus stimulated the scientific spirit of observation and experimentations, which was unknown to the Greeks and the West of that time. And indeed, those observations and experiments sowed the seeds that sprouted in the shape of Renaissance in Europe; no authority could dare to deny this fact (vide 4th. June, 2009 excerpts of speech of President Obama at Cairo—Page 138-139).

He was a great reformer. He eradicated slavery from the society and proclaimed that man is born free. He preached for the freedom of human beings and asked those who were keeping slaves to free them without demanding any ransom. Hazrath Bilal with black complexion and thick lips was a Negro and a slave. He was freed by paying ransom by Hazrat Abu Bakr. He was given the post of a Muwazzan to call Muslims for offering prayers five times a day. The day Makkah was liberated, the same slave was asked by Mohammed (pbuh) to climb over the roof of the sacred Kaa'bah and to pronounce *azan*, the call for prayers. His last sermon at his last Hajj proclaims:

> Allah is to be praised and thanked for ridding us of the vices and pride of the days of ignorance. 0 people, note that all men are divided in two categories only, the pious and God fearing, who are estimable in God's reckoning, and the transgressors and hard hearted who are lowly and contemptible in the eye of Allah. Otherwise all human beings are the progeny of Adam. Allah has created Adam from clay. Then boasting is unbecoming of a man. Hence, there is no distinction between an Arab and an Ajam (other than Arabs), between white and black, between East and West or South and North, between man and woman.

And the Qur'an vouchsafes his pronouncement about the equality of the human race. In the following verse:

> O Mankind, surely we created you from a single pair of a male and a female; and made you nations and tribes that you may know each other. Verily, the most honored among you in the sight of Allah is he who is the most righteous and God fearing. (49:13)

Emancipation of women folk from the centuries-old bondage of man was his sacred mission. The notion of man's supremacy over woman was intertwined in all the man-dominated communities of the globe, leave aside the Arab traditions. He proclaimed equality of man and woman in certain aspects. He informed his follower that the human beings are the progeny of a single pair, Adam and Eve. Therefore, there should be no distinction between man and woman. He not only defended the women folk, but he, by law, also provided share in the inheritance of their parents, which was nowhere permitted by any legal authority in that period of the world anywhere. Thus, he created provision of a legitimate right of ownership to the women folk in the properties of their parents and nearest relatives. Thus, he emphasized "Women are the twin halves of men; therefore, rights of women are sacred" since the Almighty Allah has granted those rights, which should be adhered to without any fuss.

He was the supreme commander of his armies in all the battles he fought during his lifetime and had been the greatest warrior of his time, who within ten years from AD 622 to AD 632 conquered all the Arabian Peninsula. And in most of thirty-five battles he fought, he was victorious and that too casualties had been very minimal.

The very first Battle of Badr is worth being mentioned here to exemplify his bravery and stewardship in which he, just along with 313 companions. Ill equipped militarily, he went eighty miles away from his city and fought against an enemy of more than one thousand troops well equipped with ammunition and cavalry and became victorious. Hundreds of enemies were slain against a few Muslim casualties. He was the head of a state of a vast territory and governed it merely sitting on a simple mat that from his mosque, which he built with his own hands with bricks and mud along with some companions of Medina.

He was a great legislator who constituted supreme laws for the state that he founded by keeping in view the Qur'anic dictates, which are being followed and implemented by all fifty-eight Muslim countries of the globe even today in the shape of laws of the Shariath and the Muslim personal laws are in vogue even in non-Muslim countries of the world where Muslims are in minority. He was a great orator, a great statesman, a great politician of his time who directed the political winds of the globe on a grand scale. He was the judge, protector of the slaves, emancipator of the women, well-wisher of the orphans, business magnet, and great reformer; and in spite of all this, he was a very simple man. He had no worldly belongings; he lived in a thatched house and spent his nights mostly in praying and reciting the Qur'an. During his lifetime, Medina became a wealthy city with prosperity all over the Muslim empire. By at the end time of his life, there was peace and tranquility all over the Islamic kingdom. When he passed away, his sole assets were a few coins, a part of which were paid to satisfy a debt, and the rest were distributed as charity to the poor. This was the life of a great man who changed the winds of the globe and who gave supreme laws of Shariath and whose influence after him spread to the three densely populated continents of the world (Africa, Asia, and Eurasia) and whose followers are more than 1,575 million (1.75 billion) among 6,850 million (6.85 billion) inhabitants of the globe; every fourth man is his follower.

Islam Spread in Three Continents of the Globe and Influenced Mankind

Great scholars and historians, after carefully going through the history of the Islamic world, have come to the conclusion, in the words of Edwin P. Hoyt that

> the west was stagnating. The Christian world lay in the rigidity of the un-accommodative faith. Earthly learning was despised and neglected. The teaching of the ancient authors fell into disguise and their writings were deliberately destroyed as pagans.

"At this critical moment," he says, "Arab science and culture arrived just in time since Arab civilization had respect for knowledge. It stepped in time to save what it could save the past." He further states, "There was no society other than Arabs capable of supporting scientific enquiry during the seventh to thirteenth centuries AD."

Another scholar, Robert Briffault, had conceded by writing in his voluminous book *The Making of Humanity* that

> the debt of our science in the Arabs does not consist in startling discoveries of revolutionary theories. Science owes a great deal more to the Arab culture. It owes its experience. What we call science arose in Europe as a result of new methods of investigations or the methods of experimental observations, mathematical measurements and the development of mathematics in a form un-known to the Greeks. That spirit and those methods were introduced into the European world by the Arabs.

And it is a fact that the Arabs invented the numerical systems for mathematics. Algebraic equations are their inventions; through them it was possible to calculate the unknown quantities and thus solve problems through equations. These equations and mathematical calculations helped correct the astronomical tables of Ptolemy. Their research and observations were so superb that they could formulate the solar calendar. Abu Sina is the highly revered personality of the West (they call him Avicenna) who taught medicine and wrote volumes of books on medicine, which became the textbooks in the European universities. The Arabs formulated multitudes of chemical processes and laws that were unknown to the West. They were great philosophers, poets, scholars, historians, geographers, and mystics. Their books are the reference works for the scholars of the West. The people they conquered were not simply the transmitters of the scientific ideas having inherited from the Greeks or even simply combiners who put together ideas from the Greek and sciences from India, Persia, and even China. These men were interested deeply in study of sciences and its practical implications. They were critical of what they read, heard, and saw; and they attempted to correct the errors if seen by them.

Thus, Islam spread rapidly throughout the Middle East within a thirty-year rule of the Khulaphai Rashedain (Four Companions of the Prophet); and within a century, it reached Morocco to Malaya and Philippines. It conquered Spain and penetrated into the regions of France and Portugal. It encompassed Central Asia, Asia Minor, and the Far Eastern Islands. It touched the Himalayan hemisphere and peeped into the plains of China and Mongolia just with a simple message: "Submit ye to the will of Allah."

Islam conquered many countries of the populated three continents of the globe and influenced every region and nation of the world. And through literature and scientific research, the dark period of the past evaporated into the thin air. Thus, Islam established the foundations for advancement in every walk of life and brought mankind from out of all kinds of darkness.

Illusions and fancies of the old Europe vanished through the learned scholars of the Great Mosque of Cordoba (Spain), Museum of Alexandria (Egypt), the schools of Palestine, India, and China, where hundreds of scholars from all parts of the globe came for learning and where millions of books were collected for dissemination of scientific knowledge. The West took the lead and jumped to learn and understand the Arabic language and learned it profusely for the purpose of transliterating the Arabic manuscripts written by Muslim scientists on every field of sciences into their own languages. These translations of the Arab scientists and scholars sowed the very seeds to sprout in the shape of European Renaissance, and today with that help alone, the humanity has reached its zenith by exploring the universe. Hoyt was right by saying that "the West seized the torch of science and learning from the failing East [from the Arabs, in fourteenth century] just as the Arabs had taken it from the dying Greco-Roman society [in the seventh century]."

Today the entire Muslim world consists of Muslim population of about 1,575 millions, 80 percent of which inhabit in their own fifty-eight independent homelands and the rest 20 percent is scattered and mingled in the remaining 134 non-Muslim countries of the globe.

Believe it, every fourth human being residing on this globe is a Muslim. And if our census projections are correct, in the year 2050 AD every third man of the globe shall be a Muslim! Jazak Allahu Khairun!

The Rise of the Islamic States during the Twentieth Century

The period after the advent of Islam has witnessed the grandeur of the mighty Muslim kingdoms and empires and their impact on human civilization, culture, and geopolitical affairs of the world. Islam as a religion and Muslims as a civilized nation emerged in the AD seventh century, and within the lifetime of the holy prophet, the whole of Arabian Peninsula had embraced Islam and solidified its identity as a revolutionary religion of the world. Within one hundred years it enveloped the entire Middle East and North Africa; reached the Indian subcontinent; and spread to Spain, France, Switzerland, and many parts of other European countries. They penetrated into the Central Asia and peeped into the Chinese hinterland and the Southeast Asia. During the eleventh and twelfth centuries, the entire Indian subcontinent and the Central Asia were being governed by several Muslim rulers. The thirteenth century brought the Oghuz tribes of Central Asia into Anatolia (present-day Turkey); and after consolidating their grip, they conquered European countries of Balkans, Italy, Greece, Austria, Hungary, and Romania.

The mighty Ottoman Empire then arose to dominate right from the Central and Southern Europe to East and North Africa, the Middle East, and most of the Central Asian territories and successfully governed for at least six centuries up to AD 1918. During this time, Babur the Great rose from Afghanistan and ventured into the Indian subcontinent and after the Panipath War of 1526 captured whole of North India and founded the mighty Mughal Empire, which held power until the nineteenth century. These two Muslim empires dominated almost half of the world and its population during that period.

The nineteenth century, however, brought the downfall of these two great empires, the colonial powers viz the British, French, czarist Russia, and Austro-Hungarians, with their dubious diplomacy and tactical maneuvering on one hand; and with the help of technical and naval power on the other hand, overpowered these two great empires and their subjects systematically by instigating the people to revolt against their rulers; and maliciously offered them protection against their own empires, which resulted in dismemberment and disintegration of Great Ottoman Empire, on one hand, and complete subjugation of the Moghal Empire by the British on the other.

Thus, at the beginning of the twentieth century there was no Muslim country in the world that could be rightly called to be an independent one. All were under the clutches of the French, the Italians, the Spanish, and the British. The Central Asia was subjugated by the czarist Russia. The Balkans and the remaining parts of the Eastern Europe revolted and declared independence against the Ottoman Empire. Syria and Lebanon were put by the League of Nations under the French rule. French also had authority over the Maghrib, except Libya and Egypt. The entire Middle East was under the protection of the British who were also looking after the foreign affairs of Afghanistan along with foreign affairs of Iran and Iraq. India became the British dominion. Indonesia was governed by the Dutch while Malaya and Brunei were the British territories. Thus, the Muslim world succumbed to the ruthless colonial powers of the Europe. But this situation could not continue for long for the reason of fundamental change in the politically motivated atmosphere. Amanullah Khan of Afghanistan became the torchbearer of Muslim revival and grabbed power from the British by declaring independence in 1919. Then rose Kamal Ataturk, the iron man of Turkey, who defeated the so-called superpower, the British, in the Dardanelles and proclaimed independence in 1923 followed by Saudi Arabia and Iraq in 1930, Iran in 1941, Albania and Lebanon in 1944, Syria in 1946, Pakistan including present Bangladesh in 1947, Oman and Libya in 1951, Egypt in 1952, and Tunisia in 1954. Sudan, Morocco, and Indonesia gained their independence in 1956, Malaysia in 1957, and Guinea in 1958. The year 1960 brought independence to Chad, Cyprus, Mali, Mauritania, Niger, Nigeria, Senegal, and Somalia in North Central Africa. In 1961 Kuwait, Sierra Leone, and Tanzania became independent. Algeria fought a rigorous seven-year war against France and gained independence in 1962. In 1967 Yemen attained freedom while Bahrain and Qatar and UAE gained independence in 1971, Comoros in 1972, Djibouti in 1975, and Brunei Darussalam in 1984.

The disintegration of the USSR brought independence to six central Asian countries in 1991 viz Azerbaijan. Kazakhstan. Kyrgyzstan, Tajikistan, Turkmenistan, and Uzbekistan.

Bosnia-Herzegovina declared her independence in 1992. Lastly, the tiny Palestinian state was to emerge as an independent state in 1994 under the Oslo Declaration, but to the dubious political maneuvering of Israel and the West, it is ruthlessly bleeding to declare independence. Eritrea declared her independence in 1997 and Kosovo very recently on 17 February 2008 from Serbia. Chechnya under Russia and Abkhazia in Georgia having majority of Muslim population which may come out from the clutches of their oppressors, sooner or later. The emergence of the Muslim world during the twentieth century is the landmark of the Muslims of the world, and many more may emerge in the near future. They are all the members of the organization of the Islamic Conference, which was formed in 1975.

If you go to analyze the geopolitical situation of the Muslim world, you will see that all these countries are spread over in at least five regions of the three densely populated continents, rich in history and civilization, contagious and bound with firm Islamic faith. Saudi Arabia is the adobe of two holy shrines of Islam to which millions of Muslims of all these fifty-eight Muslim countries as well as from the non-Muslim countries get together for the Hajj pilgrimage. Pilgrims assemble every year in multimillions and perform their Hajj and discuss various interlinking problems of their countries, depicting to the world as a solid political force.

From the early centuries of Islam, Saudi Arabia, Iran, Iraq, Turkey, and Egypt have exercised decisive and formidable role in the geopolitical affairs of these regions. The great battles of the past were fought in the Middle East to foster the cause of Islam. During this period of eighty-nine years (1919-2008) fifty-eight Muslim countries became independent, and their flags are fluttering among the 192 flags of the comity of the nations. Thus, the Middle East became harbinger of Islam from the very beginning. The same spirit and zeal still persist everywhere in all the regions, but the non-Muslim powers try to disturb the peace and coordinative spirit of these Muslim countries for which Muslim world must be constantly vigilant. The Western powers have a great stake in the Gulf Area on account of their oil needs, which is one of the most valuable commodities in the international market. Today the Middle Eastern countries possess more than two-thirds (2/3) of the world's proven oil and gas wealth, yet they are shy and do not dare to challenge the strength of oil as demonstrated by King Faisal during Arab-Israel debacle in 1973 and the world saw its result. If the Muslim countries can unite and start a discussion with the West based on their oil wealth, then a political equilibrium can be obtained between the West and the Muslim world. On account of the windfall gains during 2006 to 2008, the oil-producing Muslim countries alone earned more than $1.5 trillion. If the rulers of these countries believe in the Islamic teachings, then they must come forward to help those Muslim and non-Muslim third-world countries, who are burdened by the World Bank and IMF loans and whose budgetary provisions are more than 50 percent just to pay the service charges alone, leave aside the payment of the principal amount.

Let us remind the Muslim politicians once again about Saudi Arabia's oil embargo against the USA and the Netherlands in 1973 and how meaningfully it showed world the power of oil. The embargo had demonstrated that the interest of the Western powers is not safe in exploitation of the Muslim countries but in their development. Since the Muslim countries lack in infrastructure and technology, they must be respected, befriended, properly guided, and assisted by the West so that the exploitation should end once for all and mutual understanding should prevail on one hand and the West should enforce its will on Israel to adopt the "land for peace" formula forever and come to terms with the Palestinians to declare their independence. The ongoing Israel-Palestine conflict is one of the root causes of the Muslim unrest, which instigates a few fundamentalists to become suicide bombers and create Islamophobia around the world. Now President Barack Hussein Obama has announced in his historic speech on June 4, 2009, at Cairo addressing Muslims that he would help solve this terrible bloodletting dispute; and for that he warned Israel to stop settlements in the occupied territories in order to declare Palestinian State under the "land for peace" formula. Fortunately, most of the countries of the West have joined the president to pressure Israel to come to amicable already-agreed terms and solve the problem.

CHAPTER II
Creation of the Universe

Sanctity of the Holy Qur'an

Nothing could be clearer than the famous hadith of the prophet (of Islam) encouraging Muslims to seek knowledge: "Any person who goes along a course seeking knowledge, Allah will make for him the path to Paradise easy because of it" (Muslim, Sahih). Or yet in another hadith that says that, "Search for knowledge is a strict duty for every Muslim [man and woman]" (Al-Tirmidhi, hadith 74). The crucial fact is that the Qur'an while inviting us to understand and investigate science, itself contains many observations on natural phenomena and includes explanatory details which are in total agreement with modern scientific data. There is no equal to the Holy Qur'an's approach comparing to the Judo-Christian revelations. (Maurice Bucaille, *The Bible, the Qur'an, and Science*)

The literary meaning of Qur'an is that which is read, recited, and rehearsed. The very first revelation brought by the archangel Gabriel in the twenty-seventh night of the month of Ramadan (Lailathul Qadr) to Prophet Mohammad (pbuh) directs him to "recite in the name of thy Lord who created man from a clot of congealed blood. Recite for thy Lord, the Most Beneficent, who taught man [the use of] pen that which he knew not" (96:1-6).

And this particular name Qur'an was proclaimed by Almighty Allah:

"We have sent it down as an Arabic Qur'an, in order that ye may learn wisdom" (12:2).

"We have made it the Qur'an in Arabic that ye may be able to understand it" (43:3).

20

And the divine authorship of the book is attributed to the Almighty alone. which is substantiated by the words of Mohammad (pbuh) in Ayah 16 of chapter 10 (Yunus):

"It is not for me to modify it on my own. I but follow which is revealed to me. I have spent a whole lifetime among you; did you hear me any time uttering such beautiful verses?" (10:15).

It is a miracle that Allah had selected Prophet Mohammad (pbuh) who was known as ummi, an unlettered man; which is clear from the following verse:

"And thou was not able to recite a book before this book came, nor art thou able to transcribe it, with thy right hand" (29:48).

His being an unlettered man is clearer from his admission before Gabriel that he does not know how to read. Therefore, there should be no doubt that the Holy Qur'an, which was revealed to the Prophet, was not written by the Prophet Mohammad (pbuh). It is a fact that the prophet could not write because he was an unlettered man, no doubt about it. Moreover, the prophecies and the information contained in the verses are a testimony to the fact that Muhammad (pbuh) could not have possibly gotten them written from another human being of that barren remote piece of land. Thus, the Qur'an is certainly the word of Allah, revealed to Mohammad (pbuh) in twenty-three long years piece by piece. It is a fact that when Prophet Mohammad wanted to recite the words of the revelations in haste, lest he should forget, Allah's commanded him, "And we have revealed the Qur'an to you in separate chapters, so that you may recite them intermittently, and we have revealed it in intervals" (17:106).

The very word Qur'an points out to a divine prophecy that the book would be read widely, recited, and rehearsed through all the ages and in all the regions of the world. We witnessed that from the period of its origin, hundreds and thousands, rather millions, of Muslims have memorized it word by word; and if even all the volumes of the Qur'an, God forbid, are destroyed, those who have memorized it can produce new volumes. Thus, the prophecy has been working throughout all the ages in and around the regions of the world. The fact is that this degree of sanctity could not be achieved if that book had been written by any human being. This sanctity is only because it was the divine workmanship.

"Surely we have sent down this exhortation, and we will most surely safeguard it" (15:9).

This safeguarding has several aspects: preservation of the integrity of the text itself. Piecemeal revelations came in Makkah for thirteen years where Muslim literates were very few and that too when there was hostility and there had been no peace for the Muslims. Furthermore, writing material was not easily available in that remote part of Arabia of the early seventh century, which was known as the Dark Period. The fact of preservation, word by word, has been critically researched by the Westerners; and after being satisfied, they testified and proclaimed that the Qur'an is really the word of God, word for word, exactly as Mohammad (pbuh) narrated to his people, whenever it was revealed to him by God. Even a hostile critic like Sir William Muir speaking about the Holy Qur'an says, "There is probably in the world no other Book which has remained twelve [he belonged to twelfth century] centuries with so pure a text."

In order to safeguard the text of the Qur'an, Allah himself directs the Muslims to

> By no means! Indeed it is a message of instructions; therefore who ever wills should remember and record on leaves held in honor, Exalted purified, in the hands of scribes, noble and pious. (80:11-16)

"This is a glorious reading on a preserved tablet" (85:21,22).

"An Apostle from Allah recites and on leaves kept pure where the decrees of right and wrong are" (98:2,3).

Further to above, Allah directs the Muslims to

1. remember whatever was revealed,
2. write the words on leaves, and
3. keep the writings on tablets.

In many commentaries of the Holy Qur'an, it had been clarified that for want of facilities to record whatever was revealed in Makkah, the holy prophet got the revelations written on skin, leaves, and tablets. Only after migration to Madina these written and carefully saved records were transmitted properly on regular papers, which became part of the book. That is how it was saved word by word by the Prophet.

Yet another aspect is that the Arabic language in which the Holy Qur'an was revealed still continues and dominates as a living language spoken not only by the 395 million Arabs but almost all 1,550 million Muslims living in all parts of the world. Per the divine prophecy, "surely it will never die," comparing to the languages of other heavenly scriptures. The prophecy prevails when the Qur'an pronounces its literary jewels which are read, understood, and recited in larger areas (now Muslim countries count fifty-eight in the comity of the nations, and the area is not less than one-third of the globe), comparing to the early Islamic period. During the eight to fifteenth centuries, Arabic language continued to be an international language, rather a lingua franca, as that of English today. Surely this is a part of the fulfillment of the divine assurance of safeguarding every bit of the revelations. This is also a fact that there is no substantial deviation between the style and pattern of the classical Arabic language of the seventh century and the living language that has flourished in present-day Arabia.

The Qur'an has been widely translated in some thirty-five contemporary languages so far to our knowledge and the Kingdom of Saudi Arabia prints millions of volumes and distributes to the pilgrims who come to perform the Hajj every year.

Distinguishing Features:

The Qur'an bestows wisdom to the seeker and asks to maintain an attitude of reverence toward the Creator and to concentrate and ponder with open and free mind what is being directed. It expects intelligence from the reader and assumes that the seeker will exercise his/her best of ability. To test that ability, it provides metaphors, similes, and illustrations of various types. For example, in 16:68-69, Allah mentions in details the honey bee and the benefits of the honey that humans get from it. Thus, it draws attention repeatedly to the natural phenomena and asks the reader to go into the deep to understand the moral and spiritual aspects in every creation.

The Qur'an invites mankind to investigate using his/her brain and the faculty of understanding not only on the universe and the surroundings but also upon his/her life: "A book We have revealed unto thee, in order that ye may lead mankind out of the depth of darkness into light—by the leave of their Lord—to the way of him exalted in power"(14:1).

For that purpose it draws attention to every type of phenomenon and thereby reveals vast treasure of profound truth, which leads mankind to attain full wisdom and learn through it.

"Verily, in the earth are signs for those who believe firmly; and also in your own selves; do not you see?" (51:20,21).

Qur'an says that all knowledge comes only from the Almighty and warns: "Follow not that of which thou hast no knowledge; for the ear and the eye and the heart (mind) shall all be called to account for" (17:36).

Qur'an informs mankind that the earth, the skies, and the changes in the life patterns invite one to contemplate minutely and investigate thoroughly in order that he/she can understand the mystic realities of life. But pity is that man who does not care to understand them. For that he states, "How many signs are there in the heavens and the earth, which they do not care to even glimpse and simply pass on by, turning away from them un-noticed, Pity on them" (17:106).

The most important point that could be derived after careful meditation over the realities of the universe is that life functions in a perfectly balanced and a maintainable system. Everything we see around us operates under a flawlessly planned and a well-guided policy, having no fault.

"There are illustrations that we set forth for people, but only those who possess knowledge comprehend them. Allah has created the heavens and the earth for a purpose. In that surely there are signs for the believers" (29:43,44).

And those who understand these heartily proclaim and vouchsafe: "Verily, our Lord; thou hast not created all these without purpose" (3:190).

And approving this statement, Allah himself declares, "We did not create the heavens and the earth, and all that is in between them, a material for sport [purpose] only. We created them for an enduring purpose, but most of them know not" (44:38,39).

Qur'an describes the purpose of the creation in the following verses:

He has created the heavens and the earth with a true purpose. He makes the night overspread the day, and makes the day overspread the night. He has constrained the sun and the moon into service (of the mankind), each pursues its course until an appointed time. (39:5)

In another chapter, it clarifies the previous verse:

He it is who made the sun a source of light and the moon shedding luster. And ordained for its stages, that you might learn the method of calculating the years and determine time. And surely Allah has done this all under a purposeful planning. (10:5)

These verses demonstrate the very purpose of the creation. They imply that the purpose of the creation of the world is for the benefit of the mankind, and whatever has been created should benefit the human life and provide comfort and pleasure to the living beings. Thus, Allah has ordained everything that has been created in this world for the service of the mankind, and it all boils down to say:

1. Qur'an invites for understanding, meditation, and thorough investigation and contemplation.
2. Qur'an instigates to ponder, understand, and analyze the reason and purpose of the creation of this gigantic universe.
3. Qur'an explains whatever has been created by the Almighty has a purpose and has been created under a systematic planning and everything has its own value.
4. Qur'an informs that when man ponders thoroughly on all creations, he could be able to understand himself and the Creator of this universe, thereby shedding the yolk of gross ignorance and thus comes under the fold of the Creator.

With all these sublime dictates, Qur'an furnishes guidance to mankind, which leads them to the path that would bring them nearer to the Creator in a state of complete surrender and submission before him, which is the sole purpose of creation.

Cherished Goal

Qur'an guides the humanity; it draws attention to every type of phenomenon and thereby reveals vast treasures of ultimate truth, which is the goal of this entire manifestation. It directs humanity "to understand first himself then the Almighty," which is the sublime cherished goal of the purpose of this creation.

"Say: O ye men! Now truth hath reached you from your Lord. Those who receive guidance, do so for the good; those who astray, do so to their own loss" (10:108).

> This is a book that we have revealed to thee that thou may bring mankind out of every kind of darkness into the light, by the command of their Lord, to the path of the Almighty, the Praise Worthy Allah, to whom belongs whatever is in the heavens and whatever is in the earth. (14:1)

Now we have to scrutinize on what course the Holy Qur'an guides the mankind.

It is a mere wrong suggestion that Qur'an guides only religion and directs its compliance. As a matter of fact, it not only guides Shariath, Islamic jurisprudence, the norms of good and bad, but it also provides ample knowledge and understanding on worldly sciences. With some clarity we may divide its scope into five: (1) Ethics (orders and admonitions), (2) logical discussions over ecclesiastical contemplations, (3) divinity and acquaintance with religious precepts, (4) natural sciences; 5.Inspired knowledge.

The first one is the field of Islamic scholars while the second and the third are the fields of scholastic philosophers who are well versed with Islamic jurisprudence.

Fourth and fifth are the domains of those who want to ponder, investigate, and derive the realities of life from the knowledge of the Qur'anic sciences. And the book in your hands attempts to shed some light on the relationship between the verses of the Holy Qur'an and the secular scientific knowledge of today.

For that purpose, we must understand the Creator and his functions, which lead us to investigate the attributes of the Creator. When we explore his attributes, we come to understand the natural phenomena and his creation of the universe and everything that is on the surface and under the earth and in between the earth and the heavens, including man himself.

The Holy Qur'an guides us through its many verses that are basically related to matter and the orderliness in the universe. This orderliness alone is the key factor for sustenance of the universe without which the universe is bound to completely collapse. Therefore, the study of the orderliness and its components provides us the knowledge of the material world and the knowledge of the attributes of the Creator.

These attributes, in turn, lead us toward unity and oneness of the Almighty. His every attribute tells us his omnipotence and his unrestricted and divine power to control and administer the whole universe. These manifestations confirm our faith in the only omnipotent Allah and bring before us his splendid vision to be seen with our own naked eyes, and then we spontaneously proclaim, "Every changing moment of time presents a new glory, a fresh splendor and pompousness of Allah the Almighty" (55:29).

Under this guidance when we explore the intricacies of the universe, we come across the marvels of his creation. Whether we are experimenting a tiny atom or the entire space including our gigantic solar system; whether we are investigating about the animal kingdom or the agriculture maneuverings; whether we explore the instinct to work collectively in congregation by an ant, moth, or honeybee; or minutely looking to our own anatomy of life and physique; or the multifarious diversities of various types of creations, we will notice the all prevailing exquisite, colorfulness and an absorbing and eye catching beauty in them. Thus, all these phenomena will lead us to surrender to the all-existing divine power that has been embedded in everything that the eye can see, the nose can smell, the tongue can taste, the skin can feel, and the ears can hear. All these hint to an awe-striking reality that in the guise of these perceived maneuverings there exists only one alone under the veil, who is basically known as the Almighty, the all-powerful omnipotent and omniscient Allah.

In this manner we come across two features of these attributes of the Almighty: (1) attached to himself and (2) pertaining to his actions.

The first attribute denotes life, divine power, five senses, conversational and willpower; the other relates to his acts of creation, providing sustenance, maintenance, verdicts, etc. These attributes attract the thinking mind to explore further and instigate a thinking man/woman to derive essence of these attributes and draw out the formulas for the betterment of the mankind and the environment.

> He who created seven heavens, one above another no lack of proportion thou shall see in the creation of Allah, Most Gracious; so turn thy vision again: See thou any flaw? Again turn thy vision a second time; [thy] vision shall come back dull and discomfited, in a state worn out. (67:3,4)

Carefully read the verse: "Inni Jaelun Fil Arze Khalifa" (2:30). The Almighty Allah proclaimed before the angels "I am about to place a vicegerent on the earth" by fashioning Adam on his own image and breathing unto him his own self. "He taught Adam the names of all his attributes" and commanded all angels, including Satan, to prostrate before Adam. All obeyed, but Satan disobeyed and for which act of disobedience he was cursed by Allah and for his arrogance.

These verses tell us the superiority of the human race over all his creations. Thereby, Qur'an draws attention to various stages of creation of the universe.

The Creation of the Universe:

In regard to the origin of the universe, scientists propounded the big bang theory, which states that the universe was in a primordial cosmic egg in the inception. Then this egg suddenly busted with an unbelievable thrust of its own, and the universe came into being. Within seconds of that explosion also came into being an unimaginable temperature causing the thermal radiation to rise to a thousand million degrees Fahrenheit culminating into a fiery sea of radiation where particles were coming out and falling back into the ocean of fire ceaselessly and the universe thus started expanding. The explosion then created the 106 elements of hydrogen, helium, lithium, beryllium, etc. According to the propounded big bang theory, they boastfully declare that they need no supernatural being to fashion the universe and its components. George Edward Limiter (1894-1966) the Belgian astrophysicist, propounded this big bang theory in 1927, and other scientists have also suggested many hypothetical theories about the origin of the universe. Today's sciences' explanation of the origin of universe is manifested in the cosmic egg, and this very explanation was declared in the Qur'an fourteen centuries ago. The Holy Qur'an asserts that "the originator of the heavens and the Earth, when he determines the coming into being of a certain thing; He Commands the concerned to be. And it comes into existence—*kun fayakun* (2:118).

Thus, the universe came into existence with the assertion of the Almighty's commanding word "be," which is being interpreted by the scientists "the sudden bursting of the cosmic egg or big bang, which caused the existence of the universe. The Holy Qur'an declares that the Almighty Allah issues commands for any creation and it comes into being. Thus, it is inevitable that there remains the necessity of a supernatural being to control and run the universe, without whom there is no universe.

"Have not those who disbelieve known that the heaven and the earth were joined together as one united piece [in the beginning, resembling the so called cosmic egg] then we parted them asunder" (21:30).

"And the sky he has raised high and set up measure and spread the earth for his creature" (55:7).

"The process of creation is continuous. He originates the creation and then repeats it" (10:4).

The word "repeat" denotes two meanings, one being to create again and again and the second being to annihilate what has been created and again create all of them to stand before him on doomsday.

"Be mindful of the day when we shall roll up the heaven like the rolling up of the scribes. As we began the first creation, so shall we repeat it. This is our promise! We shall certainly perform it" (21:104).

"The heavens and the earth were a closed-up mass, then we split them asunder and we made from water every living being! Will they not believe? Then we have placed in the earth firm mountains, lest they should roll beneath them, and We have made wide pathways therein that they may perform journey from place to place, We have made the heaven a guarding and a protecting roof. Yet, they turn away from our signs. He is who created the night and the day, and the sun and the moon, each gliding freely in their orbits" (21:30-33).

Water has been referred necessary for the origin of life. Furthermore, Allah says in the Qur'an, "We made from water every living being," which refers to aquatic origin where water is the major component of every living cell. Further it has been verified by the scientists that every living cell consists 75 percent of water (21:30). Therefore, it is strictly in accordance with the scientific data that without water life cannot exist. When we discuss about other planets, we simply put a question whether that planet contains water or not. That means water is essential for life.

Allah even mentions the animal kingdom in regard to water in the Qur'an. It is the opinion of the scientists that the oldest living beings, which belonged to the plant kingdom, had their base in algae, which belonged to the oldest-known forest areas of the pre-Cambrian Era. Followed by animal kingdom which they too had their base in water for their growth. Thus, water may be taken to the water, which is available in the oceans, seas, rivers, tanks, springs, on the earth, and under the earth's surface or the water that comes to us through rains. Of course we may take fluid of sperm also in the shape of water. Then there should be no doubt that whether it is plant kingdom or animal kingdom or even mankind, they are all the products of water in one form or the other.

Allah is the "originator of creation of all things and protector" (39:62).

"He has created everything and has determined its measure" (25:2).

"Tell them: Travel on the earth and observe how Allah originated the creation, then he will provide the second creation" (29:20).

But the process is gradual and proceeds by stages:

"All perfect praise be to Allah who nourishes, sustains and leads stage by stage towards perfection of all the worlds" (1:2).

To understand these stages and the most recent human observations on the existence of the cosmic egg's extragalactic material, one must indeed go back to the ideas established by the contemporary science on the formation of the universe starting with the simplest and proceeding to the most complex problems:

1. Formation of the heavenly bodies and the earth as explained in verse 9:12 of sura 41 of the Qur'an required two phases. Science informs that their formation occurred by a process of condensing of the primary nebula and their separation. This is exactly

what the Qur'an expresses when it refers to the processes that produced a fusion and subsequent separation starting from a celestial smoke.

2. Interlocking of the two stages in the formation of sun and the earth, per science which confirms the statement of the Qur'an.

3. Existence of smoke, mentioned in the Qur'an as the gaseous state of the material that composes it; corresponds to the concept of the primary nebula stated by science.

4. Plurality of the heavens and the earth to an infinite number 7 of the Qur'an have been confirmed by modern science through observations by the astrophysicists who have confirmed the galactic system being in a very large number.

5. Existence of an intermediate creation between the heavens and the earth compares the discovery of material present outside an organized astronomic system.

This stage-by-stage process leads every living creation toward perfection, which we may call it an evolutionary process of creation, which is not at all what Darwin defines as an evolution. Allah declared in the Qur'an that "he is going to appoint a vicegerent, Adam on Earth for his worship" (51:56).

For Adam's sustenance he created the universe, the heavens, and the earth. After the creation of the heavens and the earth, all of Adam's characteristics came into being then Allah created Eve, for Adam's comfort and companionship. The Qur'an beautifully presents the whole universe and its unique administration, which reveals the preciseness of this gigantic universe and its functions. All that is on the earth and in between earth and the skies, the sun, the moon, the winds, the clouds, the rains, the light of the day the darkness of the earth, and the vastness of the oceans, the running of the ships, the agriculture, the cattle, and everything that is necessary for the life are the provisions for mankind. Everything is subjected unto man by the command of Allah. Allah clearly explains the purpose of his creation in the Qur'an, "You can see no fault in the beneficent one's creation, then look again. Can you see any rift? Then look again and yet again, your sight will return to you in a state of humiliation a worn out" (67:3,4).

"Do they not look at the sky above them? How We have built it and adorned it and there are no rifts in it" (10:6).

"God the one who raised the heavens without any pillars that you can see, then he firmly established himself on the throne and He subjected the sun and the moon (unto man)" (13:2).

"God holds back the sky from falling on the earth unless by his leave" (22:65).

"For you [Allah] has subjected all that is in the heavens and on the earth, all for him. Behold, in that are signs for people who reflect" (45:13).

"The moon and the sun are subjected to calculations" (55:5).

"Allah is the one who made the sun a shine and the moon a light and for her ordained mansions, so that you might know the number of years and reckoning of the time. Allah had created this all in truth. He explains the signs in detail appointed the night for rest and the sun and moon for reckonings" (10:6).

"Allah is the one who has set out the stars, that you may guide yourselves by them through the darkness of the land and of the vastness of the sea. We have detailed the signs for people who know" (6:97).

"Allah sets on the earth landmarks and by the stars men guide themselves" (16:16).

"Allah is the one who made the earth a couch for you and the heaven as the edifice, and sent down water from the sky. He brought forth therewith fruits for your sustenance. Do not join equal with Allah if you know" (2:22).

"Behold! In the creation of the heavens and the earth, in the disparity of the night and the day; in the ships which run upon the seas for profit of mankind; in the water that Allah sends down from the skies thereby reviving the earth after its death; in the beasts of all kinds He scattered there in; in the change of the winds and the subjected clouds between the sky and the earth, here are signs for people who are wise" (2:164).

Mystery of the Universe

Allah, the Almighty, had evolved life by intermixing the natural elements like hydrogen, oxygen, carbon, nitrogen, calcium, phosphorous, chlorine, sulfur, potassium, and sodium, and created protoplasm, the living organism of every created thing.

Here we would like to elaborate our discussion on the following terms used in the Holy Qur'an in relation to the creation of man:

"Allah has produced you [man] from the earth, growing [gradually like a plant]" (71:17).

"Was he [man] not a drop of fluid emitted forth? Then he became a clot of blood" (75:37-40).

"We created man from an extract of clay, then We placed him as a drop of sperm in a safe depository [mother's womb]" (23:12,13).

Thus, the creation of man is broken down into three simple steps, which science has recently discovered:

1. Created man from earth to grow (like a plant)
2. Drop of fluid that became clot of (congealed) blood
3. Extract of clay, which genetically turns into a drop of sperm

The first ayah informs that the elements for creation of man and plant are one and the same. The protoplasm, which is available for the plant kingdom, is the same one available to the animal kingdom, including man. Then what is protoplasm? "It is an organized collided complex of organic and inorganic substances [as protein and water] that constitutes the living nucleus of the cell, which is regarded as the only form of matter in which the vital phenomena are manifested" (*Webster's College Dictionary*). Thus, this collided complex of organic and inorganic substances have been scientifically proven to be based on nature's fourteen elements mentioned above, which are available in the strata of the soil in the earth. These inorganic constituents of the earth are absorbed into a living matter by way of food. This living matter reproduces itself by means of sperm. Thus, the phrase "extract of clay" befits to this organic and inorganic substances found in the earth. Therefore, it is easy to explain that the natural process that is applicable to the plant kingdom is the same process working in the animal kingdom including man. In this manner man and plant grow according to nature's program. This extract of clay, as has been described above, is nothing but the constituents of the earth, which are absorbed into living matter by way of food, thereby reproducing themselves by means of sperm, which is deposited in the ovum and in due course of time fertilizes it and rests for an appointed time (for the man it is nine months) in security passing through three stages of darkness. According to Professor Keith Moore these three veils of darkness, as mentioned in the Qur'an, refer to the (i) interior abdominal wall of the mother, (ii) the uterine wall, and the (iii) the amino chronic membrane (Islamic voice website). And referring to the creation of man Allah says that a fetus comes out from the womb "in stages one after another in three veils of darkness" (39:6).

Consider again about nature of the protoplasm. Scientific experiments reveal that protoplasm contains 75 percent of water, then read the following verse: "We made from water everything [including man]" (21:30).

And this system is repeated creation after creation, generation after generation. Its inception is one of the miracles of the Almighty Allah (the mystery of the origin of life). Thus, from the living (plants and animals) he brings forth the dead (seeds, fruits, dates, and the eggs) and then causes life in them through bringing replica just like the originals. A mango does not come from the seed of a citrus plant. A cat cannot give birth to a mouse. Rice comes from the rice seeds only and wheat from the wheat seeds only. This is the marvelous system of repetition, which is one of the attributes of (Rabbul Alameen) the Almighty Allah, the Creator of this marvelous universe. The study of genetics unravels many more mysteries. These creations imply to come to conclusion that the Creator is the only one who has the creativity to reproduce the replicas, generation to generation. To this mystery, the scientists are awestruck because they cannot understand the mystery of creation and its replica. But see how beautifully the Qur'an simplifies this mystery: "See they not how Allah originated creation, then repeats it. Verily, that is easy for Allah" (29:19).

In yet another verse he declares, "Is not he who originates creation, then repeats it and who gives you sustenance from heavens and earth?"(27:64).

From a scientific point of view, every leaf of a tree is like a factory wherein carbohydrate is produced, which is a basic constituent of food. Science has yet to explain the systematic production of food in nature, and this fact has been accepted by a reputed scientist who declares, "Unfortunately we could not understand the mechanism of this process [cell physiology and biochemistry part 3]."

This is called photosynthesis, which is a vast subject of botany. And the Qur'an has provided that knowledge when the ABC of the science was unknown some fourteen centuries ago. Based on this fact, whether scientists accept it or not, we assert that it comes from the divine inspiration. Some of these inspirations had already been revealed in the holy book to an unlettered prophet 1,400 years ago.

The Qur'an is explicit on the creation of the universe. Both have been created with a purpose.

"Allah is the Creator of all things and he is the guardian over all. To him belong the keys of the heavens and the earth" (39:62,63).

"To him belong the kingdom of heavens and the earth. He has taken unto himself no son, and has no partner in his kingdom. He has created everything and has determined its measure" (25:2).

"The process of creation is continuous. He originates the creation and repeats it" (10:4).

"And it is he who causes the break of a day and has made the night to rest and the sun and the moon the means of reckoning time. That is the measure determined by the Almighty" (10:5).

"He merges the night into the day [the decreased hours of the night are added in the hours of the day during summer] and he merges the day into the night [likewise the decreased hours of the day added into the night during winter]" (35:13).

How does it occur? The Earth is tilted to 23.27 degrees on its axis. If the tilt to the earth was not there, there would have been equal hours in the day and equal hours for the night, twelve hours each. This tilt also is the source of changing seasons, winter, summer, fall, and spring. Once again, if the earth was not placed at an angle tilting 23.27 degrees, the question of changing seasons would have not arisen. This is one of the mysteries of nature.

The secrets of this mystery and the orderliness in the happenings, day in day out, and the schedule of programmatic planning by the Almighty shall be discussed minutely in the following chapter "Modern Scientific Data and the Creation of the Universe."

CHAPTER III

Modern Scientific Data Regarding Creation of the Universe

Bringing mankind out of every kind of darkness

The Qur'an as a Guide

> This book that we have revealed to thee that thou may bring mankind out of every kind of darkness into the light, by the command of thy Lord, to the path of the mighty, the praiseworthy Allah, to whom belongs what so ever is in the heaven and whatsoever is in the earth. (14:1,2)

There are 763 verses in the Holy Qur'an that draw attention to every type of phenomenon and reveal fundamental truths that call the mankind to explore, ponder, and appreciate. The universe and its every constituent are governed under a perfect system of orderliness. It has its own natural laws, which are in vogue since inception of this vast universe. In order to understand those natural laws, prominent scientists, physicists, astronomers, mathematicians, and philosophers struggled to study the universe and its natural laws. They also devised theories and formulas, which will be presented for the benefit of the readers in the following paragraphs.

The Qur'an is a perfect guide to the humanity. It contains orders and directions. It contains similes, metaphors, historical facts of the yesteryears and prophecies for the future—matters relating to the universe, human beings, bees, birds, oceans, atmosphere, animate and inanimate creatures, celestial bodies, life and life-after-death scenarios, doomsday, and historical facts about the prophets and their people and the other chosen personalities of history. The Qur'an provides information about previous generations, communities, different forms of administration, and military strategies. The events mentioned in the Holy Qur'an are in absolute agreement with historical facts, as well as the developments that took place in the world after its revelation. However, the Holy Qur'an is not a book of the sciences, but it still sheds light on various scientific phenomena. For example, it mentions the scientific facts relating to the fields of physics, chemistry, botany, biology, anatomy, physiology, metallurgy, astronomy, astrology, oceanography, geology, and archeology. The following paragraphs will demonstrate how Qur'an clearly explains the different scientific wonders to a society that had no indication of any scientific knowledge or its related subjects. Furthermore, the Qur'an also provides knowledge relating to mankind like geography, history, politics, sociology, psychiatry, morality, economics, ethics, and scores of related fields of study, which deal with the universe and mankind.

The following few selected verses denominate the subject matter of the scientific knowledge of the human beings, but the Holy Book could not and should not be determined as the book of those subject matter as a whole.

"We created man from an extract of clay, and then we placed him as drop of sperm in a safe depository [mother's womb]. Then we fashioned the clot into a shapeless lump; then out of this shapeless lump, We fashioned bones. Then we clothed the bones with flesh; then we developed it into a new creation" (23:12,13).

The Qur'an further explains the miracle of birth by breaking down the different stages through which the fetus is formed and passed through the mother's womb.

"He, the ever Merciful, Who has created everything in the best condition and began the creation of man/woman from clay, then he made his progeny from the extract of an insignificant fluid; then perfected his/her faculties and breathed into him/her his spirit; He has bestowed upon you hearing, sight and understanding" (32:7,8-9).

1. Here, by mentioning the complex stages of the formation of a human, Qur'an clearly sheds light on what we call the field of **anatomy or obstetrics.** Today, the obstetricians have found, through the study of the anatomy of pregnancy, that

the divine verses that were revealed to the Prophet Muhammad (pbuh) about the different stages of pregnancy fourteen centuries ago are not only sound but also accurate.

For example: the human ovum was first described by Graff in 1672, and five years later the sperm was discovered by Antonie van Leeuwenhoek in 1677. It is an amazing fact that the Qur'an referred to these cells in the human body almost one thousand years before they were scientifically and experimentally confirmed by human eyes. In a series of verses (22:5; 23:12-14; 49:13; 53:45,46; and 76:2) the Holy Qur'an depicts their subsequent behavior leading to fertilization, implantation in the uterus, followed by six stages of development that have been established precisely in the same sequence by modern science.

2. The Holy Qur'an continuously refers to universal phenomena in many verses. For example, along with anatomy, it also demonstrates about the earth coming to life after it becomes barren.

"It is he who sends the winds as glad tidings in advance of his mercy, till then when they bear a heavy cloud. We drive it to the dead land, then we send down water from there, and we bring forth therewith its vegetation plentifully" (7:57).

"He it is who has caused the two waters to flow, one of the rivers and springs sweet, palatable, and potable and the other of the oceans, salty and bitter and between them he has placed a barrier, a system that keeps them apart" (25:53).

"The two waters are not alike, the one of the rivers and springs sweet, palatable and pleasant to drink, and the other of the sea, saltiest and bitter. From each you eat fresh meat and collect out article that you wear as ornaments. Thou see the vessels plough through each that you may seek his bounty" (35:12).

"He who has constrained the sea to your service that you may eat fresh seafood and may take out articles that you wear as ornaments. That you may voyage across the oceans" (16:14).

These verses inform mankind about water, clouds, rain, rivers, oceans, as well as their sweetness and bitterness, voyage through oceans, etc., which become the source of study on **hydraulic or meteorology or even oceanography.**

3. The Qur'an does not stop with anatomy and meteorology, but it continues to evoke the human brain to question the different wonders it witnesses. In the following verses, it speaks about the different benefits man can derive from the metals of the earth like copper, iron, lead, and gold.

"We bestowed our grace upon David and commanded: 'O, ye the dwellers of the mountains . . . . We have taught him the art of smelting iron ore, we commanded him to fashion full-length coats of mail; and keep their rings small . . . . We subjected the wind to Solomon . . . . We caused a font of molten copper to flow for him . . . . Experts made for him temples, statues and basins large as reservoirs and huge cooking vessels'" (34:11-12).

Furthermore, Allah mentions the great Dhul-Qarnayn and how he used "iron" and "molten lead" to create a strong barrier between "Gog and Magog" and the innocent villagers (18:94-95).

This all about iron ore and copper and their smelting technique to manufacture temples, statues, and utensils. All such were taught by the Almighty to prophets David and Solomon, directing mankind to learn the science of **metallurgy.**

4. Qur'an refers to many civilizations that arose during and prior to the revelations and that were destroyed by the Almighty for their arrogance, disobedience, and wrongdoings:
Have they not traveled on the earth and observed what the end of those before them was? They were stronger than those in power; they tilled the soil and populated the earth more than those who have populated it in greater numbers. Then came to them their Apostles with clear signs which they rejected. (30:9)
These destroyed civilizations left the archeological remains in different parts of the world and confirmed the archeological details mentioned in the Qur'an. That is how Qur'an guides us to learn a lesson from the past by studying **archeology.**

5. The Holy book also gives the details about Egyptology by mentioning the appearances of prophet Moses in the court of the pharaoh along with his brother prophet Harun. Allah mentions the details of Moses's encounter with the pharaoh.
He reminds his last prophet, Muhammad, about the influential court magicians, the freedom Israelites attained at the hand of Moses by the will of Allah from the pharaoh's bondage, and the drowning of the pharaoh along with his troops into the raging waters of the sea. The following verse demonstrates the last moments of the dying pharaoh who repented to Allah before his death: "We will grant thee a measure of deliverance by preserving thy body this day that thou may serve as a sign for those who come after thee" (10:92).
This was confirmed by the discovery of the pharaoh's body in 1919, thus inviting you to study **Egyptology, pyramids, and their art of mummifying.**

6. The following verses will denote about the astronomical features mentioned in the Qur'an. They speak about a new chapter on **astronomy or cosmology:**
"Do not the disbelievers realize that the heaven and the earth were a solid mass, then We split them asunder, and We made from water everything? Will they not believe?" (21:30).

"Have you not seen how Allah has created seven heavens in perfect harmony, and has placed the moon therein as light; and made the sun as a lamp" (71:15,16).

"He is the one who created the night and the day and the sun and the moon each gliding along its orbit" (21:33).

"He has constrained to your service, the moon and the sun, both carrying out their functions incessantly" (14:33).

When we read the book, we come across twenty-seven actual references to the Apostles of the Almighty. Whereas, the hadith and commentaries of the Qur'an by eminent scholars suggest that there must have been thousands of apostles sent to Earth by the Almighty God for the guidance of mankind. We know this because in Qur'an, in chapters 13 and 14, Allah says that "every nation had been sent with a messenger." These messengers were sent to many regions of the globe with languages of that region to guide humankind beginning from the first man on Earth, prophet Adam, to the last prophet, Mohammad (pbuh). These messengers emphasized on different aspects of the guidance. Other than the prophets, the Qur'an also speaks of prominent personalities such as the Ashab-e-Kuhaf, pharaohs of Egypt, Queen Sheeba of Yemen, Nimrod of Iraq, Zul Qarnain, Gog and Magog, and scores of personalities along with their kingdoms. Qur'an mentions their successes and failures and the many destructions that came upon them on account of their disobedience against the will of Allah. Even though Qur'an mentions the historical facts from the beginning of time, with prophet Adam all the way up until the last prophet, **it cannot be considered as a book on history** because its purpose is to guide people to infer lessons from the lives of those who existed before them.

7. Along with the scientific facts, the Qur'an also delves into the mathematical enumerations. However, it is not a book of mathematics. For example, the total number of verses in the Qur'an has been correctly calculated to be 6,666 in 114 chapters. These verses were gradually revealed to the Holy Prophet during his lifetime from AD 610 to 632. When we analyze them, we realize the astonishing orderliness of commandments and subjects, which are mathematically arranged:

Verses relating to (in numbers)

Admonition	1,000
Promise	1,000
Commands	1,000
Prohibitory	1,000

Examples	1,000
Historical	1,000
Analytical	250
Glorification	250
Sanctification	100
Other than these	66
Total	6,666

We are perplexed to see how miraculously the distribution of even number (1,000) for the first six important subjects dealing with humans have been arranged when the revelations came in installments in a long period of twenty-three years. It confirms that the Holy Qur'an already existed at the Arshe Muallah (with Allah) in a complete shape before it was revealed to Hazrath Mohammad (pbuh). Yet there are still some amazing features in the Qur'an dealing with the occurrence of equal number for opposite entities, which are listed below:

Word Meaning	No of times mentioned in the Qur'an
Al Duniya the world	115 times
Al Akhira hereafter	115 times
Al Malaika angels	88 times
Al Shayateen Iblis	88 times
Al Hayath life	145 times
Al Mau death	145 times
Al Rujl man	24 times
Al Marha woman	24 times
Al Shahr month	12 times (One year has twelve months.)
Al Youm day	365 times (One year has 365 days.)
Al Bahar ocean	32 times
Al Bar land	13 times

The ratio of ocean to land mass demonstrates another miracle of the Holy Qur'an. Amazingly the Holy Qur'an measured the ratio of ocean area to land area fourteen centuries ago through the number of times it mentioned the words "ocean" and "earth." Today the scientists have calculated the ratio of oceanic water to land mass as **ocean area equals to 71 percent and land area as 29 percent** and below.

In the Holy Qur'an the word "ocean" has come out 32 times and the land has come out 13 times:

To obtain the total mass of the earth, add 32 + 13 = 45.

To get ocean area, divide **32/45 x 100 percent = 71.111 percent or, say, 71 percent ocean area**

Likewise, to get ratio of land, divide **13/45 x 100 percent = 28.888 percent or 29 percent of total land mass**

In his book *Miracles of the Qur'an*, Harun Yahiya mentions that this ratio of the oceans and the land of the globe was revealed in the Qur'an fourteen hundred years ago but was only recently confirmed by the scientists. Is it not a mathematical miracle?

This ratio has been maintained by the Almighty since inception of the universe. It may change in the future because in one the verses of the Qur'an, the Almighty states, "See they not that we gradually reduce the land [in relation to oceans] from its outlying borders" (21:44).

Furthermore, scientists have come to conclusion that the level of the oceanic water has increased to the extent of four inches during the last century. Therefore, it may be deduced that the water level may tend to increase to the extent of some inches every century, thereby reducing simultaneously the ratio of land to oceans.

Why go so far? On the account of ozone depletion, we are experiencing warmer weather every year; and if the developed countries do not curtail their CFC level, within this century the glaciers and snows of the North and the South Poles might start melting, and the level of the ocean waters would rise to inundate the low level areas of the land, mostly the coastal areas. This fear has been emphasized very well in the Kyoto Declaration of January 2008, and the countries have accepted to reduce their CFC level by the year 2050 to check the ozone depletion at any cost. However, this is one of the prophecies of the Holy Qur'an: the borders of the land would start shrinking, giving way to oceanic waters to fill the gap and increase its ratio with reference to the ratio of the land.

In view of the mathematical accuracy in the Qur'an, one of the scientists, James Jeans, states that "the universe is more easily analyzable in terms of mathematical concepts than of those appropriate to any other science. The further we penetrate into the physical nature of things the more plainly we can see the mathematical principles underlying them." He further confirms his above statement by mentioning that "we are justified in drawing an inference as to the nature of this constructing mind; it must think and be capable of thinking mathematically."

Thus, Qur'an provides the thinking minds the basics for exploring the meticulous calculation required to master the subject of **mathematics and algebra**. Human society is a dynamic one. The dawn breaks with a new problem, and the day sets with another problem. These ever-changing problems give rise to broader outlook and fresh way of thinking. The Qur'anic guidance set forth in it proves its worth for all times and in all eventualities. Thus, the Holy Qur'an is a natural and a perpetual spring of comprehensive guidance. It seeks to convince through reason and persuasion. For example, in Qur'an Allah mentions,

"We have put forth for men, in the Qur'an every kind of parable In order that they may take heed; which is expressed in Arabic language wherein there is no deviation from the truth; in order that they may become righteous" (39:27,28).

From its first revelation in AD 610, more than fourteen hundred years ago, the Qur'an has steadily kept well ahead of man's need for guidance in every sphere and has never fallen behind, which is an impressive tribute to its mature wisdom. Guidance refers to admonition as a blessed reminder to the straight path, proper vision for uplift, piety, and restraint from evil, the healing from all ills and mercy. The following verses emphasize the cherished goal of guidance in clear terms.

"Blessed is he who sent down the criterion [of right and wrong] to his slave Mohammed that it may be an admonition to the creatures" (25:1).

"A blessed reminder which we have sent down. Will you then reject it?" (21:50).

"We have indeed sent down signs that make things manifest; and Allah guides whom he wills to a way that is straight" (24:46).

"It is true thou wilt not be able to guide every one whom thou loveth, but Allah guides those whom he will. And he knows best who receive guidance" (28:56).

"A book which makes proper visions for your understanding" (21:11).

"But to those who receive guidance, he increases the light of [guidance] and bestow on them piety and restraint [from evil]" (47:17).

"It is a clear light from Allah and a clear book whereby does Allah guide them to the right path" (5:17,18).

"Surely, this Qur'an guides to the way which is most firm and right and gives to the believers who act righteously, the tiding that they may have great rewards" (17:9).

"O, mankind, there has indeed come to you from your Lord which is full of admonition and healing for all your ills and guidance and mercy for the believers" (10:57).

Thus, the holy book is a perfect guide, a light, a healing for all ailments, and a book of wisdom to those who listen to their inner desire to ponder, to reflect, to investigate and get guidance to formulate their findings and inculcate those findings for the betterment of the mankind.

The scientific consideration, which are specific to the Holy Qur'an, greatly surprise the West. It is difficult for the Christians, Jewish, and Orientals to believe the text of the Holy Qur'an that was compiled more than fourteen centuries ago referring to extremely diverse subjects such as creation, astronomy, matters relating to Earth, animal and vegetable kingdom, human reproduction and on all other important sciences, which are totally correct in keeping with modern scientific knowledge. A careful study of the Holy Qur'an reveals the highly accurate nature of certain details that are perfectly commensurate with the present-day scientific ideas.

The relationship between the Qur'an and science is surprisingly a harmony and virtually not of discord. Any confrontation between scientific temper of Qur'an and the secular ideas proclaimed by science is perhaps, in the eyes of many people of the modern times, something of a paradox. The majority of the scientists of today—with some exceptions, of course—are indeed bound up in materialist theories that have only in deference or in contempt for religious questions, which they often considered to be founded on legend. In the West, in particular, when science and the holy book are discussed, people are quite willing to mention the Torah and Bible only among the scriptures. Unfortunately rather with prejudice, hardly they refer the Holy Qur'an. Therefore, many false judgments based on inaccurate knowledge have indeed been made about it. It is very difficult to form an exact notion in their minds about the truth and universality of the Holy Qur'an, Islam, and Muslims.

In the befitting words of Maurice Bucaille, the French scholar, "the totally erroneous statements made about Qur'an and Islam in the West are sometimes of systematic denigration. The most serious of all the untruths told about it are however, those dealing with facts; for a while, mistaken opinions are excusable, the presentation of the fact running contrary to the reality is not."

We now explore and discuss in detail what the great scientists of repute of the previous centuries have studied the universe to its entirety and formulated the basic formulas and theories concerning the vast universe in their comprehensive and painstaking deliberations, which govern the universe, in the following chapters:

Einstein Describes the Universe in a Scientific Way

Einstein's relativity theory emphasizes that evolution is the eternal principle of the nature, which is the basic principle behind this unity and diversity. He says that mass and energy are interconvertible. Through him we now know that matter is inherited with a hidden capacity to work. He explains that time-space relativity is the decisive factor for this mass-energy interconversion. According to him matter can be converted with a process of destruction into energy, and likewise, energy may be changed to matter with a process of construction. He emphasized that this construction-destruction process is continuously taking place from the very beginning of the universe, and this inherent capacity to interchange by a process of unity and diversity is the sole key gifted by nature to this gigantic mechanism of evolution. This construction-destruction cycle is going on from billions of years when the universe came into being with the so-called big bang explosion of the primordial cosmic egg, according to the scientists. However, according to the scriptures and theologians, the universe came into existence when the Almighty Allah asserted "be," and it got its existence.

Evolution Is Eternal

This inherited capacity of matter, created by the Almighty Allah, exploded on the command of Allah, with the planned program of interconversion battle of mass and energy, which was the first step toward evolution that caused an expanding universe. According to the scientists, since then there had been many evolutionary stages. Each stage lasted for at least a billion years. When the Almighty himself proclaimed that he had made the universe in six days, here days should be taken equal to a billion years. At the end of each such stage, a new entity came into being in the form of unity, which gradually went into diversity, resulting in emergence of yet another entity. This way the cycle of change and interchange, destruction and construction, unity and diversity continues in order to preserve "something out of nothing."

Scientists accept the fact that this "something" is nothing but energy, and this energy is the result of assertion caused by the Almighty who is absolute and eternal. The unity of energy created diversity in matter, which in turn gave birth to the unity of life. The life force then diversified itself to create the unity of mind, which is the source of consciousness in man and which is the sole purpose of creation of this universe by the Almighty Allah. This consciousness created such a brilliant technology, which brought the world into present stage where man feels as the dominant force in the entire universe. Is it not wonderful and amazing?

(Note: Here it is necessary to point out that wherever the word "evolution" is used, it refers to the natural way of evolution and certainly not that of Darwinian evolution. Here the evolutionary process is meant according to the "stage by stage" creation as mentioned in the Qur'an (1:2) above. For example, when one sows a seed in the earth and waters it regularly, after some time that seed sprouts into a seedling. As days and months pass on, if proper care is given, it may become a full-grown tree, which yields fruits and flowers. Then a time will come after some years that the same tree dies away. This evolutionary process is a natural phenomenon, not that which has been explained by Darwin. So you have to differentiate in these two definitions of the word "evolution" suggested by Darwin and explained by the holy Qur'an.)

Physical Forces that Govern the Universe

There are four forces operating in the universe (1) gravitation (2) nuclear strong, (3) nuclear weak, and (4) electromagnetic. While the first force operates on the large and voluminous bodies of the universe, like galaxies, stars and planets, and satellites, other three forces operate on mass of the universe in forming different elements of the universe. We shall now discuss how the gravitational force operates on large bodies:

Gravitational Force

Aristotle (384-322 BC) described universe as restless. He said that there are two kinds of motions operating on any physical body: violent and neutral. Violent force has been described as a constant force that generates a constant velocity while a resting body has a neutral force. Against this notion, an Italian astronomer, Galileo (1564-1642), declared in 1590 that speed did not remain constant but tends to increase in proportion to time when a thing would fall on surface of the earth. Thus, he asserted that instead of being constant, as Aristotle had mentioned, it accelerates at the speed of 980 centimeters per second. In other words, for each second in progress a falling body accelerates its movement at the speed of 980 centimeter per second faster than it was falling the second before. He termed this motion the law of acceleration, and he pointed out that this law operates on all celestial bodies and planets, including our Earth.

Whims about the Universe

Greco-Roman classical theory about the universe is known as geocentric theory, which was also adopted by Aristotle. It states that the earth was flat, and the sun and other planets of the solar system were orbiting around the earth. This theory, from its inception till sixteenth century, was backed by the philosophers, scientists, and the church. But Imam Jafer-e-Sadique, a Muslim astronomer of repute (702-765), declared that planet Earth is moving on its axis, first around itself in twenty-four hours, causing days and nights and around the sun once a year in 365 days. Therefore, he suggested that the Greco-Roman theory geocentric is wrong. He propounded heliocentric theory of the universe. To this theory, other Muslim astronomers like Omar Khayyam (AD 1048-1132), Naseeruddin Tusi (1201-1276), and Ibn Shatir (1304-1375) also testified by practically demonstrating trigonometrically that the earth is not the center of the universe as against the Ptolemaic geocentric theory who had proclaimed the earth is static and flat. Finally in the sixteenth century, the Polish astronomer Copernicus (1473-1543) adopted the heliocentric theory propounded by the Muslim astronomers and challenged the Ptolemaic geocentric theory, which fundamentally revolutionized the entire science of cosmology. The following are few among the many verses of the Holy Qur'an that vouchsafe the findings of the Muslim astronomers:

"He coils the night upon the day and he coils the day upon the night" (Qur'an 39:5).

The word "coil" refers to coiling of the turban around the head. Naturally if anything is round, only then one can coil it. Therefore, from this verse we may rightly infer that if the earth is spherical and not flat, then only night coils upon the day and vice versa. In yet another verse the word "merges" has been used to hint that the earth is round:

"Have you not seen how God merges the night into the day and merges the day into the night?" (31:29).

If you roll a ball in a dark room and flash a light on it, you will see that half of the ball is lit up and the half of it is black. When you rotate the ball slowly, you will notice the flash of light is merging into the dark portions of the ball with the other side of the ball, making it bright, while the lit-up portion is becoming black. Thus, both verses of the Qur'an inform us that the earth is not flat but spherical. Just imagine if the earth was flat. The light of the sun would not "merge" but would have escaped the boundaries of the earth; and since Qur'an uses the word "merges," we can surely deduce that the earth should be round. Of course, it is round. Rather, it is spherical.

Copernicus, strictly adopting the Muslim astronomers' findings, declared that neither the earth was flat nor the sun nor planets are orbiting around the earth; but instead, Earth has a spherical shape, and it, along with other planets of the solar system, are orbiting around the sun. Contemporarily at the same time, coincidentally, another astronomer Galileo was constructing his own biggest telescope, hitherto was not built anywhere in the world, and with its help he observed the universe in the light of this new theory and confirmed the challenging truth as described by Copernicus.

Moreover, in the following verses Allah mentions the balance upon which the universe is functioning:

"He is mighty, the most forgiving, Who has created the seven heavens in an orderliness, one above the other. Thou canst discover a flaw in the creation of the gracious one. Then look again: seest thou any disparity? Look again and again, thy sight will return to thee frustrated and fatigued" (67:3,4).

"It is Allah who maintains harmony between different parts of the universe and thus safeguards it against ruin. Allah holds the heaven and earth, lest they should deviate from their places. Were they to deviate, none could keep them from destruction thereafter except me. Surely, he is forbearing, most forgiving" (35:41).

"Allah has established a balance [of force] which must be respected so that it may continue to yield the beneficence which it is designed to generate. Allah it is who has sent down the book with truth and also the balance [balancing forces]" (42:17).

"He has raised the heaven high and set up the measure, that you may not transgress the measure" (55:7-8).

In the last verse the word "measure" is used to refer to the gravitational force of the earth. As stated by Allah, it cannot be transgressed, but it can be transgressed with power alone (atomic), which helps man to penetrate the regions of the space. This has been discussed in early paragraphs while elaborating the verse

(55:33) in our introduction part 1: "Ye assembly of Jin and men, if you can penetrate into the regions of the heaven and earth, then penetrate; surely you may not penetrate without the power" (55:33).

(Note: Refer to the introduction chapter for more details.)

As for penetrating into the regions of the heavens, scientists have built that energy with the help of the Einstein theory. The atomic power helps us to penetrate the far regions of the universe by rockets, and every now and then we are able to explore those regions through satellites, which are zooming around the earth and reaching beyond billions of miles from the earth encircling Saturn and Neptune, even reaching into the vicinity of the planet Pluto, the farthest planet of the solar system some four billion miles away.

The recent experiment of going deep into the regions of the earth by hundreds of scientists of the world is being conducted at the border of Switzerland and France. It is known as CERN. They have constructed a long tunnel deep into the earth and experimented to pass in the tunnel the atomic particles neutron and antiparticle electrons, which they say may collide into each other and may create something like the primordial atmosphere that was created by the so-called big bang. This experiment has created an apprehension in the public mind that this device should not pave the way for destruction of the world culminating into doomsday. But we have firm faith that unless and until the signs emerge, as mentioned by our Holy Prophet, there would be no doomsday.

Some of these signs are that Jesus Christ would appear and kill Dajjal, the anti-Christ, and Gog and Magog would come. However, the experiment of going deep into the regions of the earth confirms the prophecy of the Qur'an that one day man would explore into the regions of the earth with the help of the power

(atomic power). Apart from this, today we extract oil, natural gas, and many minerals from the strata of the earth by penetrating into the thousands of feet below the surface of the earth. Do they not vouchsafe what Qur'an emphasized fourteen hundred years ago?

In one of the verses (42:17 above), a reference to balance has been given, stating that "it must be respected." What does this mean? It's the balance created by the Almighty to be kept intact so that natural phenomena should hold a firm shape; otherwise, the equilibrium may be lost, and untold miseries to the human beings may result. Just take the question of ozone depletion, which we have discussed in the above paragraphs. If we do not adhere to the laws of nature and check the CFC level immediately, the melting of the glaciers and snows of the Arctic and Antarctic zones on a larger scale shall cause inundation of the low level areas of the earth. One more point must be kept in mind that unscrupulous deforestation is going on in the developed and now-developing countries on account of which the ecology is being badly affected. Furthermore, this deforestation is minutely changing the rain patterns. We have noticed that heavily forested areas are prone to have heavy rains, but on account of unchecked deforestation, percentage of rain has dropped to a large extent. Likewise, there are many measures for which the Almighty already hinted warnings in many verses of the Holy Qur'an. Man is asked, in many of these verses, not to disturb the natural laws relating to the phenomena for man's own material benefit. Allah has also asked mankind to "respect the laws of the nature and maintain the balance what the Almighty has maintained since inception of the universe" (67:3,4). This verse refers to the creation of seven heavens and looks like a puzzle, which I would like to discuss in the following paragraphs.

Seven Skies Are Seven Stages of the Atmosphere

When we look up into the atmosphere, we see at the last stretch of blue horizon is filled with gases, vapors, and aerosol particles surrounding the earth and reaching up to the final limit of the horizon. The composition of the atmosphere and most of its physical properties vary with altitude; certain key physical properties divide the atmosphere into seven stages, which are actually the spheres of atmosphere not related to the seven heavens mentioned in the Qur'an:

1. **Troposphere:** This is the first stage. It has 75 percent mass of the atmosphere containing 90 percent of water vapors and aerosols, which help in the generation of weather changes and where temperature falls in degrees as the altitude increases. This zone comprises about six to twelve miles above the sea level. The winds pick up water vapors from the oceans and clouds, and raining starts. Air currents move up and down while winds blow north, south, carrying warm and cold air to east and west.

2. **Tropopause:** This is the second sky or second zone where temperature stops changing as one climbs up and up. This portion of atmosphere lies in between the troposphere and stratosphere. In this zone winds reach with their greatest force and get the name "jet streams." These streams pick up a speed of more than two hundred miles per hour, and the temperature falls more in this zone.

3. **Stratosphere:** Its limit is up to thirty miles above sea level, which contains ozone layers that filter out the sun's ultraviolet rays. Without its existence life would be impossible. This is also called the greenhouse atmosphere where temperature increases on account of the ozone layers. In this zone most of the sun's ultraviolet rays are absorbed, making life on earth sustainable. Once the rays enter the stratosphere zone, they are transmitted to other gases. But the stratosphere is constantly threatened by certain chemical-based pollutants like the chlorofluorocarbons (CFCs) that are destructive to the environment. In fact,

a hole has been detected, in 1980, in this zone, which is causing ozone depletion. This matter is discussed in detail further below. This zone is very stable having no upward or downward movements of air, which is very dry.

4. **Mesosphere:** It reaches up to fifty miles above sea level. Here air becomes thinner than the abovementioned zones. On the top of this zone temperature may become lower than minus 103 degrees Fahrenheit.

5. **Thermosphere:** It starts from fifty miles to 310 miles above the sea level, where temperature falls to freezing level. Atoms and molecules of gas are bombarded by radiation from the sun. They are broken into smaller electrically charged particles called ions; thus, it is also called ionosphere. Ionosphere contains various layers of charged particles (ions) of immense importance in the propagation of radio waves used to reflect signals, transmitting to distant ground stations. This is the most important zone, which is ordinarily impossible to penetrate beyond fifty miles on account of earth's gravitation force. This fact is also revealed in the Qur'an. Allah (swt) says, "If you can penetrate into the region of the heavens and the earth, then penetrate, you may not penetrate without the power" (55:33). This region is penetrated by the rockets every now and then with the help of atomic power. It is estimated that if a rocket with a speed of seventeen thousand miles per hour is fired, it could penetrate this zone; otherwise, it will burn out in the atmosphere. Many important changes take place in this zone. The spaceships orbit around the earth in this zone; the meteors emerge and bombard the earth in this zone. This zone also generates the aurora borealis, peculiar lights on the northern polar area of the Arctic zone, seen by people living in Canada and Alaska. Like them at the Antarctic zone, the aurora Australians are seen by the people living in Australia. These are the lights caused by the collision of air molecules in the upper atmosphere. This zone also cause hail storms.

6. **Exosphere:** Over and above 310 miles above sea level, exosphere begins to comprise with rarified helium and hydrogen gases. Here the Hubble Space Telescope circles the space at the height of 612 miles above sea level, transmitting millions of photos of the space and celestial bodies of the universe. The atmosphere becomes very thin here on account of which atoms and molecules swim, and they escape the earth's gravitation so rapidly that they become part of the gases in the space.

7. **The last zone** or the seventh stage has interplanetary medium and reaches beyond to an infinite vastness even beyond man's comprehension. This outermost layer of the atmosphere continues out into space and eventually merges into the sun's atmosphere, making the air extra thin.

These zones and atmospheres create our vast solar system. The remotest planet Pluto is four billion miles away from the sun, and we are 9.30 million miles away from the sun. Out of two billion galaxies, scientists have so far investigated about eighty-eight, and it is an undeniable fact that the universe is still expanding. Allah says about the expanding universe: "The heaven we have built it with power, verily we are expanding it" (51:47).

The supreme Council of Islamic Affairs confirms expansion of universe in the *Muntakhab* by saying, "In the expansion of the universe, there should be no ambiguity."

These seven stages or seven zones have been carefully examined by the astrophysicists and cosmologists and found to be accurate and correct. There should remain no ambiguity that the universe is expanding to an infinite vastness, which is not comprehensible even by the scientists. Once again Allah reminds us about the limits of human mind by saying, "We have created above you seven paths. We have never been unmindful of the creation" (23:17). Under the assumption by the Holy Qur'an, there are many heavens as well as earths, like ours. But these multiple dimensions in which these earths and heavens exist have not been verified by scientists—yet. The Qur'an refers to the figure 7 as an infinite number of plurality. The scientists have yet to determine the actual numbers of the heaven and of the earth.

Motions are Elliptical, Not Circular

The Danish astronomer Tycho Brahe (1546-1601) and the German astronomer Kepler (1571-1630) worked together and observed that the motions of the planets are not exactly circular but they are elliptical. Kepler's laws of motion (being deeply inspired by the heliocentric theory of the Muslim astronomers) brought a new dimension in the study of the cosmology, which were picked up by an English scientist Robert Hooke (1635-1703), and he devised a new idea in terms of his laws of attraction, which states that an inverse square law operates upon all orbiting bodies of the universe, on account of which attraction decreases with the increase in distance.

Newton Adopts Musa Ibn Shakir's Law of Gravitation

Well, before the challenging theory of Copernicus, Galileo's laws of acceleration, Kepler's laws of motion, and Hooke's laws of attraction, a Muslim astronomer Mosa Ibn Shakir

(803-873) declared that heavenly bodies have force of attraction. From his calculations he propounded the theory of abstract motion, which causes the force of attraction among the celestial bodies of the universe. Ibn Shaker's theory then became the basic material for the British mathematician and physicist Sir Isaac Newton (1642-1726). The theory of abstract motion prompted Newton to derive a more accurate theory to describe the movements of the planets around the sun. The orderliness of the universe was another thought-provoking reality that tempted many minds to explore the real cause of this orderly movement. Newton was a mathematician and therefore knew that any theory, unless mathematically proved, does not appeal to the scientists. He, therefore, labored much in devising calculation methods to measure the movements of the planets arithmetically; and after being convinced with this method, he named it calculus, a new branch of mathematics. It helped him to measure the gravitational force arithmetically.

Another English astronomer Edmund Halley (1656-1742) came to his help in the voluminous task of calculations. Halley published his valuable *Principia* in 1687, which described that the intensity of the gravitational force produced by any object is proportional to its mass. Therefore, the greater the force to produce a certain change in the motion, the greater the mass of the body to which the force is applied. He declared that all the larger and smaller bodies of the universe are interlinked with each other on account of this gravitational force and due to which there exists an acute orderliness and harmony in all the galaxies, stars, planets, and comets. His theory not only describes motion of the planets orbiting around sun but also motions of the satellites of the planets.

"And the skies he has raised high; and he has set up the balance of justice" (55:7).

It is a part of the balance that an alternation is maintained between the day and night, which makes human life possible on earth, and these are the signs for understanding.

The modern rocket science has used this theory to create satellites that are constantly orbiting around the earth, covering far regions and are simultaneously recording the data used by the scientists for their research of the heavenly bodies. Thus, Newton's theory has been accepted by one and all as a dynamic and most scientific theory serving the field of cosmology.

Halley's Comet

In 1683, when Halley was of the age of twenty-seven, he had the opportunity to witness a brilliant comet with a big tail of fire behind it covering almost half of the horizon. Like others, according to the notions in vogue, he also became frightened by this comet. He was an astronomer coupled with the knowledge of a unique method of calculations given to him by his friend Newton. After witnessing the comet, he worked out calculations on the basis of the systematic record of this comet as back as 1057 BC. He verified that the same comet was regularly sighted by the world first in 1057 BC then in 240 BC, 12 BC, AD 64, AD 218, AD 455, AD 530, AD 837, and during his own life in AD 1683. Halley was fascinated by the systematic sightings of this comet. On the basis of the calculations, based on the Newtonian theory, he declared that this comet orbits around the sun in every seventy-five to seventy-six years. He further declared that, if Newton's theory was correct, this comet would again be witnessed by the world in the year AD 1758. His prediction came true, and amazingly the world witnessed the comet in AD 1758; but unfortunately he himself was not there as he died in 1742. However, he was honored by the scientist of the world who named the comet Halley's comet. This comet was seen twice in the previous century in 1910 and in 1985.

The author had the privilege to witness its grandeur on the Eastern Hemisphere illuminating the entire horizon before the sunrise. It was a spellbinding scenario, rare to witness in one's lifetime. It had illuminated the entire Eastern Hemisphere by an unimaginable brilliance. This gigantic comet had a long stretched fiery tail, which was first witnessed by us on October 16, 1985, and was continuously to be glimpsed throughout July 1986 for a long spell of nine months altogether. Although the witnessing of the comet was a natural phenomenon, viewers like me were able to enjoy it only because of Halley's theory (based on Newton's calculations), which had predicted that the comet would be seen every seventy-five to seventy-six years. Most astonishingly the world may witness it again in the year 2060 or 61; sorry, I may not be there to witness it twice in my lifespan. This perfection in calculation of the periodic appearances of the Halley's comet further testifies the perfect mechanism created by the supernatural power who controls it with utmost stewardship, and indeed we see no rift in it. The strength of the harmony, the comprehensiveness of the measured balance, and the perfection in the orderliness in the laws of the universe are marvelously depicted in the systematic and periodic appearance of this comet.

Further Test of This Theory

A noted astronomer Liverier while observing Uranus found out some unusual perturbations in the orbits of that planet. In the light of the Newton's theory, he formed opinion that these perturbations must be on account of a larger body in the atmosphere of the Uranus, and he became confident that he would witness a new planet. Another astronomer J. G. Galley caught his idea and started observing the Uranus regularly, and finally in 1846 he witnessed a large body near to Uranus. That was really a new planet hitherto unknown and was named Neptune. Thus, through his calculations of the celestial bodies and their movements around the universe, Newton established his supremacy in the field of physics. The implications of this theory were vast, and the twentieth century was witnessing amazing results through the spaceships by following the same theory.

Nuclear Force–atom Theory

The universe is full of matter. Matter consists of tiny particles that collide with each other on account of the inherent inertia hidden in them. Mass is the quantity of matter that measures inertia, as well as the gravitational attraction exerted on other particles. This tiny particle is called atom, which is so small and firm that Democritus (460-370 BC), a Greek scientist, invented the theory of atom (Greek word "a-tom" means "not divisible"), which tells that the atom is not divisible. Another Greek scientist Leucippus also supported this view. They both suggested that all the matter of the universe is filled with atoms, which are so minute that they could not be destructed and that these atoms are homogenous in substance but varying in shape.

Atoms are the basic building blocks of our world. These tiny particles make up every type of matter in the universe—solid, liquid, or gas. Matter is defined by anything that takes up space and has weight. A group of atoms that are bound together tightly is called a molecule. When atoms of the same kind combine with one another, they form the molecules of a chemical element. When different types of atoms combine them, they form molecules of a chemical compound, a substance made up of two or more elements in which the elements are always combined in exact same proportion. For example, water is a chemical compound made up of one atom of oxygen and two atoms of hydrogen (H_2O). Likewise, most of the objects we encounter in everyday life are nothing but made up of such combinations of different atoms mostly.

Atom Smashed

Twentieth century was successful in smashing the atom into subparticles known as protons, electrons, photons, and neutrons. Now an atom is defined as a tiny building block of nature. Atom is extraordinarily small and cannot be seen by a naked eye. But thanks to the American scientists who have invented a microscope that magnifies atom one hundred million times and the pictures taken out so far show the manner in which the atoms involve themselves in an inherent motion. A single drop of water contains as many as six trillion atoms (six followed by twenty-one zeroes). Through this it came to light that an atom consists an inner core called nucleus surrounded by electrons, which keep them rotating ceaselessly around their nucleus like the planets around the sun in solar system. What makes them rotate, attract, repel, push, and pull? Clearly this is a miracle given by the Creator of these atoms to them that they have the inherent capability to move in such a manner that brings motion to mass. The movement of atomic particles is a consequence of three other forces that operate on atom, namely, the nuclear strong, the nuclear weak, and the electromagnetic force. The last three forces exist in the nucleus of each and every atom. They act and interact with each other and cause formation of tiny particles of molecules, which make up the structure of universe.

Protons, Electrons, and Neutrons Discovered

A British physicist of New Zealand Ernest Rutherford (1871-1937) smashed atom and discovered protons, a positively electrically charged particle. According to him protons are massive particles of a molecule, which vary from one kind of atom to another. Yet another British scientist James Chadwick (1891-1974) discovered neutrons in 1932, which are negatively charged subparticles of atom. While James Thomas (1856-1940) discovered electrons, which carry negative electric charge. There are some subparticles called electrons, having negative electric charge, while protons having positive charge, and the neutrons having neutral charge. Thus, we get two basic groups of particles within an atom; one is called particles, and the other is known as antiparticles. Once again the nature's fundamental law of duality prevails and about which Allah has already mentioned in the following verse:

> Glory be to him who has created *all the pairs* of that what the earth produces
> as well as in their own (human) kind (male and female) and that which they
> know not. (36:36)

While the particles shape matter of the universe, antiparticles make up antimatter of the universe. The nuclear force is the strongest among all forces, which keeps protons and electrons intact in a nucleus. The electromagnetic force holds protons together. But the nature of this force is culminated in either attraction or repulsion. Where two particles have opposite charge, this force helps them to attract; and where they have similar charge, it repulses. Protons always carry a positive charge, and there will always be repulsion among them. As the presence of the protons increases, so do the effects on the repulsion force. Thus, protons always respond to both nuclear and electromagnetic charges. This is not the case with neutrons. The neutrons are electrically uncharged; hence, they respond only to the nuclear force, which is the strongest of all the four forces. However, there are weak particles in the universe, which are weaker than the neutrons, and they only respond to weak forces with some exceptions. These weak particles are called leptons. However, some of these leptons are electrically charged; hence, they respond to electromagnetic force as well as to the weak force.

Recently Discovered Fifth Force!

Till the end of 1985, it was a firm belief of almost all scientists and physicists that there were only four dominant forces, discussed in supra, which cause to remain cohesive, comprehensive, and compressed. But recently, as back as January 6, 1986, it was published in the newspapers that there exists one more force named as "hypercharge." It was claimed to have been discovered by an eminent physicist Dr. Ephraim Fishcake, professor of physics in Purdue University, Indiana, USA. It is said that during a study made by a team of scientists, this new force was discovered. This discovery challenges not only Galileo's laws of Acceleration but also Einstein's theory of relativity. According to general opinion, if that force really exists, it may be like the electromagnetic force that may be working against gravitation, which may also affect the rate of acceleration. Newton mostly relied on Galileo's laws of acceleration while Einstein reinforced his opinion on the basis of Hungarian experiment, and both assumed that all falling bodies in a uniform gravitational field have same rate of acceleration as told by Galileo. This was the basic tool of modern cosmology. Now that a fifth force has been discovered, further experiments and investigations may be necessary before accepting or rejecting it; and amendment in the science of cosmology may have to be made accordingly, of course, if necessary.

Einstein's Theory of Relativity

Albert Einstein (1879-1955) gave us a universal and dynamic theory that brought new dimensions to nuclear science and technology of the modern world. Not only did the theory help us understand universe as a whole, but it also gave a new meaning to the concepts of matter and energy, which became a source for producing the first atom bomb. However, the theory came with a baggage of the powerful bombs that were created, which were later on used in WWII. The first one was dropped on August 6, 1945, on Hiroshima, and the second one was dropped on August 8, the same year, on Nagasaki. The result of these bombings was so unimaginably catastrophic and devastating to the Japanese that the country surrendered unconditionally to the Allied Forces and brought the six-year-long horrible war to an end. Thereby, "peace" had prevailed in the war-torn world. The atomic bomb introduced a new strategy of combat, which completely changed the meaning and the dimension of war. The bomb, with the help of new technology, gave birth to the two superpowers of 1960s, the United States and the USSR, which capitalized their energies mostly upon the nuclear arsenal. This was an unfortunate aspect of this theory, but the theory also had a beneficial aspect. Einstein's theory had led to the generation of nuclear energy. Through the discovery of nuclear energy, scientists were able to get the space shuttles to orbit around the earth for further exploration of the universe. I shall discuss in detail the broad features of this theory in the subsequent paragraphs.

James Jean has rightly said that present-day science is mostly based on brain, which uses mathematical calculations. Indeed, such a mathematical genius was born in Germany in the year 1879, having attended schools in Germany and Italy. He graduated in engineering at Zurich University in 1901 and started working for a Swiss patent office in Bern. He was such a genius that while working in an insignificant office, he kept himself busy with minute calculations that searched the mathematical applicability in understanding the physical aspects of the universe as a whole. Thus, Einstein was devising new methods to study the universe with a new and different angle.

Euclid, 300 BC, an Alexandrian mathematician, discovered geometry and through it described universe to have three dimensions. His book *Elements of Axioms*, is still regarded as a final authority on geometry, except his fifth axiom. However, his fifth axiom could not be proved, so far, which states that from any point *A*, there passes on a line parallel only to point *L*. It was first challenged by Gauss (1777-1855), followed by Bolyai (1775-1856), Lobachevski (1793-1856), and lastly by Riemann (1826-1866). All of them contradicted the Euclidean parallel axiom by a hypothesis that stated that no line can pass through *A* parallel to *L*. This hypothesis became the basis of neo-Euclidean geometry, which attracted Einstein. Thus, Einstein's search for a clue to contradict three-dimensional theory of the universe had begun.

In order to prove his theory, along with Gauss, Bolyai, Lobachevski, and Riemann, Einstein also studied Ernest Mach, a nineteenth-century physicist. Mach had declared that distant matter has a profound effect on the condition of the earth and that mass of a body was generated by the effect of another matter of the universe. Many scientists did not take any notice on this point, but this short-sighted genius Einstein grasped this idea for his benefit. Before Einstein, Copernicus, Galileo, Descartes, Newton, Faraday, Maxwell, and many more astrophysicists had vigorously tried to solve the puzzle of the universe but had failed to achieve. This amazing genius Einstein followed them in letter and spirit. He observed universe in a broad sense and with convincing mathematical accuracy declared that there are four dimensions of the space instead of three. Einstein challenged the notion of space and time as being absolute; instead he argued that time and space are interrelated in this four-dimensional world and that space itself is curved. Consequently, planets have their curved paths near the sun. He proclaimed that mass, gravitation, and space time are interrelated and interdependent. He described, philosophically, that matter guides space time how to curve, and curved space-time directs matter how to behave. Einstein also challenged the positivism of the nineteenth century as propagated by the Vienna school of thought, through which Niels Bohr (1885-1962) advocated the behavior of quanta as being unpredictable. Nineteenth-century scientists had broadly accepted the principle of causation and thereby advocated the idea that **"in this universe of cause and effect, there remains no need of God at all." Einstein vigorously condemned this ideology and declared that he believed in God.**

The nineteenth century had propagated the static theory of the universe, which states that since there is no beginning to the universe, there is no end to it. Einstein was against this theory and advocated the expanding theory of the Universe, about which Qur'an says, "The heaven we have built it with power. Verily we are expanding it" (51:47).

Moreover, Einstein declared that the apparent uncertain behavior of the quanta possesses a comprehensible order, which he said is the real **mystery of the universe**. He saw an accurate, meaningful, and comprehensible orderliness in the universe. Thus, he thought "there lies the truth in the marvelous harmony between mind and orderly matter of universe." On that assumption, he declared that **"behind the causation of this gigantic, vast, and infinite universe and its high degree of orderliness, someone is there to program this universe. He asserted that without a program this universe could not exist.** Therefore, on this assumption, **he denied the chance theory of the universe propagated by Darwinians**. He differed from Newton as well. Einstein proved that **gravity is not a force but the effect of curving of space-time universe**. He informed the **scientists** that in the neighborhood of every concentration of matter, the universe is curved, and the planets therefore tend to curve their path near the sun.

New Concept of Universe

Einstein published his thesis in 1905 with a new approach in formulating the concept of electricity and magnetism with different angles that do not depend on the position and speed of the observers. During the course of this study, he was illuminated by the understanding that a new approach has to be made while observing universe. He believed that time and space are not independent of each other but are actually interrelated. He demonstrated that matter and energy are one and the same and not different. Since they are interrelated, they have the inherent capacity of interconvertibility. Thus, he declared that this is the real riddle of the universe that **on account of this interconvertibility of matter-energy, there remains the harmony and comprehensibility in the universe.** And Qur'an has a similar statement in the following verse:

> It is Allah who maintains harmony between different parts of the universe and thus safeguards it against ruin. Allah holds the heaven and earth, lest they should deviate from their places. Were they to deviate, none could keep them from destruction thereafter except Him. Surely, he is forbearing, most forgiving. (35:41)

In that sense, the approach of Einstein for understanding the universe was quite different from other scientists. He observed universe philosophically and concluded his observations logically with a unique sense of reality. Then he amended his theory in 1917, which caused a sensation among the scientists. A wide range of experimentations and observations began based on his ingenious equation theory, which provided the scientists with the ability to develop nuclear energy. Einstein proved what he understood in mathematical terms. He demonstrated his theories in geometrical and spherical figures and explained the curvature of the universe and planets.

Matter-Energy Equivalence Theory

Inertia, hidden inherently in mass, is the culmination of the abovementioned force of the universe, which generates energy. In this theory, Einstein describes that energy of the mass is equal to mass multiplied by the square of velocity of light, where velocity of light is 186,342 miles per second. His theory summarizes to e=mc2" where *e* is energy, *m* is mass, and *c* is velocity of light, being 186,342 miles per second. To understand it, we may say energy that is possessed by mass is equaled to mass multiplied by the square of velocity of light. Thus, every unit of mass that inherently possesses vast amount of energy (matter) can be converted into energy and vice versa.

According to this theory, everything in the universe is time-space related and nothing is absolute in its entirety. The equivalence of mass and energy mathematically testifies that there exists a vast amount of energy for every unit of mass. We may say that higher volume of mass may be obtained by increasing energy. He asserts that inertia is hidden in matter for all times and that time-space relativity determines mass energy interconversion. Based on this theory, modern technology has invented methods that convert matter into energy and energy is converted into matter. Thus, Einstein illustrated that the construction-destruction cycle is an ongoing process in the universe, and he adopted the same method of destruction-construction in order to obtain energy and/or matter.

Something behind the Veil

According to Einstein "matter is another form of energy" where mass-energy is convertible in this four dimensional space-time-curved universe. This inherited capacity of mass converts itself in to energy and vice versa. This mass-energy conversion causes the universe to shape itself in different forms. The abovementioned basic laws operate on every nook and corner of the space. At every stage of evolution, a new entity emerges in the shape of a unity, which gradually diminishes into diversity. From this we may infer that there is something that is eternal and under the guise of evolution wishes to remain eternal.

Evolution is the only method through which this eternal can preserve its entity. Thus, Qur'an describes the beginning of the universe:

> Have not those who disbelieve known that the heaven and earth were joined together as one united piece, before we clove them asunder. We made from water every living thing. Will they not believe? (21:30)

Scientists agree that universe is expanding. Qur'an says, "With power and skill did we construct heavens and have spread the earth as a bed and how excellently do We spread [expand]" (51:47,48).

In conclusion, Einstein's theory of relativity indirectly states that before its evolution, the universe was one single unit in the remote past. This unity then diversified, and in future the diversity may evolve into unity again, thus, coming to a complete circle. The result of Einstein's theory then is unity of everything to make nothing, and the diversity of nothing is again everything. According to the consensus of the scientists, this "something" is eternal, whose unity causes diversity of matter. The diversity of matter further resulted in unity of life, which evolved into mind. The continuous progress of mind is then manifested in the consciousness of man, which reminds us that the secret of eternity is in the continuous evolution of man.

Curved Universe and Eclipses

The relativity theory explains how the effect of acceleration and gravitation causes the space to curve. This arch in the space does not allow light to travel straight at a certain moment when there is a total solar eclipse. Einstein compellingly advised, "Let us reconsider the evidence on which our supposed knowledge of the ways of the universe specially the Newtonian laws of gravity are based." He clarified that the geometrical properties of space-time are not dependent, but they are determined by matter, where space-time directs the matter to behave. He further elucidated that gravity is not a force by itself, but it is the result of curving of space-time. He showed that, "the stronger the gravitational field, the more distinguishable is the curvature of space-time." In his general theory, he made many predictions that were confirmed through observations by other scientists within a few years. This brought fame to Einstein, and he earned the title as the genius scientist of the century. One of his predictions was witnessed in 1919 when there was a total solar eclipse. Astronomers Eddington and Cottingham went to Principi, an island in the Gulf of Guinea, while Davidson and Cormmeline went to Sobral in Brazil, the two places where total Solar Eclipse was to be witnessed. Results of their observations proved Einstein's theory to be perfect and correct in all respects than the Newtonian theory. When these observations were announced in a meeting of the Royal Society of London, the Chairman of the Society said that these observations had caused considerable sensation and he further states that, "The whole atmosphere of tense interest was exactly like a Greek Drama, we were the chorus commenting on the decree of destiny as disclosed in the development of a supreme incident. There was in the background the picture of Newton to remind us that the greatest of scientific generations was now after more than two centuries to receive its first modification."

Benefits of Relativity Theory

As a result of the relativity theory today we have the nuclear reactors that generate energy in almost all parts of the modern world, as well as the spaceships and the rockets that are continuously zooming over the skies. The amazing electronic eye is circling through endless space and has successfully tracked the so-far-unseen celestial bodies like quasars and pulsars. Brainwaves are now visible and audible, and the voices are carried around the world. Furthermore, electric tubes are transmitting pictures on the television screens. The laser beams are performing unimaginable functions, and computers are busy in mathematical calculations within fractions of a second, which the human brain, with some rare exceptions, could not do in hours. These and many others are the gifts of the modern technology developed by the atomic physics based on the theories proclaimed by many scientists and astrophysicists during the very recent twentieth century. Among all these theories, the miraculous equation ($e=mc^2$) suggested by Einstein has played a major role in the progress of present-day science. The modern world will be forever indebted to Einstein and will always be proud of him. On the other hand, the theory's dark side comes in the form of its destructive and annihilative force as demonstrated by the atomic bombs that were dropped on Hiroshima and Nagasaki on August 6 and 8 of 1945, respectively. World has witnessed the unforgettable misery of humankind in a palpable moment of a few seconds that caused hundreds and thousands of casualties along with the entire destruction of the material fanfare. Unfortunately the effects of that bombing can be felt even today by the unfortunate inhabitants of those islands.

Fundamental Elements of the Universe

From time immemorial common belief about universe was that it consisted of four basic elements: earth, fire, air, and water. These elements form the basis for the origin of life on this globe. As against this belief, the Greek physicist Descartes (460-370 BC) had declared that the universe is full of atoms, which are so minute and small that they cannot be further disintegrated. John Dalton (1903) propounded the first atomic theory. According to him, the earth and the planets are moving in the universe through the medium of Ether, which has a whirling force. Quite contrary to the indestructible atom theory, even before the Christian era, the Muslim alchemists of Alexandria (Egypt) advocated the transmutation or transformation theory of the base metal into gold through a medium of touch stone or philosopher's stone and commonly known the so-called Parus in India. They named this branch of science as "al-cheemia" (al-keemia) in which chemical formulas were devised for such transmutation of the base metal into gold. Al-Razi was the staunch supporter of this science, which later on was known as alchemy, which became known as chemistry in the English language. He wrote many books on this subject, which were translated into Latin and English. Whether the alchemists could be successful in their dreams of transmutation of base metal into gold or not, their dream of transmutation did come true during the twentieth century.

Atomic Era

The period of ten years from 1896 to 1905, the closing and beginning of the twentieth century, brought fundamental changes in the concept of the universe and revolutionized an entire generation of thinking minds. Atom was defined as indestructible by Greek physicist Descartes in fourth century BC. (The Greek word "a" means "un" or "non"; "tom" means "destructible," i.e., "nondestructible"). But the year 1897 changed that concept since in that year Joseph John Thompson (1856-1940) of the Cambridge University, London, had been able to disintegrate the atom. The very next year, in 1898, Marie Curie (1867-1934) discovered radioactive elements, podium and radium, by isolating pure metal from the mineral pitchblende. While so, Albert Einstein (1879-1955) offered his relativity theory, declaring that matter is really another form of energy, where mass energy is interconvertible.

With these fundamental changes in the scientists' outlook and in a revolutionized scenario, under the influence of radioactive and relativity theories, the scientists engineered their activities for new experiments. In Canada, professors Soddy and Rutherford (1871-1937) of the McGill University bombarded nitrogen gas with alpha particles and observed that protons were moving away from nitrogen. Thus, they became successful in disintegrating oxygen and hydrogen in 1919. In 1931, Ernest O. Laurence (1901-) of the California University materialized the alchemists' dream of the transmutation of the elements by inventing cyclotron, the most powerful machine for smashing the atom. After smashing it, he obtained certain new elements of artificial radioactivity. He also became successful in inventing elements like radio phosphorus, radio sodium, and radio iron. The very next year, in 1932, James Chadwick (1891-1974) bombarded the atom of beryllium and discovered a subatomic particle called neutron, an electrically uncharged particle. Before this in the year 1897, Thompson had been successful in obtaining another subatomic particle called electron.

Thus, atom was no more indivisible! The old concept that earth, fire, air and water are the basic elements of life was emphatically denied. Moreover, we now know that there are fourteen elements that form the complex mixtures of protoplasm to generate life.

Atoms Became the Foundation Stones of the Universe (Fundamental Basics of Universe)

According to James Clark Maxwell (1831-1876), atoms are the foundation stones of the universe. They are constantly vibrating in nature and are dynamic. Atoms are the smallest possible particles of matter composed of subatomic particles known as protons, neutrons, electrons, positrons, photons, leptons, and many other antiparticles. Basically some of them form the basic elements of matter, and the others form the antimatter of the universe. A prominent physicist, Nobel Prize winner Erwin Schrödinger (1887-1961), declared in 1933 that electrons behave like "wave patterns," lapping around the buoy (nucleus). According to him, the complex nature of these wave patterns determines the configuration and properties of the atom. He says that in each atom, electrons have inherited the ability to change the patterns and thus emit frequencies that are specific to a particular atom. Meanwhile, Niels Bohr (1885-1962) of the Copenhagen School propounded the quantum theory, through which he described these frequencies as the bursts of energy that form a distinctive feature of the atom.

Number of Protons that Determine Quality of the Element

Precisely, we may say that the elements, which are composed of atoms, are mainly distinguished by the number of protons they carry. The proportion of the subatomic particles determines the wave patterns of the electrons, which form into an orderly structure. This structure contains the chemical and physical properties of any given element. It is fact that in any given element the electrons always equal the number of protons. However, the number of neutrons can differ, and if this happens, then we get different forms of the same atom called isotopes. Radioactive elements that are found in nature are generally the mixtures of different isotopes. One hundred and six elements have been so far discovered by the scientists; out of them eighty-eight occur in nature, and the rest are prepared by bombardment of suitable chosen lighter isotopes, which are mostly radioactive. On account of these properties, the elements are classified as metals, metalloids, and nonmetals. All these elements come from the bursting of stars, which store in them the different combinations of hydrogen formed by complex sequences of nuclear reactions. Thus, hydrogen is the basic element for all the 106 elements.

Hydrogen Atoms Are Ancestors of All

According to William Proust, a distinguished chemist, atoms of all elements found on earth have a common composition representing various degrees of concentration of hydrogen atoms. From the isotopes discovered in 1919, it was established that each hydrogen atom consists of two fundamental particles: protons and electrons. It can be said that nuclei of various so-far-discovered one hundred and six elements are nothing but a combination of various numbers of elementary hydrogen nuclei. Therefore, we can say for certain that all one hundred and six elements had been actually built up during the big bang period of formation of the stars. These elements came from the mixing of hydrogen atoms by complex sequences of nuclear reaction, which is known as carbon cycle.

The Carbon Cycle

Hydrogen and helium are the lightest elements of the universe. Gravitation helped them to escape from the surface of the earth to space. The rest of the elements, which are comparatively denser and heavier than the abovementioned two, remained in the lower levels of the earth's atmosphere and on the earth itself. The heavier elements—carbon, nitrogen, and oxygen—dominated the surface of the earth and its atmosphere. The interconvertibility of the elements generated the carbon cycle. Due to the formation of the carbon cycle, the process of oxidation began, which caused the earth's volcanic activity to melt iron and nickel ores. The melting then causes the compounds of iron and nickel to drift in the shape of molten masses producing the formation of the dense core of the earth. The Earth core further motivated volcanic activity, which in due course of time released vast amounts of water vapors, nitrogen, and carbon dioxide. These vapors filled in the cavities and low-leveled areas of Earth that later on formed the oceans, which constitute 71 pecent of the surface area of the globe. The volcanoes emitted gases, 10 percent of which constituted the formation of carbon dioxide. This carbon dioxide activated calcium silicates of the rocks and converted them into quartzite, which became, in due course of time, calcium carbonates in the shape of limestone, marbles, and silica. Thus, 98 percent of the available carbon dioxide was either consumed by Earth's crust or was dissolved in the waters of the oceans. The dissolution process in the waters resulted in creation of inorganic molecules; then with the passage of time and with continuous interconversion cycle, in billions of years they changed into organic elements. According to scientists, these organic molecules finally produced the living organism, making this planet the abode of life.

This carbon cycle played yet another significant role in making the atmospheric air breathable. On account of the chemical action and reaction, carbon dioxide was automatically controlled and checked by nature, causing oxygen to become the life-sustaining property. The presence of algae and other plants helped oxygen to be liberated into air. The plants consumed carbon dioxide for their growth and then converted it into free oxygen. At this stage the organic structures began to form. Further release of oxygen by the plant kingdom helped in maintaining water balance on the surface on one hand and, on the other hand, in creating layers of zones in the higher altitudes. The ozone layers protect the living organisms from the sun's dangerous ultraviolet rays and radiation by absorbing and eliminating the concentration of the dangerous radiation and thus help life to flourish without hindrance. Thus, the fundamental elements of nature are really the complex mixtures of various atoms of hydrogen, which formed not only the planet Earth but also the constituents of the universe.

What Is Evolution?

Evolution denotes gradual development, a progressive change. For example, a seed evolves into a plant, which further evolves into a tree that gives flowers and fruits and then weathers away. The fruits and flower of that tree then bear more seeds for future growth, and thus the cycle of life continues. This cyclical change in forms and shapes to continue the cycle of life is called evolution. Evolution is the ultimate principle of universe. The secret of universe is further complicated by the many dual forms found in nature. For example, the dual concepts of unity-diversity, dark-light, and construction-destruction are some of the many examples of dualism found in nature. Qur'an says, "See they not how Allah originates creation, then repeats it and who gives you sustenance from heaven and earth" (27:64).

Evolution encompasses the entire universe. The series of evolution in matter caused cosmic evolution, in the shape of galaxies, stars, planets, etc. The geological evolution of earth caused the evolution of inorganic into organic elements, and finally the finest of all creatures was created: the thinking man. With the emergence of man's mind evolved consciousness, which caused him to evolve from the member of a nomadic life to the citizen of a civil life. Dawn of civilization is yet another form of cultural evolution, which gave birth to society, science, and religion. Modern evolutionary stage of mankind is manifested in the present-day skyscrapers touching the heights of heavens, spacecrafts that are zooming into space, and many such amenities that are enjoyed by modern man.

FIRST PHASE OF EVOLUTION

Birth of the Universe

The very word "universe" symbolizes "a distinct comprehensive system" dealing with a set of arrangement of things that are related or connected to form a unity or "a set of acts, facts, principles, rules classified or arranged in a regular and orderly form to show a logical plan, linking various entities" (*Encyclopedia Britannica*).

The Greek philosophers saw universe as constantly growing and simultaneously unfolding itself into new forms. In the words of Von Humboldt (1769-1859), "Nature constitutes periodic occurrences of the progressive development of forms, phenomena, and events," while Aquinas (1225-1274) found "God, the logical uncaused cause, the prime Reason for order in the universe"; Einstein declared, "I believe in God who reveals himself in the orderly harmony of the universe. I believe that intelligence is manifested throughout all nature." Einstein further elaborates, **"The basis of scientific work is the conviction that the world is an ordered and comprehensive entity and not a thing of chance."**

"Do the disbelievers not see that the heavens and the earth were joined together? Then we clove them asunder and we got every living thing out of water. Will they not believe?" (21:30).

"Moreover Allah turned to the heavens when it was smoke and said to it and to the earth, come willingly or unwillingly! They said, 'We come in willing obedience'" (41:11).

"What! Are ye the harder to create or is it the heaven that Allah built? He raised the canopy and raised it with harmony. He made dark the night and brought out the forenoon. And after that he spread out the [earth]. There from he drew out its water and its pasture. And the mountains he has fixed them firmly. Goods for you and for your cattle" (79:27-33).

The first verse establishes that the earth and the heavens existed together as one unit in the remotest past, and when Allah intended to create Adam and send him as his vicegerent, he created the universe out from the smoke and then created the earth and heaven and other amenities. The last verse is self-explanatory as to how Allah has provided all earthly gifts to man in the shape of night and day, water and wind, mountains, and pastures and cattle. These are the means of sustenance and comfort for man. This all came into existence with Allah's intent to create, and for that, he asserted "be," and it came to being. Modern scientific data is compatible, and it is in no way against the assertion made by the Almighty in the holy Qur'an.

How Wonderful Is Our Universe

A very splendored thing and a spellbound scenario of the dawn and dusk, the fragrance of the ever-blooming flowers, the heart-touching enchantments of the multifarious birds, the sudden flouting clouds pouring alleviating showers, the morning somniferous winds, the snow-clad peaks of the mighty mountains, the ever-flowing waters of the raging rivers, the awesome ever-green valleys, the multitudinous of the fauna and flora; the vast and boundless bluish horizon, the scintillating rainbows, the magnanimity of the space and vastness of the skies, the ever-orbiting stars, the life-energizing radiant sun, our beautiful Earth and her sister planets ever roaming in the Milky Way, their satellite moons, and the ever-changing and untenacious seasons are some of the enamoring facts that we see, visualize, hear, and witness day in and day out during our tenure of life—the glory of the universe and of nature! Are they not wonderful and amazing? These are all the attributes of the Almighty manifested in different shapes in and around the universe, which attract the thinking mind to investigate further and further!

Behold the Glory during Night

"We have indeed illuminated the lower heaven with beauty of the stars" (37:6).

"Did you see how Allah has created seven heavens one above another and made the moon a light therein and made the sun a lamp" (18:12,13).

"Allah is the one, who made the sun a shine and the moon a light and for her ordained mansions, so that you might know the number of years and the reckoning of time. Allah created this all in truth. He explains the signs in detail for people who know" (10:5).

With this conception and background of the universe, if we look into the depths of the curved vastness of the skies in a moonless night, we are amazed with the grandeur of the constellation of the Southern Cross; the beauties of the Magellan clouds and the guiding stars in the constellation of the bear; the magnificent swarm of bright and twinkling stars in the Milky Way; the luminous constellation of the Sagittarius, that of the Orion, and of the Crab Nebula in the constellation of Tarsus, the fading away Andromeda near the Double Stars; and the big luminous stars less in number compared to the scores of other dimly shimmering stars. How wonderful are the depth of the earth and the curvature of the skies! Thus, we witness the venerability of variance of the phenomena. The diversified unity of the environmental changes, the longitudinal and latitudinal diversities of the surface of the globe, and the succession of cyclic intervals of the seasons create a terror-stricken sense of the all-powerful unity of natural forces and reveal the contiguous unanimity linking together the visible and invisible phenomena wrought together masterly. At a moment all phenomena appear to be isolated, but through deep concentration and observation, we find the meaningful and mutual relationship existing between them all. This is the complexity of nature that is hidden in it. Qur'an says, "Should they not prostate before Allah who brings to light what is hidden in the heavens and earth" (27:25). And further it states, "It [Qur'an] has been sent down by him who knows the mystery hidden in the heaven and the earth" (25:6).

And this mystery has simultaneously been a pushing force constantly provoking man to explore the mysteries by diving deep into the depths of the earth and by zooming high over the heights of the heavens. Thus, Qur'an demands from the intelligentsia:

> Do they not look into the dominion of the heavens and the earth and all
> things that Allah has created and that it may be the end of their lives is near.
> In what message after this will they believe? (7:185)

"Even if we opened unto them a gate to heavens and they were to continue ascending therein, they would say: our sight is confused as in darkness. Nay, we are people bewildered" (15:14,15).

This phenomenon is wonderful because if any person goes into space, he will not witness the sky bluish as we see from the earth, but actually the viewer from the space will catch the glimpse of the sky darkened and the earth will be seen as wrapped in a bluish mantle circling in space. The viewer himself would be puzzled to see darkness all around him. That is what Yuri Gagarin, the first Russian astronaut, had witnessed when he first traveled into the space in July 1961. While still on the spaceship, after witnessing the wonders of the space, he immediately contacted the then-Russian president Khrushchev and, being overwhelmed by the space panorama, exclaimed to him and expressed in a state of utter bewilderment that he was witnessing nothing but darkness around him, and he was puzzled. Those feelings Yuri Gagarin expressed are exactly the same from what we read in the abovementioned verse of the Holy Qur'an! How amazing! An astronaut traveling into space in 1961 had given the same description of the heavens about the skies expressed in the Qur'an fourteen centuries ago! Thus, with the curious instinct, man has been constantly gazing stars, first through his naked eyes and then through the eye of the telescopes.

North Pole Star Guides the Direction

"Or who guides you from the depth of darkness on land and seas; and who sends the winds as herald of good tidings" (21:63).

"[Allah Sets on the earth] landmarks by the stars which guide men" (16:16).

For example, you are in a ship sailing from Sydney, New Zealand, to London, and suppose the ship does not have its compass, just a guess, and suddenly it loses its way on account of heavy storm. Then behold! The stewardship of the Almighty pragmatically visualizes itself. Allah the Almighty has illuminated the lower sky with brilliant stars, and in the midst of them one will notice a combination of seven stars called the Big Bear or the Big Dipper. Now, to find the direction for the ship, one needs to gaze at the two stars ahead of the Dipper, Merck and Dobie. If one draws the line in mind that links these two stars then the projected line, towards the small dipper which holds a big, brilliantly shinning, North Pole star. Thus, if all else fails, one can always rely on the shimmering star that, as mentioned above, "guides one from the depth of darkness on land and seas" (21:63).

Theories of the Universe

Fred Hoyle (1915), Hermann Bundy (1919), and Thomas Gold (1920) formulated the steady state theory of the universe in 1948, which states that the universe has an infinite extent in the space or an infinite future in time. Therefore, there is no beginning and also no end to it. In opposition to them, Alpha, Better, and Gamow propounded their evolutionary theory in 1953, which is known as alpha, beta, and gamma theory of the universe. According to the alpha, beta, and gamma theory, the universe initially consisted of a uniform distribution of protons and electrons, which gradually formed into a gaseous primordial cosmology. About this Qur'an says, "Then he turned to the sky, when it was still gas and smoke, and said to it, and to the earth, come into existence, willingly or unwillingly. They said, 'We come willingly'" (41:11).

"Have not those who disbelieved see that the heaven and the earth were joined together as one united piece, then we parted them asunder? and we made from water every living thing. Will they not then believe?" (21:30).

Originators of this theory state that under the influence of the inter-convertibility, matter burst out with an un-imaginable explosion causing evolution of the universe. Similarly, a time will surely come in the infinite future when on account of the natural forces, repulsion will start and entire universe will contract back to form into a cosmic egg again. The Holy Qur'an describes this fact as a contraction of the universe heralding the Doomsday in the following verses:

"O Mankind: Be dutiful to your Lord. Verily the earth quake at the hour of judgment will indeed be a terrible thing" (22:1).

"When the sun will lose its brilliant light. When the stars will lose their luster and when the mountains will perish into dust"(81:1-3).

"And remember: The day when we shall roll up the heavens like a scroll rolled up for books. As we began the first creation, a Promise we have undertaken. Truly we shall do it" (21:104).

"This will be the day when mankind will be like scattered moths, and the mountain will be like carded wool" (101:4,5).

And thus an endless cycle of expansion-contraction shall be continued forever. This theory was accepted as the most appropriate theory of the universe by all scientists, astrophysicists, and astronomers of the twentieth century.

Difference of These Theories

The main difference between the steady state theory and the theory of evolution is that while the latter puts the creation of matter in a different moment of time (the remotest past, beyond human conception), the steady state theory offers no solution to the fact of the creation of matter. The theory of evolution states with certainty that universe was created billion of years ago and it has to still pass on another lengthy period of billions of years. Under the theory of evolution, the universe is to attain an age of eighty billion years before it contracts back to become again a cosmic egg. Thus, by expanding and then contracting back to its original form, the universe would end its cycle of life. However, under the steady state theory, this is not the case. This theory assumes that the life of the universe is eternal.

Impact of the Fundamental Laws on Universe

Newton's law of gravitation tells us that attraction between spherical bodies of universe varies inversely according to the square of the distance between the bodies. If this is true, then there must be a center for the universe. In that case, the galaxies that are (as pointed out by an American astronomer Hubble in 1924 that the galaxies are receding farther) receding farther away from the center as well as from each other allude to the fact that a time might come when their spatial density will diminish. But astronomical observations show that this is not the case. Due to the forces of uniformity, of attraction, and of contraction of mass, the galaxies will first expand and then recede.

Based on Euclidean axioms, Newton proposed a theory of a three-dimensional universe where time and space are absolute. However, Einstein proved Newton wrong by demonstrating the fact that we live in a four-dimensional world (as stated in the previous pages of this book) that is governed by a space-time curvature. Moreover, through the relativity theory, Einstein confirmed that our universe is constantly expanding, which is the most imposing discovery of modern science. The fact that the galaxies are parting away from the center of the universe, as well as from each other, at an imaginable speed is a proof to this theory. Qur'an speaks about the expansion of the universe as well:

"The heaven, we have built it with power, verily we are expanding it"(51:47).

Furthermore, Einstein proposed that space and time are not absolute, but they are interrelated and they make universe curved. The celestial bodies are shaped spherically according to the environmental force. Hence, the Euclidean axioms do not apply or operate on this space-time-curved universe. According to Einstein, these celestial bodies are condensed to a spherical shape due to the surface tension. This adaptation allows the celestial bodies to survive for billions of years without crashing and collapsing. Thus, based on this curvature of the cosmic bodies, Einstein concludes that gravity is nothing but the effect of the curvature on the four-dimensional universe. Many observations and experiments were conducted by many noted astrophysicists on the basis of this theory. Thus, after satisfying himself with his own observations and after relying on the observation of others, like Eddington, De-Sitter, Hamsun, and Hubble, Einstein finally declared at Pasadena Observatory in California that "new observations by Hubble and Hamsun concerning the red shift of light in distant nebula, make it appear likely that the general structure of the universe is not static, but expanding."

Along with Einstein, other scientists also observed the universe and concluded in favor of the theory of expansion. Christian John Doppler (1803-1853) observed in 1842 the red shifts in the spectra of the distant galaxies, and on this basis he propounded that the phenomena indicate that universe is expanding. In 1927,

George Edward Lemaitre (1894-1966), a Belgian astrophysicist, worked on red shifts of galaxies and came to the same conclusion as Doppler. Lemaitre further suggested that the origin of universe lies in the explosion of a cosmic egg in the unimaginable remotest past. Another astrophysicist, George Gamow, adopted and advocated the theory of expansion based on nucleosynthesis, a method of recreating nuclei from the existing subatomic particles. Thus, not only Einstein but many other scientists had subconsciously agreed to the Qur'an statement on the expansion of the universe.

Big Bang Theory and Afterward

"To him is due the primal origin of the heavens and of the earth; when he decrees a matter, hE says to it: 'Be!' And it comes into being" (2:117).

"That the heavens and the earth were joined together as one united piece, then we parted them asunder" (21:30).

"Then we diverted our attention towards sky which was nothing but a smoke. And said to it and to the earth: 'come ye together willingly or unwillingly' both of them responded willingly" (41:11).

"With power did we construct the heaven with our own hands, verily it is we who create vastness [expansion] of space" (51:47).

Thus, the Qur'an is explicit about the creation of the universe in the above verses, and the big bang theory fits this explanation. According to the big bang theory, the primordial cosmic egg busted with an unbelievable thrust and the universe came into being within seconds from that tremendous explosion. The explosion created high temperatures, which cause the thermal radiation to increase to the temperature of approximately one thousand million degrees Fahrenheit. At this point, the universe became a fiery sea of radiation, causing the particles to bounce violently. Einstein further explains the rapid expansion of universe in the following manner. Once the density of the radiated matter cooled down to the density of water, fundamental building blocks of the matter—the protons, electrons, neutrons, and other antimatter particles—condensed to form hydrogen and other 106 elements. Meanwhile, neutrons and protons of hydrogen atoms stuck together in groups of four to form helium nuclei. According to the calculations of astronomers, roughly 30 percent of hydrogen was thus converted into helium. During the formation of helium, temperature and the density further decreased resulting in the creation of the basic materials needed for the formation of stars and the galaxies. Then through condensation, gravitational forces combined with the powerful magnetic fields and radiation causing the stars to illuminate as they contracted. This is called the thermonuclear reaction, which led to the occurrence of heavier atoms formed by fusion. Thus, the transition that began from the conversion of hydrogen to helium then to carbon and oxygen ended with metals and metalloids. After the formation of the stars, Earth and other planets formed through a separate process from the surrounding primary nebula. We shall discuss about the formation of galaxies, stars, and planets in detail in the subsequent chapters.

Thermodynamic Theory

There is one more theory called the thermodynamic theory of the universe, but it is an ancillary theory to the theory of expansion. It upholds the same narration of other scientists who told that a time will come in infinite future when all the galaxies would be very close to each other because of the gravitational pull, which is constantly increasing the moving speed of galaxies resulting in an overall increase in the temperature. Qur'an says, "Surely, when the stars become dim; when the heavens are cleft asunder; when the mountains are scattered as dust" (77:8,9).

"When the sun with its spacious light is folded up; when the star fall losing their luster; when the mountain perish into dust" (81:1,2,3).

"O Mankind, fear your Lord for the convulsion of the hour will be a thing terrible" (22:1).

Consequently the stars shall change into a uniform gas, which will cause the temperature to increase to millions of degrees Fahrenheit, which will be followed by radiation. This radiation will cause the stars to fall into the black hole. There are many black holes in the universe. A black hole is a place in the space where gravity is at its strongest. Nothing can escape the pull of the black hole, including light and radiation. Astronomers say that black holes ruthlessly swallow the dead massive stars. Once swallowed by the black hole, the expanding universe will eventually be brought to a halt. Then, due to the gravitational force, the universe will begin to contract, which will increase until the cosmic egg is formed perhaps to explode once again.

Quantum Theory

Quantum theory predicts that the fireball created via the condensation in the black hole will never collapse but emerge again creating a new universe or universes ceaselessly, thus, bringing into life new generations of organisms in a new environment. Thus, an eternal cycle of evolution-dissolution shall continue forever.

That day (doomsday) we roll up the heavens like a scroll, rolled up as books, even as we produced it at first creation, we shall produce a new one. A promise we have undertaken. Truly shall we fulfill. (21:104)

The verse points out that as Allah had created the universe in its present form, he would then roll that up and then create afresh a new creation. The scientific theory of quantum agrees that a new creation would emerge after the first one collapses. Thus, quantum theory's assertion is compatible with the verse of the Holy Qur'an.

Men May Come!

Such is the story of the universe! It began with the big bang and shall end in a black hole. According to an American astronomer Allen Rex Sandage, the estimated lifespan of this universe is around eighty billion years. And whereas the universe has approximately crossed thirteen billion years or more, so far, thus, it has yet another sixty-seven billion years (80-13 = 67) of expansion. Man's age, unfortunately, is too short to imagine that length of time. Who knows what would happen at that moment of time? As the saying goes, "Men may come, men may go, but I go forever!" Likewise, I shall go but not the universe. As far as I am concerned, all the grandeurs of this universe—it's marvelous civilization, high culture, science, and technology—shall diminish with me at the moment of my last breadth. That moment will be my doomsday but surely not of the universe indeed! This is the fate of a man and in future will be of the universe too. Both of them shall go into the oblivion to rise again in another atmosphere, in another environment, maybe in the heavens!

SECOND PHASE OF EVOLUTION

The Black Holes

New York, October 09:

Cambridge researchers, led by an Indian-origin scientist, have discovered a new population of enormous rapidly growing supermassive black holes ever seen in the early universe. The black holes were previously undetected because they sit cocooned within thick layers of dust. The new study that used cutting-edge infrared surveys of the sky has shown that they are emitting vast amounts of radiation through violent interactions with their host galaxies.

The study findings are published in the journal of the Royal Astronomical Society.

The most extreme object in the study is a super-massive black hole called ULASJ1234+0907.

This object, located in the direction of the constellation of Virgo, is so far away that the light from it has taken eleven billion years to reach Earth, so we see it as it appeared in the early universe.

The monster black hole has more than ten billion times the mass of the sun and ten thousand times the mass of the supermassive black hole in our own Milky Way, making it one of the most massive ever seen.

The research indicates that that there may be as many as four hundred such giant black holes in the part of the universe that we can observe.

"These results could have a significant impact on studies of supermassive black holes," said Dr. Manda Banerji, lead author of the paper.

"Most black holes of this kind are seen through the matter they drag in. As the neighboring material spirals in toward the black holes, it heats up. Astronomers are able to see this radiation and observe these systems," she said in a statement.

"Although these black holes have been studied for some time, the new results indicate that some of the most massive ones may have so far been hidden from our view," said Banerji.

The newly discovered black holes, devouring the equivalent of several hundred suns every year, will shed light on the physical processes governing the growth of all supermassive black holes.

Supermassive black holes are now known to reside at the centers of all galaxies. In the most massive galaxies in the universe, they are predicted to grow through violent collisions with other galaxies, which trigger the formation of stars and provides food for the black holes to devour.

The team from Cambridge used infrared surveys being carried out on the UK Infrared Telescope (UKIRT) to peer through the dust and locate the giant black holes for the first time.

PTI   (With courtesy to NASA)

According to George Gamow, "the embryo of this universe freed itself by shattering the fetters of gravitational force and exploding like an artillery shell in the surrounding space." The fragments thus scattered by the force of explosion constituted galactic gases, which are said to be still flying apart against the gravitational bondage and some time in the future will tend to be pulled back toward the common center. It is said that when the embryo exploded, its metamorphism began, and the first things to come out were the stellar clouds, which later on condensed to form galaxies. The stellar clouds are also mentioned in the Qur'an in the form of smoke. Allah states, "He comprehended in his design the heavens when it was smoke" (41:11) (actually the whole universe was filled with smoke).

Although the term "stellar clouds," like many scientific terms used above, is not mentioned specifically in the above verse, we know that after the so-called big bang, the first thing that might have occurred was the smoke, the term that is used in the Qur'an. This smoke is used as an all-encompassing term by the Almighty God for the stellar clouds, the subatomic particles, and all the other basic materials that were crucial in the formation of the universe.

Continuing with the subject of the formation of galaxies, it may be pointed out that the galaxies came into existence due to the strong gravitational forces. By nature the gravitational force is the strongest of all the four forces. However, the curvature of the space makes the gravitational force a weak force. Due to its weakness, the gravitational force was slowly working its way up to form the galaxies. Meanwhile, the other three forces—nuclear strong, nuclear weak, and electromagnetic forces—operated upon the mass and formed the 106 elements of the universe at the burst of the big bang. Thus, for billions of years, the universe was a gaseous mass, primarily composed of hydrogen and helium gases that were slowly rotating in space. According to the law of gravity, the weaker the force, the larger the structure; hence, massive bodies of galaxies came into being from the gradual workings of the gravitational force. According to, *The New Book of Knowledge*, volume G, there are three types of galaxies: spiral, elliptical, and irregular. Our own galaxy, the Milky Way, is a spiral galaxy. All this and more came into being with one command, about which Allah says, "To him is due the primal origin of the heavens and of the earth; When he decrees a matter, he says to it, 'Be!' And it comes into being" (2:117).

The galaxies formed by the gravitational forces are huge and unimaginably gigantic. For example, if we gaze toward the sky during a summer dark night, we can spot multitudes of shimmering stars. Among these only about three thousand or more can be seen by naked eyes and the rest are invisible. Combination of millions of these stars form one galaxy. For example, the sun is a huge star in our galaxy, the Milky Way. According to *The New Book of Knowledge*, volume G, the galaxies closest to us are the Canis Major, which is forty-two thousand light-years away. The Andromeda is 2.5 million light-years away, and the Magellan clouds are ten times closer than the Andromeda galaxy (where one light-year is equal to six trillion miles). Moreover, it has been calculated by powerful telescopes that not a single bright star among these galaxies is located less than one thousand light-years away from us, and many small galaxies exist between the big ones. Thus, the distance between the galaxies gives us a clear idea of the vastness of space.

Moreover, recent discoveries have shown that these galaxies are expanding with an incredible amount of speed, and they are constantly rotating and receding. Out of the two billion galaxies that are known to us, the astronomers have measured the speeds of about

620 galaxies through Hubble and other large telescopes. It is estimated that 75 percent of these galaxies are spiral galaxies. Galaxies are the largest individual objects in the universe. The stars and nebulas (a group of stars) rotate around the center of the galaxy in millions of years. The guiding star Big Bear belongs to the galaxy Ursa Major. This peculiar galaxy is the third largest of the eighty-eight constellations. It is visible below the horizon all around the year. It is also known as the Big Bear sometimes because of the guiding star. Ursa Major (Big Bear) has two northern stars, Merck and Dhobe, which determine the North Pole star. The North Pole star is the guiding star of the North, which forms part of the Small Bear (refer to page 78). The Small Bear is heavily surrounded by luminous clouds, gases, and dusts, which are said to be the result of a recent explosion, as reported by NASA. Small Bear is located ten million light-years away from the earth. Thus, among many galaxies Milky Way is just another part of this vast universe.

The Milky Way

Our galaxy is a typical spiral galaxy, which measures up to one hundred thousand light-year miles in diameter. It is composed of swarms of bright and faint stars covering at least half portion of the sky. It circles almost entire space, half of it is visible in northern and other half in southern hemispheres. German-born English astronomer Hershel (1738-1822) states that "he observed Milky Way to be bulging at the center like a convex lens." The photographs taken in Pasadena, California, by the one-hundred-inch telescope at Mount Wilson Observatory and another by a two-hundred-inch powerful telescope at Mount Polaner Observatory show a swarm of stars in cloud-like image. In comparison to the Milky Way, our solar system lies somewhere at the corner of one of the spiral arms. The ultramicroscopic photographs of the Milky Way show a vast spiral structure of more than one hundred billion stars. In the midst of the stars lies a concentrated core of the oldest stars that form a part of three distant arms rotating majestically around the center of galaxy carrying shockwaves that compress the interstellar material. This compression triggers every now and then only when there is a new star about to be born.

The core (innermost central part) of the Milky Way itself has the distance of about thirty thousand light-year miles from the earth, and its thickness is fifteen thousand light-years from its center. Our magnificent and radiating sun is one among these one hundred billion stars, whose diameter is 835,200 miles, and its distance from the earth is 93,870,000 miles.

Even though our galaxy is so large and huge, the solar system lies in a distant part of the heavens, which once again reminds us about the vastness of Allah's universe.

During the year 1986, American astronomers Mark Morris and Farhad Yousuf Zahade of Columbia University found faint threads in the Milky Way. They say that these threads are weaving their way through the center of the Milky Way, which is more than six hundred trillion miles long. The movement of these threads creates enormous radio waves according to them. Furthermore, our galaxy rotates once in every 230 million years around its center, which lies somewhere in the constellation of Sagittarius. Thus, we may assume that our solar system too revolves around the center in every 224,000,000 years with a speed of 160 miles per second.

The mass of the Milky Way and other galaxies is another astonishing factor. Milky Way consists of billions of stars, which were nothing but gas and smoke, before they joined large groups of stars called the nebulae. Science expresses with certainty that, billions of years ago, the universe was filled with gaseous mass mainly composed of hydrogen and helium. The nebula, formed out of this gaseous material, slowly began to rotate and suddenly split into multiple fragments. The weight of these fragments has been estimated by the astrophysicists to be anywhere from one to one hundred billion times the present mass of the sun that is three hundred thousand times bigger than the earth. Moreover, apart from the galaxies, there are also quasars and pulsars that add to the mass of the universe. Each one is separated by billions of light-years from the earth. Thus, the galaxies are not only a huge part of the universe, but they are dynamic and constantly moving apart from each other, enhancing the dimensions of this vast universe even bigger and bigger!

THIRD PHASE OF EVOLUTION

Birth of the Stars

After formation of the galaxies, a different atmosphere and a different environment dominated the universe for another billion years. Galaxies were rotating and floating freely into the vastness of space. The atoms of abundant hydrogen were strongly struggling for survival. Each atom was flying away from each other under its own gravitational force, giving rise to enormous heat and energy. Mass-energy interconvertibility caused construction-destruction cycle and created chunks of gaseous clouds all through space, and a time came when under the gravitational force these clouds began contracting. It is estimated by the astronomers that in a period of more than two million years, the dense center of the gaseous clouds shrank, and the atoms were attracted by the gravitational pull at the center of the clouds. This increased the energy and the temperature of the gaseous clouds rose to one hundred thousand degrees Fahrenheit, which temperature seemed necessary for the birth of a star. It is said that this enormous temperature was sufficient to start a nuclear reaction in which atoms of abundant hydrogen fused to form helium nuclei. This process released further energy resulting in the birth of a new star on the horizon. Our sun was born in the same manner as well. It may be pointed out that the sun's brightness is the result of burning fuel provided by hydrogen. Fresh hydrogen is the main source of energy that makes stars shine. The moment a star is born, it starts consuming hydrogen as its fuel under the nuclear chain reaction through a continuous flow caused by carbon-nitrogen cycle. This cycle helps hydrogen to transform into helium, which then forms enormous volumes of energy and light. Thus, carbon and nitrogen became a medium for transforming hydrogen into helium. In this way, the release of energy and light in the form of photons coupled with a flood of neutrons reaching the surface of our planet Earth every day since its inception.

Facts about the Sun

Our sun has a predominant place in the Milky Way, our galaxy. It is about thirty thousand light-years from the center of the Milky Way and is located in one of the spiral arms of the constellation of Orion. It is the nearest star to Earth, with a distance of 93,870,000 miles away. The diameter of the sun is 865,400 miles, roughly 109 times larger than Earth, whereas the earth's diameter is only 7,926 miles. Light travels from sun at a speed of 186,283 miles per second and reaches Earth in 8.20 minutes, whereas the light coming from other stars takes billions of years to reach us. The sun rotates around the center of Milky Way at every 224,000,000 miles with a speed of 160 miles per second. It rotates at its own axis, west to east, in every thirty days. It has been calculated that the sun has orbited around the center of the Milky Way so far just twenty five times. God knows best!

The sun, as per scientific calculations, is supposed to have a lifespan of about ten billion years, and so far, it has only consumed half of its fuel. Thus, it may be inferred that the sun will burn its full quota of fuel in another five billion years, and after that, it would surely collapse! Its collapse is supposed to be the death of the mankind as per Qur'an: "The sun [with its spacious light] folded up and veiled; and the stars fall and lose their luster on account of fading of the sun's light) and the mountains are moved away from their place" (81:1-3).

Thereby annihilation of all living organisms on the surface of the earth is a must. According to the relativity and quantum theories, this has to happen, and no force on earth could stop this catastrophe. According to George Gamow and Dr. Schoenberg, the very beginning of the emanation of neutron radiation from the contracting sun should be taken as the red signal for such a catastrophe (Gamow, *Birth and Death of the Sun*).

Our sun is a fireball that contains 69.5 percent hydrogen, 28 percent helium, and the rest, 2.5 percent, is a combination of carbon, nitrogen, sulfur, silicon, iron, nickel, calcium, magnesium, and gold, all in a gaseous form because of the tremendous heat within the sun. The heat, energy, and light produced within the sun are the results of a series of thermonuclear reactions. The sun's interior temperature is estimated to be about thirty-five thousand degrees Fahrenheit while the surface temperature is supposed to be about eleven thousand degrees.

Light Is the Source of Life on Earth

The sun's brilliant light contains seven distinct colors: violet, indigo, blue, green, yellow, orange and red (called VIBGYOR). These colors are visible in the rainbows often during rainy season on the hemisphere. Each divided with a black line, which is the absorption line. The light and radiation are main forms of energy, which reach the surface of the earth from the sun. These energies include gamma rays, X-rays, infrared rays, cosmic rays, and radio waves, which cause life-sustaining organisms on earth. The sun is encompassed with free protons and electrons, which are continuously involved in thermal nuclear reactions that constantly emanate life-providing energy to us.

The sun is a principal source of energy on Earth. Sunrays are also used by plants for processing photosynthesis. Sunrays can also be converted in to electricity using the photoelectric cells. Present-day technology is being diverted to capture solar energy in electric cells to be used as electricity. Today, solar energy has become a reliable source of energy that can be used as an alternative to energy sources that may cause environmental hazards. Solar energy can also stimulate the development of energy-producing industries that create jobs.

Marvels of the Total Solar Eclipse, a Unique Occasion of One's Lifetime

The sun's atmosphere consists of several layers of gases. The surface layer is called photosphere. The layer next to the surface is ten thousand miles thick; it is known as chromosphere. Above the chromosphere is the corona, which is fully visible during a total solar eclipse. A vision of the total solar eclipse is the most wonderful event of one's lifetime. At that auspicious period, a very short period indeed, even during the day, darkness surrounds the atmosphere, causing birds and animals to rush toward their nests and sheds, as if the sun has actually set. Then the moon disc starts to move slowly to cover the face of the sun. This creates a brilliant ring that seems it is studded with a million-carat diamond. After a few seconds, the corona appears in a fully illuminated circle having full radiation of the sun. Really a unique scene is witnessed by the viewers of Earth when shadows of the mountains of the moon, as if rushing on the surface of the earth, in a pale yellow light, peep out through the slowly moving disc of the moon. Just after four minutes, full light of the sun again spreads over the earth as if bathed in the cosmic showers. On February 16, 1980, at 2:33 p.m. at Hyderabad, India, a spellbinding scenario of nature was witnessed by the author. On that day from all over the world, hundreds of prominent astrophysicists and astronomers came along with their sophisticated equipment in Hyderabad, and a grand gala function was celebrated at a hillock some thirty-two miles away south from the city of Hyderabad, where complete eclipse was sighted. It may be pointed out that a similar occasion was witnessed in 1919 in Brazil and New Guinea. Prominent astronomers—Eddington, Cottingham, Davidson, and Cormmeline—observed it and found that the beams of light passing near the sun at the time of the total solar eclipse were deflected from their usual straight path. The beams were curved because the space through which they were traveling is curved, which could be witnessed only when there is a total solar eclipse. Thus, the astronomers proved Einstein's theory to be accurate, and the eclipse of 1919 brought worldwide fame to Einstein as the century's best-known physicist of the world.

Luckily this year also, very recently, on Wednesday, 22 July, 2009, the world had again witnessed the total solar eclipse. On that day at 1.30 Universal Times, the shadow of the moon started at 6.23 a.m. in India, exactly in Surat city of Gujrat. NASA has predicted that this would be the longest eclipse of the century, which would last for six minutes and thirty-nine seconds. The shadow of the moon from India had proceeded to Nepal, Bhutan, Bangladesh, Myanmar, Indonesia, China, Japan, and many Islands of the Pacific Ocean. Unluckily, this eclipse could not be seen in California as this area does not lie on the path of the shadow of the moon that day.

Sunspots and Solar Storms

The most effective striking feature of the sun lies in its spots, which are dark and turbulent regions of large areas covering its surface. The presence of these spots is a result of solar bursts created by the auroras. The effect of these spots is felt in radio and telegraphic communication on earth. They occur in every eleven years in repetition and last for few weeks, but sometimes they last for a longer period as well. During this period sun sprays solar winds, which are a continuous flow of charged particles of protons and neutrons in space. These are known as solar storms. It is a period when magnetic field near the poles reverses by itself. Thus, once again an order in the universe is witnessed as the solar storms periodically occur every eleven years causing an electromagnetic effect on radio and television and telegraphic communications.

Scientists have found out recently that the sun has been unusually "quiet" lately. It has produced fewer sunspots and weaker magnetic fields than the previous century. They say this behavioral change of the sun is good for us. On account of which GPS systems is more accurate, satellites stay in orbit longer, and even the effects of human-caused global warming are marginally reduced. They are unable to describe why this change occurs but declare that whatever happens is good for humankind (*Los AngelesTimes*, 04-04-09).

FOURTH PHASE OF EVOLUTION

Planets Formed

When the sun was born, it was surrounded by a cooler and denser region of gaseous clouds, but slowly its heat and radiation increased due to which the surrounding clouds began to condense and contract from the internal gravitational force. Then, the atoms surrounding the sun rushed toward the center of these gaseous clouds. The gravitational force acting upon these atoms forced them to move on a curved passage, and thus, the atoms began to rotate in elliptical orbits around the sun. The fundamental laws of universe finally transformed these gaseous clouds into planets, which are constantly revolving around the sun. Thus, the planets came into existence. The temperature during the formation of the planets was low, and it was during this time that all the lighter atoms of hydrogen and helium escaped to space. The heavier and denser elements remained in space, for example, carbon, nitrogen, oxygen, iron, sulfur, nickel, magnesium, gold silicon, etc. These heavier elements, with passage of time, contracted and formed the crusty regions on the outer surface of the planets. However, the inner regions remained warm, and the inner magma of the planets melted. Thus, in this panoramic maneuvering our planet Earth came into existence: "The earth, we have spread it out. How excellently we did that"(51:48).

"For you Allah made the earth a carpet so that you travel along its roads and the paths of valleys" (71:19,20).

"The mountains, how they have been pitched [like a tent].The Earth it was made even" (88:19,20).

"Have we not made the earth an expanse and the mountains stake?" (78:6,7).

(Here "stakes" refer to the pegs that anchor a tent in the ground firmly.)

Along with the formation of the planets, it was necessary to have something that would hold the land mass in its place and keep it partitioned from the sea. Thus, if we take a look at 78:6-7, Allah (swt) speaks about mountains and their role on the planet Earth. Scientists have discovered that mountains have foundations as well. These foundations go deep within the ground, according to the height of the mountain. For example, if a mountain is five thousand feet high, then the foundation will also be five thousand feet deep below the earth. It is necessary for the foundations of the mountains to be as deep as the mountain's longevity itself so the mountain can remain stabilized on the surface of the earth.

Realm of the Solar System

That is how our solar system came into being, having its own independent atmosphere, a gigantic gravitational field, and a unique orbital organization, which is not found in any other galaxy. The solar system consists of nine huge planets: Mercury, Venus, Earth, Mars, Jupiter, Saturn, Uranus, Neptune, and Pluto in seriatim. The planet closest to the sun is Mercury, which is about thirty-six million miles away from the sun, and the farthest planet is Pluto, which is 3.7 billion miles away from the sun. In this way the solar system almost stretches to an orbital circumference of more than four billion miles. The sun provides heat, light, and energy to all the nine planets. Furthermore, some planets have their own moons, and so far, we know of thirty-eight satellites called moons of these nine planets. Earth has one moon, whereas other planets have more than one, and some do not have any moon at all. Thus, all the planets, comets, moons, and other celestial bodies such as the asteroids and meteoroids rotate around the sun on their own axis and at different speeds.

There are billions of comets, meteorites, and asteroids under sun's hemisphere, which crash with the surface of the earth and other planets and moons every now and then. This system has a predominant impact on the sustenance of life on earth. Now we will discuss how our planet, the earth, progressed evolutionarily and how life emerged on the earth alone.

Mother Earth: Our Beloved Planet

Earth, the civilized abode of mankind, had undergone innumerable turmoil, catastrophes, and devastations in the shape of earthquakes, typhoons, floods, inundations, glaciating epidemics, man-made wars, and scores of other upheavals; but it has somehow survived. The same Mother Earth bestowed mankind with an everlasting impulse and a provoking instinct to explore further. This brought inventions and an ultramodern technology with whose help and assistance man-made satellites that are orbiting around our planet and as well as other planets in the vast space. These satellites are tracing out the hidden secrets of the universe to solve the puzzles and riddles of the universe and to gain control over nature's devastative forces hopefully for the betterment of mankind. However, this blind technology has also become a source of amassing enormous quantities of nuclear weaponry, which if, deterred, shall annihilate the entire race of mankind, along with its thousands of years of marvelous civilization, golden history, and the very valuable technology. Even after these upheavals, yet unmindful of all these occurrences, Mother Earth will remain in this universe without us and without our pomp and glory—ever orbiting as before, around the glorious sun—in the hope to generate a better crop of yet another living organism, perhaps on a better scale with a better understanding. With this background of construction and destruction, we shall see how Earth became the abode of life. Among all the nine planets, life only exists on Earth, which makes it not only a unique planet but a unique heavenly body. Regarding this Allah says, "God is the one who made the earth a couch for you and the heaven an edifice and sent down water from the sky. He brought forth therewith fruit for your sustenance. Do not join equals with God" (2:22).

"Behold! In the creation of the heavens and the earth; in the disparity of the night and day; in the ships that run upon the sea for the profit of mankind; in the waters that God sent down from the sky thereby reviving the earth after its death; in the beasts of all kinds he scatters therein; in the change of the winds and the subjected clouds between the sky and the earth; here are signs for people who are wise" (2:164).

"God is the one who spread out the earth and set therein mountains standing firm and rivers. For every fruit He placed two of a pair. He covers the day with the night [and the night with the day, vice versa]. Verily in this there are signs for people who reflect" (13:3).

"God is the one who has made for you the earth a cradle and inserted roads into it for you. He sent water down from the sky and thereby we brought forth pairs of plants, each separate from the other. Eat! Pasture your cattle! Verily in this are signs for people endued with intelligence" (20:53-54).

"God is the one who made earth docile to you. So walk up on its shoulders. Eat of his sustenance! Unto him will be the resurrection" (67:15).

Like these, there are several verses dispersed throughout the Qur'an. These verses invite the reader to reflect on the divine beneficence by pondering on the examples provided therein. They contain instructions of a general nature not restricted to time, place, or human being. This is the mark of Qur'an universality.

Apart from this, Qur'an invites the reader to pay attention to things around him that he may take for granted such as the facilities of water, pastures, pairs of plants, roads, seas for running the ships for voyages, rivers, and mountains provided by the Almighty for the benefit of mankind.

Water Cycle and the Seas

"We sent down from the sky blessed water whereby we caused to grow gardens, grains for harvest, tall palm trees with their shoots of fruit stock, piled one above the other, sustenance for [our] servants. Therewith we gave new life to the dead land" (50:9-10).

"We sent down water from the sky in measure and lodged it in the ground. And we are certainly able to withdraw it. Therewith we gave rise to the gardens of palm trees and vine yards from which you have abundance of fruits and of them you eat" (23:18-19).

"And we send the fecundating winds, then cause the rain to descend from the sky; there with providing you with water [in abundance]; though you are not the guardians of its stores" (15:22).

"Hast not thou seen that God makes the cloud move gently, then joins them together, then makes them a heap. And thou seest rain drops issuing from within it. He sends down from the sky mountains of hail. He strikes therewith whom he wills and He turns it away from whom he wills. The flashing of its lightening almost snatches away the sight" (24:43).

"Hast thou not seen that God sent water down from the sky and led it through sources into the ground. Then he caused sown fields of different colors to grow" (39:21).

"God is the one who subjected the sea, so that you eat fresh meat from it and you extract from it ornaments which you wear. Thou seest the ships plowing the waves, so that you seek of his bounty. Maybe you will be thankful" (16:14).

These verses tell us how water comes from the skies and revives the dead earth to life for sowing of seeds and harvest. The rain that comes from the skies not only harvests the fields but also drenches the soil. The water that remains after the harvest goes down into the strata of the soil and remains there as a reservoir for future use. The rivers flow from various fields and provide water for harvest and other purposes. The heat of the sun evaporates the water of the oceans, and the winds take away these evaporations and convert them into thick clouds. Then the Almighty directs the clouds to pour the raindrops on the dead earth wherever he wills. These clouds sometimes condense into hail, and the winds bring hail storms out of them. These waters help Earth to grow various sorts of food grains and fruit gardens and pastures for the benefit of mankind and their animals. The ships plow on the waters for benefit of humanity.

All Planets Formed with a Like Matter

Formation of earth and other planets is very much indebted to the gravitational forces; but as far as Earth is concerned, its unique placement in the solar system, its distance from the sun, and its axis play a vital role in the structural, environmental, and geological evolution, which ultimately helped it to become the abode of life, unique in the universe.

The data obtained by the space probes on the materials found in the meteorites and asteroids that are falling upon earth from time immemorial and the fossil records of the billions-of-years-old preservations in the strata of the soils of various regions of the earth, mountains, and oceans confirm the fact that at least four out of the nine planets are composed of identical mixture of rocky material. These four planets—Mercury, Venus, Mars, and the earth—that are nearer to the sun than other five planets (Jupiter, Saturn, Uranus, Neptune, and Pluto) all mostly wrought up with iron, nickel, calcium, magnesium, carbon, nitrogen, sulfur, gold, mercury etc. Recently the rocks brought back of the lunar surface by the *Apollo 10* in 1969 also confirm this fact. Another common feature of all these planets is that they all rotate on their respective axis, all orbit around the common sun, and all are nurtured and nourished with the sunrays. These rays supply them all with its light, energy, and heat. Still, it is amazing that no life is traced on any of the planets except on our planet, the Mother Earth. Why it is so? That is what we are going to discuss here.

Distinct Feature of Planet Earth

As has been said in the para supra, Earth's unique placement, its axis, and distance from the sun definitely created that particular atmosphere. Climate, presence of ample breathable air, formation of ozone at a higher level to protect Earth from the sun's radiation, proper heat, and needed energy all have led the earth to evolve such structure on its surface that is benevolent and inevitable for sustenance of life patterns over it.

Mercury is the nearest planet to sun, with eight hundred degrees Fahrenheit temperature sufficient enough to melt all the material of the planet, and the result is that the planet is the densest among all. Water is one of the necessities of life, but this planet is barren without water, since all water becomes evaporated if available anywhere in that planet. On the other hand, Venus has the same temperature as Earth's; still water is not available on it. It lacks in water and sulfur resources. While Earth is enriched by both water and sulfur in abundance, other planets lack them utterly. On account of availability of water on Earth, iron sulfide and hydrous silicates condensed on Earth very quickly, and Venus lacks them all. On account of presence of water and sulfur, Earth could melt iron ore very quickly at any time during its life tenure, and since Venus could not perform this melting job, consequently it becomes lifeless forever.

Formation of Magnetic Field

Apart from water and sulfur, radioactivity of barium also helped Earth in melting iron and iron sulfide in its early stages of life some four billion years ago. On account of smooth condensation, iron and nickel core emerged to create a magnetic field. This field further generated internal reaction in the earth's interior core. The gravitational force, coupled with magnetic field and the internal heat and energy of the earth, caused earthquakes and volcanoes that gave birth to mountains, rocks, and boulders on the surface of the earth.

> The heaven and the earth were a closed mass, then we split them asunder and We made every living being from water. Will they not believe? We have placed on earth firm mountains, lest they should shake with them; we have made wide pathways thereon that they may journey from place to place. We have made the heaven the guarding and a protecting roof (from the ultraviolet rays of the sun by providing ozone layers, some thirty to fifty miles above the surface of the earth) yet they turn away from our signs, he is who created night and day, and made the sun and the moon each gliding freely in their never changing orbits. (21:30-35).

This lengthy passage in the Qur'an tells us a brief synthesis of the phenomena that constituted the basic process of the formation of universe as well as the earth. The verse 33 particularly refers to the solar system, as well as beyond the solar system, which has been discovered recently, which relates to the orbits of the sun and moon. As regards mountains, it is an expression of the idea that the way the mountains are laid down ensures stability and it is in complete agreement with geological data obtained by the scientists recently. Volcanoes and earthquakes generated high volumes of gaseous vapors and, coupled with the vapors of water, changed the entire atmosphere. Seasonal changes brought heavy rains, floods, and storms, which however, internal temperature still remains to more than three thousand degrees Fahrenheit below a depth of about thirty miles, sufficient enough to melt the metallic matter and rocks under the ground.

Role of the Axis

Earth's axis is tilted 23.27 degrees away from a perpendicular to the orbit, which played a basic role of a unique cyclic system of the climatic changes, which flourished a healthy atmosphere in every nook and corner of the globe to taste hot and cold effect of the temperature with an evenness. The tilt of the axis, with respect to the sun, determines seasonal changes. Had there been no tilt at all, then there would have been equal division of day and nights of twelve hours. And also the temperature of all regions would have been one and the same: either hot or cold. The present-day scenario is just the gift of this tilt and tilt alone. Due to its slow turning, only two days, one on 21 March and the other on the 21 September, each year, have equal duration of exact twelve hours of days or night; and the other 363 days have a systematic decreasing or increasing of one or two minutes every day, making larger days in the summer and larger nights in the winter. The following verse probably clarifies the existence of the axis:

> He merges night into day (the decreased hours of the night are added into the hours of the day) and he merges day (likewise, the decreased hours of the day are added to hours of the night) into night and he has subjected the sun and the moon (to his law) each one runs its course for a term appointed. Such is God your Lord" (35:13).

How did it occur? Because the earth is tilted 23.27 degrees on its axis. Just think over the following verse in which two easts and two wests have been mentioned: "Lord of the two East and two West" (55:17).

Whoever watches the daily timings of the sun's rising and setting (timings) knows that it is a recorded habit of the sun that it rises at different points of the east and sets at different points toward west each day. This is on account of the tilt of the axis of the Earth, just mentioned above. Except for two days in a year, all 363 days of a year have a change of one or two minutes, so also we notice a minute change in the rising and setting points of the sun on the horizon. Therefore, the Qur'an tells us that each day has a different point in the horizon for the rising and setting of the sun. The plurals of "east" and "west" are used in describing this phenomenon. This denominates the existence of axis without which such changes would never occur.

Moon's Behavior

Earth has only one satellite called moon, which orbits around it in every twenty-seven days, seven hours, and forty-three minutes; but on account of the motions of Earth and moon, being common around the sun, the lunar month has twenty-nine days, twelve hours, and forty-four minutes. Moon's mean distance from Earth is 238,857 miles, and its diameter is 2,160 miles.

Full moon attracts waters of oceans and rivers on account of its gravity, causing levels of water to rise. This is called the tidal effect caused due to its nearness to earth. These effects played an eminent role in origin of the living organisms on Earth. In the primitive stage of Earth's life, these tidal effects brought waters to a higher level and filled the cavities on Earth's surface. When the effect of the tide was gone, the water levels receded to their original position, but the cavities retained that amount of water.

"See they not that we gradually reduce the land from its outlying borders" (21:44).

This verse informs that when there is a full moon, because of moon's gravity, water rises upward, reducing the borders of the Earth, which later come to their previous position once the water levels get back to normal. This is called the tidal effect. The tidal effects cause the water to absorb the radiating waves of the sun and turn the water into a medium for chemical activity. The organic and inorganic material mix up with the water and cause molecules to appear, and later on these molecules originate living organisms. Moreover, the moon revolving around the earth creates a cooling effect on the high-temperate zones of the globe. The scientists have witnessed that sometimes these tidal effects cause some perturbation due to which the axis becomes inconsistent.

"We have created everything from water" (21:30).

The Impact of Carbon

In the early stages of formation of the earth, hydrogen and helium escaped to space, leaving behind the weighty elements. Volcanoes and earthquakes caused by the magnetic field produced carbon, nitrogen, and oxygen and helped them to form into hydrogen molecules like methane, ammonia, and water vapors, which oxidized the atmosphere. Carbon, nitrogen, and oxygen activated themselves in an organic manner. These elements then mixed with the atmosphere and led to the formation of various compounds. The various compounds formed are necessary for the fertilization of soil. For example, the iron-nickel compounds that come from the eruption of the volcanoes are extremely crucial for the upper strata of the soil. These compounds harden the earth's crust, thereby causing a dense core. This dense core in turn is essential for the eruption of volcanic activity, which releases large quantities of water vapors, nitrogen, and carbon dioxide. Thus, the carbon cycle helps in formation of various compounds.

Although all three elements—carbon, nitrogen, and oxygen—are essential for the formation of various compounds, carbon plays a more important role in the formation of these compounds due to its versatile nature. The volcanic eruptions produce at least 10 percent carbon dioxide. When carbon comes into contact with calcium and silicon that is available on surface, quartzite is formed. Another good example is when the activated carbon comes into contact with silica and sand, calcium carbonates are formed. These calcium carbonates are later molded to produce limestone, sand stone, and marbles. Furthermore, when carbon dioxide dissolves in oceanic waters, corals, shells, and carbonic rocks emerge in the interiors of the oceans. Thus, 98 percent of the carbon dioxide produced by volcanoes and quakes is consumed in these processes, leaving only 2 percent of the total carbon production in the atmosphere. Another beautiful feature of carbon comes across when we compare coal and diamond, which are made of 100 percent carbon. While coal is easy to break, only diamond can cut a diamond. Thus, carbon has multitudes of important features that produce compounds that are necessary for the chemical activity of the atmosphere, necessary to maintain life on Earth.

Greenhouse Atmosphere

Apart from this, carbon dioxide also helps in the vegetative growth, bringing about a greenhouse atmosphere on Earth. The infrared rays produced by the sun are daily absorbed by the vegetation on the earth, producing a pleasant and cool effect on Earth's atmosphere while making the temperature bearable. Carbon has the ability to mix with other atoms easily; on account of this ability, it forms most complex as well as simple organic compounds, which finally evolve into complex molecules. Thus, we may infer that perhaps nature itself selected carbon and gave it the ability to freely mix with others and generate organic and inorganic compounds on Earth.

Ozone Depletion

We have discussed the seven layers of the atmosphere in earlier paragraphs. One of the layers is called stratosphere, which is formed thirty to fifty miles above the surface of the earth, filling it with a bluish gas formed due to the presence of the atoms of oxygen. These layers act as a natural shield against sun's radiation and the dangerous ultraviolet rays so cannot penetrate the earth's atmosphere due to the layers of ozone. This layer of ozone absorbs sun's ultraviolet radiation and helps in generating a favorable atmosphere for the survival of plant and animal kingdoms. Today this atmosphere is under threat due to the industrialization and capitalization of the world industries. For example, some environmentally ignorant industries emit CFC (chlorofluorocarbon)—molecules, which have a devastative effect on the ozone layers. These molecules produce holes in the ozone layers that directly affect the atmosphere. For example, in 1980 scientists discovered the holes in the ozone was causing the ice caps of the Arctic and the Antarctic to melt. The melting of the ice caps poses a threat to the environmental equilibrium because when the ice caps melt, the water levels of the lower-level areas of the earth, particularly the ocean front areas, rise, causing an inundation of the lower-level areas. Thus, the ozone depletion disrupts God's established equilibrium and has a drastic effect on the ecology.

It is the responsibility of the highly industrial countries to curb the emission of the CFC gradually. The matter has been widely discussed internationally. Under the Kyoto Protocol of 1995, many countries agreed to curb their level of emission and a time frame was adopted to adhere to the international dictates. But unfortunately George W. Bush, U.S. president, did not accept that mandate since he did not like, unscrupulously, to disturb U.S. industrial hegemony. Thus, the matter was not solved. During this stalemate period, the situation worsened, and the international community came together in Bangkok on April 5, 2008, to solve this acute problem. One hundred and sixty countries joined the international forum in which Prince Philip of Great Britain took the lead and stated that "scientists are saying that climate change is now very grave; and we have less than ten years to slow, stop, and reverse the greenhouse gas emission. Common action is needed by every country to protect the international inheritance that has been given to us by our Creator." In 2008, UN's International Panel on Climate Change (IPCC) reported that no practical steps have so far been taken by member countries; and on account of this human error, global temperature is enormously rising to plus four-degree Celsius in the overall worldwide temperature. Moreover, the report suggests that the change in temperature has affected the food production resulting in a 10 percent loss of food production internationally, and it has caused droughts in Africa and resulted to inundation of the low-level coastal areas like London, New York, Tokyo, Bangkok, Hong Kong, Calcutta, Karachi. Almost two million people are at risk of coastal flooding. Half of the Arctic tundra is at risk. In 2008 Europe lost 80 percent of Alpine glaciers. Once again, if the ozone depletion is not stopped, then the Arctic and Antarctic ice sheets may begin to melt, causing an inundation in low-level coastal areas.

Recently, in March 2009, California's Interagency Climate Action Team issued a warning that hundreds of thousands of people and billions of dollars of Golden State's infrastructure and property would be at risk if ocean level rose fifty-five inches by the end of the century. The warning comprises the state's two-thousand-mile coastline, which would be affected severely, particularly in San Mateo, Orange, Alameda, Marina, Santa Clara, San Francisco, and Los Angeles counties where more than four hundred thousand people and $83.4 billion worth of property would be affected. This warning has been based on a computer model (*Los Angeles Times*). If such model has some value, then we must get such models for all the low-level areas around the world, and only then we can figure out the catastrophe that will occur if the Bangkok Declaration of 2008 is not fulfilled. Recently we tasted the tsunami upheaval. God forbid, if measures are not taken, then perhaps this catastrophe would be a hundred times greater.

In these times where the average lifespan of a human being, man or woman, is expected to increase, consequently the problem of overpopulation should create an imbalance in the nature. Along with the ozone depletion, the unscrupulous deforestation of the formidable forest areas all around the world poses another threat to the balance of nature. The schemes undertaken by many countries for the deforestation of many densely populated areas in order to accommodate the increase in population will eventually cause further disruption in the already disturbed balance. However, deforestation is dangerous because lack of trees means less rain, which in turn results in higher temperatures, drought, and famine due to a loss in natural equilibrium. In these circumstances, we have to check and curb the production of the CFC by the developed and the developing countries on one hand, and simultaneously, we need to ban the deforestation of further areas. Secondly, for the already deforested areas, governments should enforce schemes of reforestation by providing facilities and monetary help.

The G8, at the time of this writing, met at L'Aquila in Italy on 10 and 12 July 2009. Hopefully they embraced the high-sounding goal of reducing their CFC emissions by 50 percent by 2020 and 80 percent by 2050 at the base level of 2005. Unfortunately, a few of the developing countries like China, India, and Brazil reacted by rejecting the package. If that undertaking is strictly followed by all the developed and developing countries, we may hope to successfully cure the dangerous problem of ozone depletion forever by reducing the rest 20 percent during the years following 2050. Most important was the push by President Barack Hussein Obama who, in contrast to his predecessor Bush, wasted no time in proclaiming a fresh befitting U.S. policy on climate change and also induced other G8 dignitaries to bring together the nation's most responsible for greenhouse emissions to work against warming and share the cost of emission-curbing technologies to those developing countries that lack finances to take up the measures.

If that is not followed and the countries who are responsible for such drastic emissions of CFC, God Forbid, the situation shall become alarming and unbearable, viz; by 2050 population of the world would become more than nine billion and to feed them, sources are meager, and no country would be able to feed comfortably, resulting arson, loot, bloodshed, strikes and hooliganism everywhere in the world. Those countries that produce surplus and export to the needy nations shall try to stop exports and hoard for their own population. Thus, the most effected shall be Asian and African countries whose rate of population growth is comparatively higher than the European and American countries. Further, malnutrition and lesser unit of supplies of food grains per capita will create unspeakable problems for the inhabitants of the world and will introduce more health problems and early deaths; childbearing ability of womenfolk will deteriorate, causing juvenile deaths. That is the punishment from the Almighty for disturbing the natural equilibrium that maintained so far moderation of the environment for mankind. If mankind is against the plan of the Almighty, no one in nature will save us except man himself by adhering to the laws of nature, which had been so far described in detail.

Apart from this, on account of high-temperature melting of glaciers and snows of both Arctic and anti-Arctic, inundation of low-level areas will happen, causing casualties, damage of properties, and other unimaginable damages and health problems as well. Such is the untold misery, devastation, and catastrophe that will be our fate if we do not take early and timely measure as elaborately explained and planned above.

Oxygen: Life-sustaining Property

Plants require a minimum quantity of oxygen for their life process as they mainly consume carbon dioxide. Plants use carbon dioxide to produce organic molecules, and they release oxygen as an end product. Not only does the oxygen released into the atmosphere help balance the water levels on Earth, but it also helps in the formation of the ozone. Had these ozone layers not been formed by oxygen, Earth would have been deprived of water because it would be continuously absorbed by the radiating sun. Water is an important medium for chemical reaction, and if it would have evaporated, then sustenance of life would not be possible. Our Earth too would face the same fate as that of other planets. Hence, the distance of Earth from the sun plays a major role for generation of living organism and for maintenance of sustainable atmosphere. Thus, because of the carbon cycle, oxygen plays a vital role in formation of the ozone, keeps water balance on the surface of Earth, and acts as a valuable life-giving property to all living organisms, making the Earth a cradle for mankind.

Earth as We See Today

All the factors mentioned above make the earth a unique planet in the universe. Geologically, its outer crust has evolved to become cooler than its interior. As we go deep into the earth's crust, it becomes hotter and hotter; and below thirty miles, its temperature is more than three thousand degrees Fahrenheit, which is sufficient enough to melt metallic matter and rocks of the underground. The mass of Earth consists mainly of rocks and metal, of which 97 percent is in a molten condition, and only 3 percent of the outer crust is solid and cooler, which is made up of all the one hundred and six, so far, known elements of the universe, which have been converted into rocks, sands, and salts. The rocks have three categories: igneous, sedimentary, and metamorphous. It took a billion years for this formation after which the planet was ready for a further step toward geographical evolution. Volcanoes, earthquakes, and internal combustions caused mountain building.

Storms, floods, and oceanic waters were activated by carbon, oxygen, and other gases, which caused further contraction and resulted in the formation of wrinkles and ridges on the surface of the earth. While ridges developed, hills and mountain depressions created the inland seas and rivers on surface of the earth. The periodic vomiting of magma from the interior of the earth with a thrust caused further development of hills and rocks. With passage of time, these grains of rocks grew to larger sizes under the force of gravity, and the larger rocks became huge and high mountains. With this mountain building process, continental boundaries became visible. All waters flowed down in the low-leveled areas of the surface to become oceans. Thus, slowly but steadily, in another one billion years, Earth attained a continental shape, duly divided by mountains and oceans. Yet the evolution has not stopped, and the Earth continues to evolve further.

Formation of oceans, mountains, and continents changed the entire atmosphere. The sun's heat and radiation vaporized waters of oceans and built up thunderous clouds over the atmosphere that generated heavy and turbulent rains, storms, and typhoons back to the surface of Earth.

"And in the alternation of night and day it is he who sends down rain from the sky, whereby he revives the earth after its death, and in the changing courses of the winds are signs for people who use their understandings" (45:5).

"Allah is he who sends the winds, so that they raise the vapors in the form of clouds, which he spreads in the sky as he pleases, layer upon layer, and thou sees the rain coming forth from their midst. When he causes it to fall on whom he pleases on his servants, they rejoice there at; though before its coming down, they were in despair. Observe, then, the token of Allah's mercy; how he revives the earth after its death" (30:48,49).

Thus, under the doctrine of the Almighty, the winds and the clouds provided enough water that resulted in roaring rivers, streams, and lakes. Waters of these rivers, streams, and lakes carried away with them sediments, sands, and nutrient salts to make the upper strata of the soils of Earth fertile to cause vegetative growth in abundance. These storms, floods, tidal waves, tornadoes, hurricanes, blizzards, glaciations, and rivers all jointly help in production of Earth's upper strata with chemical salts and their solutions made the soil loose. Natural weakness of rocks also helped waters to submerge by infiltration, producing a complex system of underground water channels, sinkholes, caverns, tanks, and springs.

"Of stones there are some out of which gush forth streams, and there are some that cleave asunder and water flows out from them and others which sink for fear of Allah and he is who not unmindful of what you do" (2:74).

This cycle of occurrences is so systematically arranged by the Almighty that it ensures a balance between the supply of freshwater and its maintenance. In this manner, the scheme of supplying water to the living beings is chalked out by providing fresh potable water from the rivers, springs, and pools while the oceans have saltiest waters.

"He it is who has caused the two waters to flow, one of the rivers and springs, sweet and potable and the other of the oceans, saltiest and bitter, and between them He has placed as a barrier, a system that keeps them apart" (25:53).

This system had been instituted by Allah, and nature had brought it into operation, and the Almighty has complete powers on and over this pragmatically adopted system, and he alone has the power to repair the system if it fails. Therefore, human beings should not disturb this equilibrium at any cost; otherwise, we have to suffer as has been warned in the Bangkok Declaration of 2008. The effect of deforestation shall produce drastic results in drought and famine.

"Say: See you? If your stream is lost in any morning [in the underground earth] who then supply you with clear flowing water?" (67:30).

Formation of Atmosphere

We know that gases are made of molecules that have an inherent force to always be in motion. This rapid motion is called velocity. When velocity escapes the gravitational force of Earth, it is called escape velocity. Earth's gravity is so powerful that velocities of the gaseous can never escape from the earth's surface. These gaseous molecules also help in the formation of the earth's atmosphere and the ozone at a higher level, creating a breathable atmosphere.

The Qur'an contains several verses that deal with the phenomena that occur in the atmosphere.

"Whomever God wills to guide, he renders his chest wide open to submission. And whomever he wills to send astray, he renders his chest intolerant and straitened, like one who climbs towards the sky God thus places a curse upon those who refuse to believe" (6:125).

Centuries after the revelation of the Qur'an, we learned that the proportion of oxygen diminishes as we climb toward the sky, and we gasp for air.

The words "He renders his chest intolerant and straitened, like one who climbs towards the sky God contracts his chest as if he is ascending the skies" denote the discomfort felt by a person when he ascends the high altitude. Thus, by linking the two together, Qur'an mentions the usefulness of oxygen to man, a phenomenon that was unknown at the time the Qur'an was revealed. As one rises in altitude, a time comes when man feels weightlessness and feels the pressure with the simultaneous lacking of the oxygen. Thus, verses like these are a proof to the fact that unlike many religions of the world, there is absolutely no contradiction between science and Islam.

Electricity in the Atmosphere

"God is the one who shows you the lightening with fear, and covetousness. He raises up the high clouds. Thunder glorifies his praise; and so do the angels for awe. He sends the thunderbolts and strikes with them whom he wills while they are disputing about God. He is the almighty in his powers" (13:12).

Qur'an and science both agree that electricity does not come alone; but it brings with it thunderbolts, thunderstorms, and hail storms. It has the striking power, which, when struck, burns the target to its entirety. These verses speak about the power of rain coming forth from the clouds and the hail storms that bring thunder and awesome lightning on places with the permission of the Almighty.

"Hast thou not seen that Allah makes the cloud move gently, then joins them together, then makes them a heap, and thou seest rain drop pouring from within it. He sends them mountains of hails. He strikes therewith when he wills. The flashing of its lightning almost snatching away the sight" (24:43).

These two verses explain an obvious correlation between the formation of heavy rain clouds, as well as the hails, and the occurrence of lightning. The present-day scientific knowledge vouchsafes the authenticity of the occurrences of electricity in the atmosphere.

We may conclude part III discussion by recalling the true meaning of the verse "to bring the mankind from the darkness to the light." We hope from the foregoing paragraphs that the reader sees the divine connection between the making of this universe and the absolute necessity for the presence of a Creator. I have tried my best to enlighten the readers by drawing connections between the basic scientific knowledge and the relevant verses of the Holy Qur'an wherever necessary. I have tried in length to describe the scientific theories, formulas, and cures in furtherance of my goal to bring to light the correlation between Qur'an and the latest scientific data, which are complimentary and not at all contradictory to each other.

CHAPTER IV
Origin of Life

Science: Creation or Evolution

There is a fundamental difference between creation and evolution as stated in Darwin's *Theory of Evolution* (1859). Creation refers to the process that has been described in the Holy Scriptures. Another notion is evolution is filled with scientific deliberations mainly propounded by Charles Darwin of Great Britain. Evolution as explained by Darwin is a materialistic theory of the origin of the species. It says that matter alone has the capacity to evolve itself into different stages. Evolution uses the same explanation to explain the emergence of man on Earth. It contradicts the very existence of God. Although the theory of evolution has explained the emergence of all the organic and inorganic matter, it has yet to satisfactorily prove the coming of first man. Thus, the theory of evolution is just another theory, based on assumptions and hypotheses, which cannot answer many of the questions on the origin of the universe and of man in particular. Furthermore, the Darwinians assert that matter is evolving itself without any supernatural help. The matter itself came into existence of its own and gradually evolved first into living organism, then evolved into a life cell, and then changed into simple cell, then further developed into complex species, giving birth to botanical manifestations and then to animal beings. Finally this life cell, without any supernatural help, evolved into present-day man. Thus, they say that man is the product of so many complex sets of evolutions, which took billions of years whereas, according to the Holy Scriptures and particularly the Qur'an, man did not evolve as per the theory of evolution but was rather created by Allah. There is a distinction between the creation of the universe and the creation of man. The Qur'an proclaims that the creation of universe took billions of years whereas Adam came into existence instantly after Allah proclaimed that he would "create A vicegerent on earth, then Allah shaped Man on his own image and then breathed unto him his own spirit" (2:30-39).

Allah does not mention a timeline for the creation of Adam, as mentioned for the universe. For example, Allah says that he "created the heavens and the earth, and all that is between them, in six days" (7:54).

The term used in Arabic is *yaum*, which denotes different time measures. For example, in one verse Allah says that "a yaum [a day] in the sight of your Lord is like 1,000 years of your reckoning" (22:47), and in another verse yaum refers to fifty thousand years (70:4). Thus, according to the Islamic scholars, the word "yaum" refers to a long period of time. Hence, we can conclude that when Qur'an states that the universe was created in six days, it means a really long period of time rather than just six twenty-four-hour days. Therefore, as mentioned above, according to Qur'an, Allah created the universe over a long period of time, whereas man was created instantly with Allah's will. Allah asserted "be," and Adam came into being.

The Darwinians proclaim that the life of our planet comprises of more than four billion years, and man's emergence on this Earth accounts to about a billion years. As a proof, they submit geological, archeological, and anthropological remains of fossil materials and promote the theory that man's ancestors are apes and chimpanzees! The theory denies that Allah is the creator of this universe and stresses that there is no need of any God for the creation of this universe as life emerged by chance from inanimate matter. But he failed to explain the sudden generation of life from the so-called inanimate matter. His fabulous theory did not stand on the scientific crucial experimentation and thorough analysis. Therefore, it miserably failed to establish its claim that man's ancestors are apes and chimpanzees. Moreover, he himself confessed in his another book *Difficulties on Theory* in which he concedes his failure to convince many objections put forward by the antievolutionary scientists. Many scientists from the United States and Europe—and from different fields of study such as, biology, biochemistry, and paleontology—recognize the invalidity of this theory and instead lean toward the concept of "intelligent design." Intelligent design or the theory of creation accepts the fact that life could not have originated by itself. As described in the Holy Scriptures, it clearly asserts to be the act of the Creator who has a perfect plan and scheme for this universe. Accordingly, in chapter 10 of the Qur'an, Allah affirms that "surely Allah has done this all under his purposeful planning." If we analyze Darwinism, many unanswered questions come to mind. For example, how could a single cell evolve to generate millions of complex living species on Earth? Even if we assume that such an evolution did really occur, then where are the fossil records of the intermediary stages? If every living being has evolved into its present form, then, likewise, there must have evolved hundreds of intermediary species, but fossil records have no bearing on this matter. This fact itself is enough to nullify and reject this deceptive and unrealistic theory.

The most problematic part of Darwin's theory is his claim that man emerged from monkeys and chimps. Darwinism substantiates itself on the latest archaeological, anthropological, and paleontological discoveries and asserts that man did not emerge a few thousand years ago as asserted by the Holy Scriptures but billions of years ago. Darwinians prove their theory by showing fossilized skeletons, which hardly resemble man. Thus, he proclaimed that man is the descendant of a tailless, long-handed monkey, which, after various complex evolutionary stages, became a two-legged animal and was named *Ramapithecus*, a creature that walked on its two legs and lacked a tail. Then after hundreds and thousands of years, that two-legged animal evolved to walk erect and was named *Homo erectus*. This creature was able to manufacture instruments for hunting and for his own safety. The Java Man or Heidelberg Man came from this species and had a bigger brain than the previous species. After passage of hundreds and thousands of years, a new species appeared, which was known as *Homo sapiens* consisting of a bigger brain. These skeletons were excavated in Germany and were named as Neanderthal Man. There were still others that were found in France, and they were named Cro-Magnon Man. Many other fossils were excavated in different parts of the world like Asia, Africa, and Europe; but these fossils do not hold enough weight to prove that the man evolved from creatures that looked like chimps.

Darwin's theory poses a big problem to the religious thinking as it falsifies the concept of creation and the Creator. But unfortunately the theory is very popular in the West, and it seems as if the entire Western Hemisphere is thrilled with this unscrupulous theory only because it rejects the existence of any supernatural being and states that man is a product of chance and that spontaneously everything has come to being without any plan or program. Let them be in their own fool's paradise, but the tragedy is that the effect of this theory has enveloped the thinking minds of the entire world. Rather, it has become an international issue where the intelligentsia is at the crossroads and the thinking mind is questioning and cross-questioning the sanctity of this theory. Disputable arguments are filled in the literary circles and are purposely and erroneously adopted in the syllabi and the curriculum of the schools, colleges, and universities, dangerously affecting the minds of the learning generations. The imprint of this theory can be seen in every walk of life, whether it is art, science, or philosophy. Fortunately, the ongoing debate of evolution forces the thinking mind to question the origin of man and makes one delve into the quest for truth. While the academia struggles to put forth an end to this debate, there are many who are turning away from religion, calling it a tale of the old generations. As far as Islam is concerned, it is the duty of every conscious being to search for the truth and proclaim it a theory based on false imaginary record. Hence, only through works like these can one bridge the growing gap between religion and science in order to prove that the vacuum between the two is a myth and hope to give a convincing reply to the

Darwinians.

Harun Yahiya, a prominent Islamic scholar and a staunch critique of Darwinism, has opined:

1. The theory cannot explain how life originated on Earth.
2. No scientific finding shows that the evolutionary mechanisms proposed by this theory has any evolutionary power at all.
3. The fossil record proves the exact opposite of what the theory suggests. Many evolutionists continue to research the validity of Darwinism. Many try their best to explain the correctness of the theory through scientific experimentations, but those experiments failed to produce results. Finally the biochemist Jeffrey Beda of San Diego Scripps Institute accepted the defeat and reported in the *Earth Magazine* (1998): "Today as we leave the twentieth century, we still face the biggest unsolved problem that we had, when we entered the twentieth century. How did life originate on earth?"

Similarly, Professor Leslie Orgel, an evolutionist of repute from the University of San Diego, confessed in 1994 issue of *Scientific American Magazine*: "It is extremely improbable that proteins and nucleic acids, both of which are structurally complex, arose spontaneously in the same place at the same time. Yet it also seems impossible to have one without the other. And so, at first glance one might have to conclude that life could never, in fact, have originated by chemical means."

Finally I would like to conclude this chapter with Harun Yahiya's statement that when it has become impossible to ascertain that life could not be created by chemical means or natural causes, then what is the problem if they accept the divine concept of creation by supernatural way (excerpts from *Secret behind Our Trials* by Harun Yahiya)?

Qur'anic Version Regarding Creation of Man

No doubt we cannot establish a particular date of the emergence of man on the earth, and Qur'an is silent about this matter. However, according to the Judeo-Christian texts, the nomadic times when man was still using stones to hunt can be traced back to eighteen to twenty thousand years ago or even a bit remote. The period when he learned to domesticate animals and raised crops and cattle to feed himself and his family can be traced back to about eight to ten thousand years or so. Thus, we can assert that according to the Judeo-Christian traditions, the early man emerged on the earth only about eighteen to twenty thousand years ago. However, according to the popular version of the scientists, the first man came about at least a hundred thousand years ago. Either way, all the Abrahamic faiths agree that the first man to emerge on the face of this Earth was Adam. If we take a look at the sacerdotal text of Genesis, we find a timeline that can be traced back to prophet Adam. Genesis says that prophet Ibrahim passed away after 2,123 years from the passing away of prophet Adam. From that year, three centuries after Abraham came prophet Jesus. Now after 2,009 years, if we calculate the date of creation of prophet Adam, we may safely conclude that 2,123 + 3,000 + 2,009 = 7,132. Thus, man emerged on the earth between seven thousand and eight thousand years, or we may assume even ten-thousand-plus years. This also is vouchsafed from the ancient historical record mentioned in the timetable of history, third edition; from the chronicle record of Baithul Muqaddas (Jerusalem); and also from the chronological record prepared by Tabri that our Holy Prophet Mohammad (pbuh) was the forty-ninth descendant of prophet Adam. That period of forty-nine generations has been reckoned as 7,163 years dating from prophet Adam to the birth of prophet Muhammad. If we add 1,438 years to 7,163 (the date of birth of the Prophet Mohammad [pbuh] is AD 571, hence, 2,009-571=1,438), we get 8,601 years, or we can round it to eight thousand to nine thousand years. Either way, as we have suggested according to the Judeo-Christian texts, it has been ten thousand or so years since the emergence of the first real man on this Earth. Thus, the Judeo-Christian sources differ from the scientific data. Moreover, because the Holy Qur'an is silent on the exact dates of the emergence of Adam, any solid conclusion is not possible, and neither can the Judeo-Christian sources be rejected. However, we can safely say that Allah knows best, and we believe in the Holy Qur'an.

According to the Holy Qur'an, the Creator of the universe asserted to populate the earth by declaring, "Inni Jaelun Fil Arzi Khalifa [I am going to create man as my vicegerent on the earth]" (2:30), and for that, he shaped man in his own image under a perfect program and breathed unto him his spirit "Nafakhta Ruhi [I have breathed unto him my spirit]" (15:29).

For Adam's comfort, he created Eve; an opposite gender, with fair, tender, and attractive complexion, and made her his companion who in course of time became his spouse under a perfect program to populate the earth. Allah decreed them to live together and enjoy all that was available in the universe and taught them all the necessary knowledge. Allah says, "Allamal insaan ma'lam ya'lam" meaning "We taught man that which he knew not" (96:5).

Thus, Allah, through his might and glory, taught Adam and Eve how to live a blissful life and empowered them with knowledge and wisdom to control the universe. For their sustenance, he had already created all the living species in pairs and gave them the sense to multiply. But Allah did not leave man alone; in order to educate him, he selected his messengers among them and sent them to teach and guide mankind. This continued for thousands of years from prophet Adam to the last prophet Muhammad, peace be upon them. Prophets were sent from time to time to all regions of the world. The prophets taught their followers the right way of worship. They showed them the difference between good and evil so that man would be able to lead a righteous life. Thus, man was given the freedom to choose between good and evil. Along with the prophets, he also bestowed Holy Scriptures to the selected few to teach and reprimand men and women against the evils of the society.

The Holy Qur'an, which is the word of Allah, asks us to ponder on the creation of the universe as well as the creation of man himself. When we study man, we come across a perfect order and a high system of organization that is reflected in the creation of the universe. For example, we have flesh that covers the entire body; bones that keep us strong; contracting muscles that control the body movement; a heart that cleans and pumps the blood through veins to every part of our body; and the brain that understands, considers, thinks, infers, and distinguishes between good and bad virtue and evil and controls the entire system of the body. All the different and complicated systems of the body wonderfully coordinate and react as a whole constituting a complete microcosm. This complete microcosm is genetically engineered by Allah alone. All the information is contained in less than a minute's fraction of a drop of fluid, sperm; then in due course of time, every being, human and nonhuman, shapes into a very different personality (23:12-14). Every human, with a different personality and capability, matures into a human being whose prime mover is the soul, which is breathed by the Almighty Allah into the mechanism of the man. Thus, the body and the soul together constitute a single unit to enjoy life at many different stages. At each stage of his/her life, from infancy, to childhood, adulthood, and old age, every man and woman evolves and lives to his/her hopes to achieve and fulfill the purpose with which he/she thinks he/she was born. Everybody has a limited period of time; and after a while, the body disintegrates; and the soul, which is invisible, merges into its source from where it was breathed by the Almighty.

"Does man think that he is to be left purposeless? Was he not a drop of fluid emitted forth? Then he became a clot of blood, then Allah shaped and proportioned him, and that he made him from a male and female. Has He not the power to bring the dead to life? And vice versa?" (75:37-40).

Secret of Nature

Nature's secret lies in its duality. The principle of multiplicity reflects everywhere in nature. For example, we have day-night, sweet-bitter, intellect-simpleton, male-female, unity-diversity, etc. Yet no two faces, no two fingerprints, no two voices are exactly the same. Even no two minds coincide completely. But the truth is that even with this diversity there exists a broad similarity among all human faces, voices, feelings, and thinking. This similarity-duality is the dominant feature of nature.

Our universe is the superb craftsmanship of the Almighty Allah who has enveloped the whole universe in many splendors and spellbinding scenarios. The dawn and dusk, the fragrance of ever-blooming flowers, the heart-touching enchantment of the multifarious birds, the sudden flouting clouds pouring alleviating showers on the earth, the morning somniferous winds, the snow-clad peaks of the mighty mountains, the ever—flowing waters of the raging rivers, the awesome ever-green valleys, the multitudinous of the fauna and flora, the vast and boundless horizon, the scintillating rainbows, the magnanimity of space and its supportless skies, the ever-orbiting stars, the life-energizing radiant sun, our beautiful Earth and its sister planets and their satellite moons, the powerful lunar and solar eclipses causing beneficial tidal affects, the ever-changing and tenacious seasons, the limitless waters of the oceans and the mountain-like ships roaming over these waters, the milking animals and the domesticated cattle, and the honeybees are some of the enamoring facts that are seen and visualized, heard and witnessed, day in and day out, during one's tenure of life; who chalked out experiences and results of his or her experiments as theories notifying the glory of the universe and of the nature. Finally they declared, "Verily, thou whatever hath created is not in vain" (3:191).

"And the earth: we have spread it out [in a spherical shape] and set thereon mountains standing firm, and produced therein pairs [of buds, flowers and fruits] of beautiful growth" (50:7).[20:53]

"He is the one who made the earth habitable for you, and paved in it roads for you. And he sends down from the sky water with which we produce many different kinds of plants" (20:53).

From the above few verses, one has to be convinced that whatever is in the universe is created by the Almighty with a purpose and nothing is in vain. When we study Qur'an, we come across two types of scientific facts that are directly related to the universe and its material phenomena. First are the unquestionable statements regarding the universe and second the secrets and mysteries that require thorough investigation by sophisticated advanced techniques.

While the animal kingdom is made up with males and females, the plant kingdom also has the male and female parts in the plants. These are referred to as zauj, meaning pairs, contemplating exactly to husband and wife, or male and female. Rather, correctly speaking, they are spouses of each other.

"Glory to him who has created all the pairs of that which the Earth produces as well as their own kind [male and female] and of that which they know not" (36:36)

Botanists have researched and come to conclusion that the plant kingdom does possess male and female parts. For example, in Qur'an Allah mentions: "[God is the one who] sent water down from the sky and thereby we brought forth pairs of plants [zauj] each separate from the other" (20:53).

"O people, if you have any doubt about resurrection, [remember that] we created you from dust, and subsequently from a tiny drop, which turns into a hanging [embryo], then it becomes a fetus that is given life or deemed lifeless. We thus clarify things for you. We settle in the wombs whatever we will for a predetermined period. We then bring you out as infants, then you reach maturity. While some of you die young, others live to the worst age, only to find out that no more knowledge can be attained beyond a certain limit. Also, you look at a land that is dead, then as soon as we shower it with water, it vibrates with life and grows all kinds of beautiful plants" (22:5).

"We caused to grow [on the earth] every noble pair [of plants]" (31:10).

"Of all fruits [God] placed [on the earth] two of a pair" (13:3).

The term used for pair in Arabic is *zauj*, which means "spouse," to be exact. Thus, fourteen centuries ago the Holy Qur'an accurately furnished this knowledge to mankind when man knew nothing about botany.

Allah further states, "We have neglected nothing in the book" (6:38).

Thus, the Holy Qur'an provides information about everything in the universe, including the history, present, future, and the things that did not happen and, if they were to happen, how they would turn out to be. Islam is the only religion, to our knowledge, that directs humanity to contemplate over the creation of the universe the natural phenomena and religion's compatibility with the natural laws. Thus, Islam demands mankind to postulate over these facts with utmost curiosity.

"Ask them to stroll over the land to know how this creation took place" (29:20).

"In your creation and the way the animals are scattered on earth have visible signs for those who believe" (45:4).

"It is the sign of his existence that he has created skies and the earth and scattered therein different species of living beings" (42:29).

"And we have created opposite genders of each and every species so that you can understand" (51:49).

Imam Ghazali, an eminent Muslim philosopher and theologian, compiled a book under the title *Jawaherul Qur'an* (*The Essence of the Qur'an*) in which he selected 763 verses, almost one-eighth of the whole text of the Qur'an, that deal with material substances and the phenomena governing the functions of the universe.

A deep study of these 763 verses will clearly point out to the divinity, exaltation, providence, compassion, nourishing, protective capacities, unique sagacity, and systematic planning of the Almighty who directs and instigates mankind to investigate, analyze, and infer realities of the universe to deduce scientific and academic theories for the betterment of mankind. It must be clearly understood that there is no difference between the realities of the universe and the teachings of the Qur'an. Both are compatible to each other.

Necessities for Life

Here we have to see what are the necessities for life to sustain and nourish in this world of mud and slush. First and foremost is air to breath, second is water to drink and cleanse, and third is food to be healthy and strong. Regarding this, Allah says, "He it is who sends down water from the sky; from it you drink and from it grow the vegetation on which you send your cattle for their grass to eat. With it he causes to grow for you crops, the olives, date palms, grapes and every kind of fruit. Verily! In this is indeed a sign for people who think over these manifestations of Allah" (16:10,11).

The atmosphere is full of free air everywhere in every nook and corner of our surroundings. We have ample air to breathe without paying anything for it. Along with this free-flowing air, the nature is filled with streams of sweet and potable waters that run underneath the strata of the soil and over the ground gushing in the shape of rivers providing water to the surrounding soils and finally merging into the oceans. And the unique manner in which Earth provides grocery for us to feed ourselves and our domesticated animals.

"These are all the provisions provided by the sustainer and every bit of these provisions demonstrates that they are meant for sustenance not only to the mankind but for each and every thing which is created by the Almighty. And each and every thing which is created has been ordained to serve the mankind."

"Allah is he who has subjected to you whatever is in the heavens and whatever is in the earth, all of it" (45:13).

"Seest thou not how Allah makes the cloud move gently, then joins them together, then makes them into a heap; then you will see rain issues forth from their midst. And he sends down from the sky mountain like masses [of clouds] wherein is hail; he strikes there with whom he pleases and he turns it away from whom he [dis] pleases the vivid flash of His lightening, well nigh blinds their sight" (24:43).

"There is an abode for you and a provision for a time on earth. Thus, we did indeed establish you on the earth and provided therein for you means of sustenance" (7:24).

"It is we who have placed you with authority on earth and provided you therein with means for the fulfillment of your life. Small are the thanks that you give" (7:10).

All the above mentioned verses interpret each other. They refer to many natural processes that take place around us daily. For example, they mention the sun and the manner in which it provides heat to create vapors, which then cause the formation of the clouds. Then the winds spread the clouds to pour rain on earth, which help vegetation of different varieties to feed both humankind and the animals. The earth becomes an abode and produces crops as provision for the living beings. All are subjected under the control of mankind. This empowerment, given by Allah to man, includes authority over all the elements of the universe like air, water, oxygen, hydrogen, nitrogen, carbon, forests, mountains, rivers, oceans, all living and animated and inanimated creatures of the world; and all these are the means of sustenance for mankind and for other living beings on the earth. However, this has been provided to each human being for a limited period only, and then death emerges, and then emergence from the graves is imminent to face the Day of Judgment.

The verse 87:1-3 is a very comprehensive one, which elaborates divine principles under which the universe has been created; it declares, "Glorify the name of your Lord, the Most High; who has created [every material being] and then proportioned it [through a well-designed system] and determined for it [a natural order] then guided it [to adopt that system under which it is created]" (87:1-3).

Thus, Allah the Almighty is the sustainer and provider to all that he has created. All creation is governed by the following principles:

1. Creation: to create from nonexistence to existence
2. Orientation: to give proper shape and proportion to which he has created
3. Divine Order: all creation is strictly governed by physical laws under the authority of Allah's divine orders
4. Guidance: all created material objects are governed by strict guidelines to adopt a perfect system, which has been chalked out, in DNA, by the Creator adjustable to the environment.

While studying Qur'anic concepts of the universe, we have to keep these four factors in mind, under which the universe and its every creation is governed. If one wants to study the sustaining powers of the Almighty, then he/she has to study the creation that is a proof to Allah's greatness and his perfection. For example, Allah's creation of plant kingdom bears testimony to the very existence of a pragmatic planner whose creativity is manifested in the creation of colorful growth of various kinds of plants that cover the space of the earth. The verse 16:10-11 clarifies the plan under which the creation took place:

> It is he who sends down water from the sky which you drink and which grows the vegetation on which you feed your cattle. With it he causes to grow your crops, the olives, date palms, grapes and every kind of fruits. Verily, in this indeed are the signs (of the divine existence and providence) for people who contemplate on it. (16-10,11)

Qur'an is not a book of botany or biology, but it reveals the philosophy of the origin of a living thing. A life can only originate from another life. A cell is a unit of life that contains protoplasm, which is an absolutely essential force for the emergence of life. It is the perplexity of nature to determine from where and how this living matter emerges from the dead matter. No branch of science has been able to solve this puzzle. The Holy Qur'an solves this problem very exhaustively in one of its verses (6: 95): "Verily, it is Allah who causes the seed-grains and the date-stones to split and sprout. He brings forth the living [protoplasm] from the dead elements and he brings forth the living from the dead [like eggs of the birds] from the living. Such is Allah, then how are you deluded away from the truth." Science has come to conclusion that life cannot emerge from a dead thing. Instead, they say that life emerges from a living cell alone. The above verse is self-explanatory in the sense that Allah is the one who causes a lifeless seed or a date stone to split and sprout in a full blossom tree and from the dead egg creates a living being. In a detailed study on the living cells, French scientist Pasteur came to conclusion that every cell is made up of protoplasm, a jellylike movable material. Why can't we name it water-like matter? Yes, why not? And sperm is also a jelly-type water; hence, everything comes from water. That is what Qur'an says!

This protoplasm is common in both animal and plant kingdoms. Protoplasm is the source of life, and science has accepted this fact that protoplasm is a living matter. Yet they are dumbfounded to realize that a dead seed or a dead egg is endowed with that ability to generate life. Many other important functions occur in the protoplasm. For example, it also controls the task of copying information from one generation to another. Thus, science needs to accept the fact that there is *someone* behind the veil who administers these dynamic forces and fills the world with colorful fauna and flora. For example, the same qualities that Adam and Eve had at the time when they were born thousands of years ago are being carried by their progeny today after passage of thousands of years. Is it not a miracle of Allah? Today's man is the same who had been created by Allah after he declared, "I am going to fashion Adam as my vicegerent on the earth"—a beautiful creation on his own image.

"Indeed we have created man in the best of moulds" (95:4).

Pity on Darwin who was happy to declare himself to be the descendant of an ugly-looking chimpanzee and who miserably failed to establish his theory and gloomily passed away by telling that there were some "difficulties in the theory."

It is a fact that the Allah is the one who combined these inanimate or lifeless elements of hydrogen, oxygen, carbon, nitrogen, calcium, phosphorus, chlorine, sulfur, potassium, sodium, and some such other elements and asserted them to "be"; and they miraculously became a jellylike, watery material, scientifically known as protoplasm, the living cell, with the inherent capacity to copy generation to generation. Thus, the whole world of fauna and flora of hundreds and thousands of species along with mankind came into being and filled the world.

Microbial Organism

"Is it not he who originates creation, then repeats it and who gives you sustenance from heaven and Earth?" (27:64).

"And in the alternation of day and night and the fact that Allah sends down provision from the sky, whereby he quickens the earth after its death, and in the courses of winds are signs for people who use their understanding" (45:5).

Allah has created every animal from water. Some of them move on their bellies (worms and microbes), some of them on two feet (man and birds), and some on four (animals like horse, camel, bulls). These are the three creatures living all around the world simultaneously.

And in the earth are diverse tracts adjoining one another and gardens of vines and fields sown with corn and date palm trees, growing from one root and others from separate roots watered with the same kind of water, yet some of them are made more excellent in the quality of their fruits than others with a different taste. "Verily, in these things there are signs for people who understand." This is a miracle of Allah, that a simple kind of water with no taste or color or smell produces so many things that have different tastes, colors, and odors.

"Then let man look at his food, that we pour forth water in abundance. And we split the Earth in clefts, and produce therein corn, and grapes and clover plants [green fodder for cattle] and olives and dates, and gardens with many trees, and fruits and herbage—for enjoyment and convenience to you and your cattle" (80: 24-32).

From the above verses, we can infer that the repeated creation of the microbes is inherently deposited in the strata of the soil. During the rainy seasons, these deposits then lead to the production of life cycles of various kinds of flora and vegetation.

Furthermore, fresh rain water irrigates crops, renews the subsoil reservoirs, and supplies minerals to the parched earth, trees, and shrubs. This water is also stored up in huge quantities in the form of snow on the mountains, higher plateaus, and glaciers, which form a permanent reservoir of freshwater and reinforce the supply to the earth in the form of rivers, springs, and ponds.

> Seest thou not that Allah wafts the clouds gently, then joins them together, then piles them up so that thou seest the rain issue forth from the midst thereof? He sends down from the clouds volumes of water, part of it in the form of hail and causes it to fall on whom he displeases and turns it away for whom He pleases. (24: 43)

This is a constant cycle of life and death, which has been elaborately discussed in the above verses. The following paragraphs deal with this perennial feature of life hidden in the earth, which comes to life when rain falls and vice versa dies when there is no rain.

Everything created or caused to be created has its own value and nothing is a waste. The oxygen we breathe is the product of the living organism, which is microscopic algae of ocean plankton continuously releasing oxygen in a free form in the atmosphere while the plant kingdom and other nature's organism of the microbes generates carbon dioxide continuously along with other gases and chemical emissions. Thus, Earth's surface is filled with microbes, insects, ants, termites, earthworms, and scores of other creatures, which move on their bellies and derive food from the substrata of the soil and convert the soil chemically fit for generative qualities. These visible and invisible creatures make up the texture of the soil fertile in all aspects for the growth of the plant kingdom. The humus contains billions of living microbes of various different varieties each of which is transferring and decomposing several kinds of organic materials basically derived from the animals, plants, and other microbes and insects. Thus, soil contains a large percentage of this microbial organism. When animals and human beings die, they are consumed by this organism rapidly, and cycle of change and interchange takes place. This interchangeability fragmentizes slowly into simpler forms of compounds, and all the dead stuff returns to nature, and thus, a cycle of change and interchange continues in the living cells and cause life to start in different shapes.

How beautifully a great Urdu poet of India, Mirza Asadullah Khan Ghalib, has elaborated this cycle of phenomenon of life and death in one of his poems (in Roman English):

Sub Kahan, kuch, Lala—o—Gul mein, numayan hogaien
Khak mein kya soorthein hongi jo pinhan hogaein.

Translation:

Not all, but a few had converted into roses and lilies;
Those beauties when buried underneath the soil.

An eternal cycle of life and death is going on in nature on account of this microbial organism since nature's inception.

This is an accepted fact by the scientists that any dead material or lifeless thing cannot produce life and that life comes only from a living being. This fact was emphatically denied by the French scientist Pasteur who determined that life inherits in a cell, which is full with jellylike dynamic material called protoplasm, commonly found both in the animal and plant kingdoms. As a matter of fact, bodies of both animal and plants are full of these cells, which enjoy full life energy, and that is the sole miracle of Almighty Allah who according to the abovementioned Qur'anic verse causes grain and the date stone to split and sprout into a full-blown tree and these trees produce seeds (seemingly lifeless) and the eggs from hen or birds to give life to the chicks of their own breed. This is such a riddle that science has no answer. That therefore we have to accept the providence of the Almighty who brings life from the dead and who brings death to the living being.

Let us repeat the function of the microbial organism that has encompassed the present surface of the earth to enrich through the microbes, insects, earthworms, ants, and scores of other creatures, which derive food from it and convert the soil chemically and physically. These visible and invisible creatures make up the texture of the soil fertile in all respects. The humus contains billions of living microbes of various different varieties each transforming and decomposing several kinds of organic materials basically derived from the animals, plants, and other microbes and insects. Soil of the earth consists of a large percentage of this organism. When the animals and plants die, they are consumed by this organism rapidly, and a cycle of change and interchange takes place. This interchangeability fragmentizes slowly into simpler forms of compounds, and all the dead material returns to nature again, and then again further creation of the living cells emerges, and a new life starts in different shapes. Thus, the eternal cycle of life and death is going on in nature on account of the microbial organism.

Since then there have been many evolutionary stages, and each stage lasted for billions of years. At the end of each evolutionary stage, a new entity came into being in the form of unity, which gradually went into diversity, resulting in emergence of yet another entity and so on; the cycle of change and interchange, destruction and construction, unity and diversity, continues in order to preserve something out of nothing according to the systematic engineered program of the Creator.

Main elements like hydrogen, oxygen, carbon, nitrogen, magnesium, and sulfur played a vital role in evolving organic compounds of methane, amino acids, carbon compounds, carbonates, bicarbonates, hydrogen cyanide, and so many other oxides, which actually have been evolved only from the inorganic bases; and these compounds generate protoplasm, the living cell, that completes the origin of life to this planet Earth.

For example, let us study our physical structure and body. Its analysis tells us that thousands of complex organic compounds surround it. Our food is nothing but a bi-product of hydrogen, carbon, oxygen, nitrogen, sulfur, and phosphates. For maintaining our health, we eat proteins, carbohydrates, fats, and minerals. Glucose is the simplest form of carbohydrates, which is nothing but a complex compound of hydrogen, carbon, and oxygen. Thus, we may understand that how hydrogen, carbon, oxygen, nitrogen, sulfur, phosphates, and phosphorus after being organically combined could be able to produce the amino acid molecules, which in turn evolved into protein. So also all fats and oils are the complex compounds of these elements only. We use so many vitamins orally and intermuscularly to maintain our health and replace deficiency caused by exertion and labor; they also are the complex forms of those elements.

Earth: The Nursery of Life

When Earth cooled down to the normal temperature, inorganic evolution spurred, and different elements stuck together to form inorganic molecules. Thus, Earth became the nursery for free atoms of hydrogen, oxygen, carbon, and nitrogen to act and react and to immerse in various forms of molecules of carbohydrates, water, methane, ammonia, hydrogen cyanide, etc. Natural harmony among these elements wove the fabric for basic life patterns. When methane mixed with water, they jointly produced sugars and fatty acids.

"We created every living thing out of water" (21:30).

It means that every living thing originated in water. Life is, in fact, of aquatic origin in accordance with the scientific data. That means water is the major component of all living cells. Modern data leads us to think that the oldest living being belongs to the vegetable kingdom. Algae, the oldest known aquatic organism that belongs to the animal kingdom, probably came to life in the sea.

"God is the one who sent water down from the sky, and thereby we brought forth pairs of plants, each separate from the other" (20:53).

"God created every animal from water" (24:45).

There are several verses in the Qur'an that denote the aquatic origin of life of the vegetables, animals, and men; and they are strictly in accordance with the modern data.

As has been said supra, when methane mixed with water, they jointly produced sugars and fatty acids. When carbohydrates-cyanide acids affected them, they became nitrogen-based organic chemicals known as thymine, uracil, cytosine, and adenine. Sugar molecules formed carbohydrates, and the fatty acids produced fats and oils, which when combined with amino acids produced proteins. These organic molecules of sugars, phosphates, and the nitrogen-based compounds joined together to form most complex molecules of DNA (deoxyribonucleic acids) and RNA (ribonucleic acids), which are the fundamental molecules of the living organism. This has the sanctity of the laboratory tests. The experiments conducted by the biologists prove that DNA is a gene and a self-duplicating machine. It is a unit of life whose molecules not only contain almost all properties of the living organism but also the ability to pass or transmit them on. These living molecules generate a nucleic acid known as RNA. When DNA forms the nucleus, RNA helps organic compounds to surround the nucleus, and then they evolve to form cytoplasm. Cytoplasm carries duplicating characteristics for subsequent generations. The cytoplasm later evolves into a thin membrane, which ultimately becomes the cell.

This fact has also been confirmed by two important experiments. Heinz and Robles of the Virus Institute of California, in 1955, separated a tobacco virus TMV into two nonliving pieces of RNA and protein. A like experiment was conducted by Spiegalman of the University of Illinois. In both of these experiments, a virus that links the nuclei, atoms, and molecules of the physical universe was discovered. This virus rests in a stage between life and death. From this discovery, the scientists declared that life evolved out of the moving organic substances. Thus, the amino acids and the nucleotides are the essential molecules that generate building blocks of life. Each of them plays a different role in the building process of proteins. There are different types of proteins that are processed for different functions in the body. For example, the structural proteins build the structure of the body walls, hair, muscles, and bones while enzymes control the chemical reactions in it. Francis Creek and Watson, eminent physicists, found out in 1950 that our body contains twenty free-flowing amino acids and five nucleotides. They also discovered the genes that pass on correct information on proteins from one generation to another. Thus, DNA molecules control assembly of proteins that determine the nature of organism, and each living organism represents its own special set of DNA molecules.

CHAPTER V
Stages of Man's Creation

Life Is Still a Riddle

Despite the fact that it has been proven that life did, miraculously emerge from lifeless elements, as in the case of the basic elements of protoplasm and DNA, scientists still continue to question the presence of God. Allah says in the Qur'an surely it is he who can bring life from the dead.

"Surely, it is he who causes the seed grain and the date-stone to sprout. He brings forth the living from the dead and it is he who brings forth the dead from the living" (6:95).

This verse clearly mentions that it is Almighty Allah who generated life from the inanimate elements on one hand, and repeats it for generations to generation on the other hand. Is it not a miracle that the Almighty God infuses life into the dead things like seeds, date stone, and eggs? From the same seed and the egg, he then creates the same species of bird and plant and that too for generations together. This infusion of life is the manifestation of the Almighty's dominating providence of the universe. To this fact a renowned scientist declares, "To say that the body form is controlled by the genes is hardly scientifically illuminating than to say that it is controlled by God" (*Encyclopedia of Ignorance, Oxford*). The fact is that the protoplasm, DNA, genes, and the chromosomes are themselves a riddle for the scientists who could not determine the origins of all abovementioned and particularly about the DNA and its molecules. This fact was accepted by scientists in 1978, and even today the origins of the formation of DNA are unknown. In 1978, a scientist claimed that "it is still not known, exactly how these four kinds of building units are joined to form DNA" (Ruth Well, *Human Genetics*, 1978). Furthermore, in his book *A Guide to Science,* Asimov, a renowned scientist, asserts that in the creation of the DNA and the origin of life, religious beliefs manifest their sanctity. Without DNA, living organism cannot reproduce life. All the substances of living matter—protoplasm, enzymes and all others—whose production is catalyzed by enzymes, depend on DNA. How then, did DNA and life, started? This is a question that science has always hesitated to answer, because the religion's claims on the origin of life are much stronger than the religion's claims on the origin of Earth and universe.

The power that comes from life helps one to carry out the basic functions of living. For example, it helps the body to excrete, breathe, move, grow, reproduce, respond to the external stimuli, etc. Metabolically speaking, life is a property surrounded by a definite boundary. It is capable of exchanging materials with its surroundings. The chemical analysis declares that life subsists in cellular system containing nucleic acids and proteins. Genetically, it is said that it belongs to systems that are able to perform complex transformations of organic molecules and to produce its copies from the raw material, which are, more or less, identical and possess the ability to evolve further. To be more precise, life is an individual's animate existence, which distinguishes a living being from a dead one. Theologically, life is an "order of God." Allah says in the Holy Qur'an addressing his prophet Mohammed (pbuh): "When they ask you about the soul, tell them it [cometh] by command of my Lord, about which you know very little" (17:85).

Our firm belief is that Allah ordered life and it came into existence. However, a consensus of the scientific world about life is that "the possibility to explain a living organism, exclusively in terms of chemical and physical processes, at least, is a great faith than the theories which postulate a directing force" (*A Guide to Science*). Either way, somehow finally life came to Earth. Was it not a wonderful event? Indeed, it is in the history of the earth as well of the universe!

Description of Man/Woman

Man has many distinguished qualities, traits, and habits. He possesses a flexible, resilient, and well-coordinated erect stance, skilled hands and legs with opposable thumbs, oppressive countenance, powerful and sharp eyesight, sensitive ears, and communicative tongue and lips. Moreover, he/she is able to invent and use time properly; he/she is inherited with a developed massive brain, which is conscious, reflective and imaginative, courageous, and pragmatic to face any eventuality. These are all the benevolent qualities embodied in a single creature of the planet Earth called man, the crown prince of this gigantic universe. Allah says in the Qur'an, "Glorify the name of thy Lord who created and made man flawless, who determined the measure of his faculties and guided him accordingly" (87:1-3).

"He is who fashions you in the wombs as he pleases. There is no god but Allah, the exalted in might, the wise" (3:6).

"We have created man in the best of the mould" (95:4).

"We created you from dust, then from a sperm drop, then from clotted blood, then from lump of flesh, formed and unformed, then we caused him to stay in the womb for an appointed time, then we bring you forth as babes, then we cause you to grow that you may attain to your full strength. Then some of them die, and some of you reach to a feeblest old age" (22:5).

"We have created man from an extract of clay, then we placed him as a drop of sperm in a safe depository [womb of a mother], then we fashioned the sperm into a clot of congealed blood; then we fashioned the clot into a shapeless lump; then we fashioned bones; then we clothed the bones with flesh; then we developed out of it distinct new creation [man/ woman] so blessed is Allah the best to create" (23:12-14, 40-63).

Six Stages of Man's Creation

When the sperm of a man attaches to the seed of a woman's ovary, in her womb, it persistently joins to it; and from that moment of time, both start developing in six stages:

1. A combination of both male and female extracts remains in the womb for a week or so.
2. After a week, it develops into the shape of a ball, around which a combination of cell gathers and helps them to mix each other to become one.
3. It takes the shape of a horseshoe.
4. Then it develops into a shape of a fish and converts into an amphibian. Within a month from conception, glimpses of head, brain, heart, and backbone are visible.

Here the fetus develops the gender, but sex organs do not develop until the final stage.

5. Then it changes into a mammal, which has a tail also; it looks like a monkey in the beginning of the second month.

   (Is that the monkey in the womb that caught the attention of the learned Darwin, who postulated his unworthy theory that man is the descendant of a monkey-like creature?)

6. Then, suddenly it changes into an altogether very different shape of a man or woman by the end of the second month of the conception. (This is the stage Darwin denies to accept.)

Thus, all the genes are copied from the parents to the fetus, leaving no room for Darwinian evolution.

Qur'an had already informed mankind about these stages when the world had no knowledge of the science of embryology. When inquisitiveness to know about the creation of human being became inevitable, then scientists started to find out the mystery.

In the year AD 1677, Leeuwenhoek, a Dutch scientist, was working on a project to build a powerful microscope. While he was building it, he discovered that the sperm of a man contained living germs that made the sperm the life source for conceiving a child in the womb of a mother. Later, German scientist Fredrick Wolf declared that male's sperm only cannot conceive, but it has to merge and mix with the female's extraction in ovary at the time of mating and, on account of their interconvertibility, forms the basis for further development of the fetus. Finally in the nineteenth century, Ernst Haeckel established the foundation of embryology and wrote two books on it: (1) *Natural History of Creation* and (2) *Evolution of Man*. These books gave complete details of the creation of man. Qur'an revealed the mystery of the development of the embryo 1,400 years ago, and scientist confirmed and established the sanctity of the Qur'anic verses through their research in the seventeenth and nineteenth centuries. Qur'an says that man develops in six stages, which finally shapes up to a fully fashioned creature. This creature is gifted with all his abilities to see, hear, taste, feel, walk, eat, think, and visualize at the time of birth. These faculties later help him/her to question and ponder over the purpose of his creation, thus, leading him toward his Creator. Now comes the question of gender. In previous century, on account of acute investigation and experience, midwives could guess the gender of the baby; but in most cases, that too was just a guess. Today, an ultrasound machine is able to predict the gender of the fetus much more accurately and faster. Before that, it was practically impossible to predict the gender of a fetus. However, even with this machine things are not a hundred percent correct. The field of determining the gender is the sole domain of the creator of this universe. In Qur'an Allah relates the case of the mother of Mary, who wanted a boy so that she would devote him to the service of Allah. After listening to her prayer, Allah grants her a female child and consoles her by saying that "and Allah knew very well what she had given birth to, male and female are not the same" (3:35).

One needs to ponder deeply on this! How meticulously, pragmatically, and even arithmetically God has chalked out the plan of repeating the regenerative cycle of production with a complete balancing act. Under this program, from the time of Adam on the earth to this date, so far to our knowledge, no society, no region, and no country of the world has experienced the catastrophe of an acute shortage of either males or females. Thus, God continues to balance the male-to-female ratio for the purposes of mating and reproduction. This balance is maintained throughout the world in everything that can be divided into males and females.

Once again science is dumbfounded. No doctor, no scientist, and not even the most expert Darwinist can explain the balanced gender ratio maintained by God since the birth of this universe. Only the Almighty who alone is the master craftsman of this gigantic universe where everything is running on a preplanned program that can balance the gender ratio of the fetus that is enfolded in the "darkness of three veils" of a mother's womb (Qur'an 39:6).

Can the Darwinists dare to explain this arithmetically driven formula of the creator of the universe?

But it is very unfortunate to know that in an Indian province of Harayana, this gender equilibrium has been disturbed leading to a man-made disaster according to a report published by the Urdu newspaper, the *Siasat Daily*, of Hyderabad, India. On August 7, 2009, the ratio of man to woman had drastically fallen to 1,000 versus 618 in that particular province. The reason shown is very pathetic. The report says that on account of poverty, pregnant ladies have been constrained to abort female babies. This horrible situation is not the outcome of a year or two years, but such decrease in ratio must have been a matter of more than a decade. We have to question the authorities who have horrendously neglected since more than a long time to check this grim situation and willfully allowed the killing of the unborn female babies at a grand scale. Thus, although nature provides a balance between the population of men and women, this dangerously increasing gap in the ratio of males to females is the result of man's lack of belief on the Almighty who had issued clear admonition in the Holy Qur'an: "Do not destroy your offspring for fear of poverty. It is we who provide sustenance to them and for you too. Surely, destroying them is a great sin indeed" (17:31).

What a pertinent and befitting admonition has been given by the Almighty. If still proper education is not provided, the situation would become dangerous. This is not only an Indian problem, but many such instances may be occurring in poverty-ridden countries of the globe whose information is lacking. Since the problem of gender preference may be occurring on a global scale, we address also the authorities of the United Nations to take proper measures against these horrendous episodes.

Man inherits much from his/her ancestors, but if there is any part of the human body that has the ability to evolve at different stages, it is the mind. Man's common inheritance lies in his vertebrate structure, round head and skull, backbones with limbs hooked symmetrically, upright erect stance, a jaw that enables him to talk, a developed brain on top of the body with a developed sensitivity, an imaginative and understanding capability, a powerful stimuli and excitement to act and react promptly, and a complex nerve pattern with the ability to sense, send, and receive messages from outside, convey commands to the parts of the body for prompt actions according to circumstances, etc. Apart from all the other marvels of the body, Man's thinking ability distinguishes him from the animals. It gives him power over the entire animal and plant kingdom, as well as over the universe. A person's mind allows him/her to think and ponder over the purpose of his/her creation so that he/she can understand self and the Creator. Being able to recognize God and the purpose of one's creation is the sole reason behind the creation of this vast universe. It all boils down to say that man is the supreme commander of this vast and gigantic universe. He has an awesome power to modify his environment without changing himself.

"It is he who created for your benefit all that is in the earth and subordinated everything unto you whatever is in the earth and below the heavens" (45:13).

"And he has subjected unto you the night and the day, the sun and the moon, and the stars and subjected them unto you by his commands. These are signs for people who understand" (16:12).

"Has not man passed from space of time when he was not anything to mention of [from nothing] we created man from a sperm drop comprising many qualities; that we might try him, so we made him hearing and seeing and we showed him the way; he is either appreciative and follows it or is ungrateful and therefore gets punished with burning fire" (76:1-4).

"We have created man into toil and struggle" (90:4).

"Have we not made for him pair of eyes; and a tongue and a pair of lips; and showed him the two highways [virtue and evil]" (90:8-10).

"Indeed we have created man in the best of moulds" (95:4).

Thus, these verses nullify Darwin's theory that man is the descendant of monkeys, apes, chimpanzees, and whatnot.

The brain is man's directive force. It is a mini-working space with four different portions; each of such portions called lobes is designated to perform certain functions. They are the following:

1. Frontal Lobe—associated with reasoning, planning, parts of speech, movement, emotions, and problem solving.
2. Parietal Lobe—associated with movement, orientation, recognition, and perception of stimuli.
3. Occipital Lobe—associated with visual processing.
4. Temporal Lobe—associated with perception and recognition of auditory stimuli, memory, and speech.

Thus, all these lobes function together and evolve from the experiences that a man/woman comes across in his/her lifetime. Furthermore, because of the mind, man has the awesome ability to modify and adapt to his/her environment without changing himself/herself (http://serendip.brynmawr.edu/bb/kinser/Structure1.html).

Human Brain Works like a Telephone Exchange

The human nervous system consists of a brain, spinal cord, and a vast network of nerves, which run in the body, near and far. The human body consists of trillion cells, arranged in a supporting network for the body. While some of the cells fight diseases; some generate blood; others filter and pump blood to every nook and corner of the body through veins and arteries. These trillion cells are the offspring of a single soma cell to which the various other little connections, called dendrites, are entrusted. The brain controls functions of all these cells, and its communicative system carries impulses to every part of the body.

The nerve system of brain provides communications, which links senses through skin, eyes, nose, and tongue. It coordinates the activities of every part of the body. It stores memories and holds patterns of habit and behavior, thereby permitting us to learn. It records dreams and composes our thoughts. The nervous system carries the incoming impulses to the spinal cord and the brain. The brain has a set of electrically charged cells, known as neurons, which link sensory and action nerves. They are like dynamos conducting messages through electrical impulses and synapses.

The nervous system resembles a telephone exchange, where receptor organs receive messages and pass them onto the nerve fibers that act as the wires of this system. The spinal cord plays the role of the main cable, and the brain becomes an exchange system. The spinal cord is the relay center that contains substation cables as well. These stations help in handling simple reflex transactions without informing the higher level and, when required, notify the headquarters of what has been done.

One and half-pint of blood runs through the nerves of the brain per minute. It is experimentally proved by the biologist that the higher the supply of blood to the brain, the better the brain cells function. Thus, this may be taken as a hint to understand the brain structure of a genius. According to a study done in 1999 at McMaster University in Ontario and many other research projects, people who are smarter have some parts of the brain that are bigger when compared to a person with average IQ. Research affirms that the arteries of the gifted people should be larger in diameter to bring greater volume of blood to the brain than the others. However, practice and hard work also change the dimensions of the brain, and thus not everything is related to the size of the brain (http://www.scientificamerican. com/article.cfm?id high-aptitude-minds).

Brain versus Computer

The brain constantly receives impulses from human senses that are simultaneously seeing, hearing, tasting, smelling, and touching. The brain controls and responds to thousands of these messages every second and strives to coordinate them perfectly. However, apart from all these five senses, there is one more sense called the sixth sense; it relates to the subconscious. Some actions are coordinated by the subconscious only. This capability is not available to the computers. Receiving thousands of messages per second would overload the computer, and it would not be able to react as fast as the brain is able to perform.

The brain receives bulk of information from these senses through which it learns, adapts to environmental surroundings, and responds instantly. The ability to produce an output based on the input it receives allows the human brain to learn by trial and error. It induces conclusions from past experiences and creates new methods to deal with new situations while computers lack this ability. The human mind's genius also lies in its ability to adapt and automate daily functions. In other words, the brain has an excellent tool called forming habits. Once a habit is formed, it does not require too many resources to carry out the function, and more resources can be used to form new habits or for new situations. For example, a person who takes route 405 to work daily does not have to put much effort after a period of time. Automatically his arms will turn the wheels in the direction of his workplace. Or in the case of typewriting, it becomes a habit; and without giving much attention, the fingers start working subconsciously and get the work done without difficulty. The negative aspect of this is that habits (if unhealthy) do not change easily. In order to change habits, a particular alternative program must be repeated for a particular period to adopt the new procedure and to exit from the old habit. Computers here too are inefficient in handling such situations.

The memory of the brain is not absolute. That is why it takes time to adapt to new systems. This is also because the brain handles general purposes and not specific jobs. On the other hand, computers are meant for specific jobs, and their memory is absolute. Computers need no adapting as they are loaded with specific programs with specific output. The brain is dynamic and can adapt quickly when compared to the computers. However, the computer defeats the brain when it comes to specific functions. For example, calculations and charts. Thus, we may say that the brain is a general purpose processor compared to computer. However, while the computers are fed with specific programs by mortal experts, the immortal expert of the entire universe feeds every brain with specific programs to act according to the circumstances by inspiring them.

What Is Consciousness?

The awareness of self as individual being in called the consciousness. How amazing is it that in this complex vast universe man alone is aware of his being—only man knows that he knows. The moment he discovered himself, he became free to discover others and to think of others, to feel the emotions of others and visualize their thoughts. Consciousness links one not only with the fellow beings but also with the entire creation of the universe. It is the greatest and the most exclusive gift from nature to man. Therefore, man bears the responsibility for using it as a guide for the betterment of mankind and other living beings. Through consciousness men/women have been able to discover themselves. Men/women who follow their consciousness think, reason, plan, and discover through it. They also know what is right and what is wrong; feel pity; grant mercy; accept guilt and offer apology; program their income and expenditures; chalk out their plans; take care of themselves, family, relatives in need; offer charity to the needy and goodwill to friends and neighbors; and have the courage to sacrifice for good causes. This is the definition of consciousness upon which human culture and behavior have built giving rise to civilizations! For maintaining balance in one's life. Allah commands "to do good and liberality to kith and kin, and forbids all shameful deeds and injustice and transgression. He admonishes you that you may be careful" (16:90).

The following eight verses from thirty-one to thirty-eight of chapter 17 are a few moral injunctions from the Almighty:

1. "Do not destroy your offspring for fear of poverty. It is we who provide sustenance for them and for you. Surely, destroying them is a great sin" (17:31).
   Thus, abortion is strictly prohibited in Islam.
2. "Do not even approach adultery, surely it is a foul thing and an evil" (17:32).
   Thus, Allah provides a solution to preserve the progeny.
3. "Do not destroy the life which Allah has made sacred, save for the just cause; the heir of one who is killed wrongfully has our authority to demand compensation, but let him not transgress the prescribed limits in demanding compensation; for within the limits he is upheld by law" (17:33).

4. "Do not approach the property of an orphan when he is a minor, except for the purpose of his betterment, and fulfill every covenant; for you shall be called to account for" (17:34).

5. "Give full measure when you measure out, and weigh with a true and perfect balance; which is best and most commendable in the end" (17:35).

6. "Do not follow that of which you do not have knowledge; for the ear and eye and the heart shall be called to account for" (17:36).

7. "Do not tread haughtily on the earth, for thou canst thereby reach its confines nor reach the mountains that are in height" (17:37).

8. "Of all such things, the evil is hateful, in the sight of thy Lord" (17:38).

These verses are a few that provide guidance for doing right things. Now these are few that direct humanity to avoid wrongdoings:

"Say: Come, I will rehearse what Allah hath [really] prohibited you not to join anything equal to him; be good to your parents; kill you never your children, on a plea of poverty, since we provide sustenance to you and to them; avoid doing shameful things; whether open or secret; take not life, which Allah has made sacred; except by way of justice and law"; Thus, he commands you that "you may learn wisdom" (6:151).

"Whenever you speak, speak justly; even if a near relative is concerned" (6:152).

"Wherever you see good thing, pursue it zealously; and where ever you see anything wrong, avoid it persistently" (3:110).

This is a cornerstone of good civilization and culture of a society of the human beings. From the above few verses, we come to understand the ways to establish a good society. These basics have been inserted as a program for a better society by the Almighty into the spheres of conscience and subconscious mind of human beings. They act as a guidance for man's day-to-day life in maintaining order and peace in the society.

With all these attributes of man, now it is time to explore God's plan for man's civil life. In the following paragraphs, we shall try to analyze how and when man ventured into a civilized life, which became his greatest adventure for human generations to come.

The family institution was, according to Islam, established in heaven when prophet Adam and Eve met in paradise. By the blessings of Allah, they were given the sense to hide their private parts with fig leaves. Thus, man was taught to clothe himself and protect his body. Slowly and steadily the merits of the family life became visible, and they adopted what was best for them at that time of inception of the human history.

Then, as per program of the creator of the universe, when the population multiplied and many parts of the world were inhabited, Allah sent his wise and pious messengers to different regions of the world. They reminded human beings, in their language, the difference between good and bad, how to live in the society, and how to administer the available natural resources for the betterment of the society. That is how social justice evolved for the welfare of the human beings.

CHAPTER VI
The Islamic Renaissance

Marvels of Islamic Renaissance

Then there followed a dark period during the first six centuries of the Christian era as Edwin P. Hoyt, the author of *Arab Science: Discoveries and Contributions*, emphasizes that the West was stagnating. The Christian world lay in throes of the age-old faith. Earthly learning was despised and neglected. The teachings of the ancient authors fell into disguise, and their writings were sometimes deliberately destroyed as "pagans." Wars raged among the Romans and the Byzantines. While the Wild Barber Tribes were devastating the Northern Europe. Cities were raged, and the great libraries went into flames. Another century of warring and wasting and perhaps all the learning of Greece and Egypt would have been lost. At that critical moment, he says, at that time. Arab civilization had respect for knowledge. "Arabs brought science and culture. It stepped in and saved what it could save from the works of the past." He further states, "There was no society other than Arabs capable of supporting scientific enquiry during the AD seventh and thirteenth centuries." He says that during this time the concept of exact sciences of the ancients was based on metaphysical observations and speculations hidden in the mysteries. "But the Arabs ventured into the Greece and other ancient cities, and they went far towards developing the objective attitude that we regard in the modern world as scientific."

Islamic science took some time to attain its zenith. It lacked the means of information exchange. Muslim scientists were left at first to their own meager resources. At that time there was no such thing as Islamic science but only Greek, Roman, Persian, Indian and Chinese sciences existed. The Arab conquerors were the first to give science the international character, which I consider one of sciences' fundamental characteristics. Neither Alexander nor the Romans made as profound an impression on their subject races as did the Arabs. Arabs taught them the sacred language of the Holy Qur'an as a profound religious duty.

Arabic became the international scientific language. Any important scientific text was written in Arabic and was read or caused to be read all over the cultured world.

The rise of Islamic sciences was the result of individual as well as collective will to inculcate teachings of Islam in every sphere of cross sections of the society, both ethnic or diverse religious groups. This is not limited to the Arabs only; the newly converts like Turkish, Iranian, and even Indians joined the mainstream. Since Islamic science got an international appeal, other religious groups also entered in the arena to flourish their individual cause. Thus, Islamic science became a subsisting and lucrative business for them all.

It was drawn on a rich and varied heritage and sustained by many groups of people. One more important point is that knowledge as a whole was deeply rooted in the Islamic tradition, which was taught by Qur'an. It derives from the central belief that Allah is unknowable. To know about Allah, one must study his signs of the natural world. Perception of nature was regarded as a necessary prelude to the awareness of Allah. Thus, the pursuit of knowledge is nothing but faith and a religious duty. It is because the obvious stimulus was provided by theHoly Qur'an.

Second, Islam was in a transitional period, making inroads to the bygone-days civilizations and creating its new civilized image all over the world, which attracted highly nourished intelligentsia, which gave Phillip further to establish the supremacy of Islamic sciences, which in turn helped systematically dissolution of the classical legacy as a whole.

Arab scientists, geographers, and scholars had contributed much to the world of knowledge and science. The Arab scientists and men of learning had introduced the Indo-Arab numerical system. They invented algebra to calculate the unknown mathematical quantities and thereby solved problems via equations. They made astronomy their grand career and became able to correct Ptolemy's astronomical tables. They invented the solar calendar. Under the alchemists' influence, they formulated various laws of chemical processes. They were great historians and also geographers and cartographers.

According to Edwin P. Hoyt, "the Arabs and the people they conquered were not simply the transmitters of scientific ideas inherited from the Greeks, or even simply combiners who put together ideas from the Greek world and sciences from India, Persia and even from farthest part of the world, China. These men were interested in efficiency and advancement. They were critical of what they read, heard and they attempted to correct the errors found in Greek works."

The period of Islamic Renaissance brought scientific learning to its height and found bases for advancement in every walk of life. Illusions and mysteries of the past vanished under the influence of the "house of learning" of Baghdad, the Museum of Alexandria, the Darul-Uloom (university) of Cairo, the Great Mosque University of Cordoba (Spain), and the schools of Palestine, China, and India where hundreds of scholars from all parts of the globe came for learning. There were millions of manuscripts collected for imparting scientific education to those who came in search of knowledge. The stream of learning spread everywhere, and thus, the West took deep interest in learning the Arabic language. Many students from the West visited the Islamic universities and translated the knowledge of various sciences into their languages. The process of intensive translations from Greek, to Syrian, Persian, Sanskrit, and Arabic, between the eighth and the tenth centuries, led to an unprecedented accumulation of scientific and medical learning; and it also synthesized knowledge and thereby refined the Islamic civilization.

Thus, "the West," says Hoyt, "seized the torch of science and learning from the failing East [in AD fourteenth century] just as the Arabs had taken it from the dying Greece-Roman Society [in the AD sixth century]." Another scholar of fame, Robert Briffault, also accepted this fact in his voluminous book *The Making of Humanity*, in which he says, "The debt of our science to the Arabs does not consist in startling discoveries or revolutionary theories. Science owes a great deal more to the Arab culture and owes much to their experience." He further states, "What we call science arose in Europe as a result of new methods of investigation, or the method of experimental observations, measurements and the development of mathematics in a form unknown to the Greeks. That spirit and those methods were introduced into the European world by the Arabs." Thus, the summations of Hoyt and Briffault, like many other works on the Islamic Renaissance, testify to the scientific legacy of many Muslim scientists. Without this legacy, many important works upon which science is based today would have been lost and long forgotten. Surprisingly, this fact has justifiably been bravely acknowledged by the strongest leader of the world, President Barack Hussein Obama, in his befitting oratory from the podium of the elegant

Al-Azhar University, Cairo, Egypt, in his historical address to the Muslim world as a whole on June 4, 2009, in which he narrates:

> As a student of history, I also know civilization's debt to Islam. It was Islam—at places like Al-Azhar University—that carried the light of learning through so many centuries, paving the way for European Renaissance and enlightenment.

While furnishing Muslims' contributions and innovations in present-day sciences, he rightly applauded by saying:

> It was innovation in Muslim communities that developed the order of algebra; our magnetic compass and tools of navigation, our mastery of pens and printing, our understanding of how disease spreads and how it can be healed." Praising art and architecture and artistic beauties of Islamic culture and universal equality propagated by religious teachings of the Holy Qur'an, he further emphasizes that, "Islamic culture has given us majestic arches and soaring spires; timeless poetry and cherished music; elegant calligraphy and places of contemplation. And throughout history, Islam has demonstrated through words and deeds the possibilities of religious tolerance and racial equality. (*Los Angeles Times*, June 5, 2009)

These befitting remarks vouchsafe what professors Edwin B. Hoyt and Robert Briffault have opined about the Muslims' contributions to the present-day sciences. And that is what we are stressing in our lengthy sermons in these pages before you.

Impact of Qur'an and Its Teachings

The Muslim scientists, philosophers, astronomers, and physicists studied the Qur'an with integrity and learned how to reflect, infer, and understand the natural phenomena embedded in the universe. They studied various elements of universe and the human body. They scrutinized the universe, the earth, the heavens, the moon, the sun, the stars, the planets, the mountains, the plant world, the animal kingdom, the fauna and flora, the minerals, the flowing and raging waters of the rivers, the breaking of the day, the enveloping darkness of the night. They pondered at the beautiful and systematic design used to create the universe and everything in it. They contemplated also upon their own creation and arrived at the fundamentals through logic and scientific points of view. The following verses invite the reader to ponder, to investigate, and to formulate into understandable formulas for the betterment of the society: "In the creation of yourself and the fact that animals are scattered throughout the Earth are signs [physical and biological proofs] for those who believe" (45:4).

"In the alteration of the day and night and in all that Allah has created in the heavens and he Earth are signs for those who fear him" (10:6).

"On the Earth are clear manifestations of Allah regarding the universe for those who have faith and also upon your own self" (51:20, 21).

The natural laws are the fundamental laws of the universe that govern the natural phenomena, and they never change. The creator of this universe has drawn a natural system that controls the universe and has devised carefully the governing rules for the natural phenomena, which will never change. The following verses describe those fundamental rules:

"Heaven and earth are his domain; who had not bigoted any one as son, and no one is his associate; and has created all things and ordered them in due proportions and with balance" (25:2).

"Verily, all objects we have created in proportions and with proper measures" (54:49).

"He rules and governs from the heavens to the Earth, and you shall not see any change in the system, which runs the natural phenomena" (2:255). (Refer to part 3 above to rehearse the natural laws and their never-changing attributes as mentioned above.)

Qur'an respects the intelligence of the seeker and assumes that he/she will exercise it to the best of his/her ability. Qur'an is full of metaphors, similes, and illustrations of various types. It draws attention repeatedly to natural phenomena and argues from the physical, material, spiritual, moral, and many different angles calling man to the right path, forcing him to deduce laws based on logic and practice.

Renowned Islamic Scientists "the Pioneers of Islamic Renaissance" of the Medieval Period

The following renowned Muslim scientists, mathematicians, astronomers, astrologers, physicians, geographers, historians, and philosophers left behind many works of great importance that were in use until the late eighteenth century. These thinkers found no conflict between science and the dictates of the Qur'an. Instead they found great inspiration from the teachings of the Holy Qur'an and the traditions of the holy prophet of Islam. Among scores of Muslim thinkers of the past who amassed their experiences in an analytical formulation with research, investigation, and enthusiasm, a few of them are going to be introduced further in this chapter. Through their research, these thinkers gave the mankind a lofty treasure of wisdom, which emanated scientific theories and solved intricate problems of the nature. Thus, the Muslim thinkers became the pioneers not only for the fundamental change from the age-old beliefs of the Christendom to a new and practical outlook on the world of science, art, philosophy, engineering, etc., but practically founded the foundation also for the fourteenth-century European Renaissance. There is no doubt that had they not struggled to attain mastery over the natural phenomena and understood the underlying truth, there would have been no renaissance at all in Europe. The Muslim world is proud of its venerable heroes who sowed the seeds that sprouted in the glorious European Renaissance. Thus, the Europeans are indebted to these Muslim scholars, philosophers, scientists, astronomers, and physicians for the modern scientific, philosophical, and art works.

A few among them, approximately in chronological order, are mentioned below:

1. Jafer Al Sadique: **Jafer Al Sadique** (664-732) is one of the imams of Mehdavi sects of Islam. He was a great astronomer and studied the experimental designs of the movements of the earth, sun, and moon and came to conclusion that Earth was not flat but was rotating around the sun. He also concluded that the earth is spherical and not flat. Thus, he refuted the geocentric model of the universe common at a time when Earth was known to be stationary; and the sun, moon, and the planets were believed to be orbiting around it. He was the first to refute Ptolemy's theory of the sun, which stated that the sun had two movements, one going around the earth in a 365 days year and the other going round the earth in twenty-four hours, causing day and night. Al-Sadique argued that if the sun moves around the same Earth for 365 days, which consists of twenty-four hours per day, then it would not

be possible for the same sun to change its orbit and complete a rotation in another direction to complete the 365-day cycle. Instead, Al Sadique suggested that Earth's movement could be explained with a heliocentric theory in which the earth rotates on its axis in twenty-four hours and around the sun in 365 days. He also wrote a theory on the expansion and contraction of the universe. He stated that every object in the universe is always in motion including objects that appear to be inanimate. However, most of his scientific works were not recorded exclusively but were only narrated through his students. A famous student amongst his many students was **Abu Musa Jābir ibn Hayyān al azdi.**

2. **Abu Musa Jābir ibn Hayyān al azdi: (c. 721-c. 815) Jabir was a famous astronomer, philosopher, physician, and pharmacist. In the West, he was known as Geber. He was keenly interested in chemistry and is often known to have separated alchemy from superstition, turning it into a proper science. Many take Jabir to be the "father of chemistry."**

   It is said that once Geber (Jabir ibn Hayyan) asked Hzt.Jafer-e-Sadeq the following question on the movement of stars: "How does the movement of the stars keep them from falling?" Al-Sadiq replied, "Put a stone in a sling and swing it round your head. The stone will stay in the sling so long as you are rotating it. But as soon as you stop the rotation, the stone will fall down on the ground. In the same way the perpetual motion of stars keeps them from falling down."

3. **Al Asmi** (739-831) was the first Muslim scientist who contributed to zoology, botany, and animal husbandry. His famous writings include *Kitab al—Ibil, Kitab al-Khalil, Kitab al-Wuhush, Kitab al-Sha*, and *Kitab Khalq al-Insan.* The last book on human anatomy demonstrates his considerable knowledge and expertise on the subject and explains the six stages of birth of a child in the mother's womb. He based his work on the teachings of the Holy Qur'an, which was later on acclaimed by all physicians of his age.

4. **Musa Ibn Shakir** (803-873): He was a mathematician, astronomer, astrophysicist, and engineer. He was educated under an able teacher Yahiya bin Mansur. He was the pioneer in the science of astrophysics and celestial mechanics. In his book *On the Motion of Orbs*, he has described how the heavenly bodies and the spherical bodies are subject to the same laws of the physics that govern the earth. Thus, he refuted the classical theory that the celestial spheres follow their own set of physical laws other than Earth. As regards astronomy and mechanics, he discovered that there is a continuous force of attraction between heavenly bodies. He thus propounded the

abstract motion theory between the heavenly spherical bodies. On this discovery, Newton based his laws of universal gravitation.

5. **Ali Ibn Esa** (803 B): He was an astronomer. Together with Khalid Bin Abdul Malik in 827, he measured the earth's circumference, getting a result of 40,248 kilometers (or, according to other sources, 41,436 kilometers).

6. Mohammad Ibn Moosa **Al Khwarizmi** (died 840) was born in Persia. He was the first outstanding Muslim mathematician. He studied first in Baghdad and then went to India to master the Indian sciences. The word "Al Jebra" is derived from his use of the word "Al Jabr" ("coercion," "restoration") in his book *Al Meqala fi Hisab Al Jabr wal Muqabila*. He used the Indian system of counting including the zero. Thus, he introduced the Arabic numerals in mathematics, which are still in use internationally. His influence in the West was so great that his name was Latinized "Algorism." For a long time his calculations were used in the European world. Even today, his work is used for any recurring method of calculations. It has entered into the technical vocabulary—"algorithm"—of modern computation technique. He is also a master astronomer and geographer who introduced astronomical tables in Islamic astronomy. (See also item 31 of the list of part 2.)

7. Abu Kamil Shudja bin Aslam bin Mohammad **al Misri** (died 850) is a great name in the Islamic world. He influenced the development of Western algebra by building upon the foundations laid by Al Khwarismi. He solved systems of equations involving up to five unknown quantities and coined the theory of algebraic identities. Thus, his major contribution came when, based upon his calculations, he turned the theory into a powerful tool used for geometric research. (See also item 33 of part 2.)

8. Abu Baker Mohammad Ibn Zachariah **Al Razi** was born in Iran (850-925). He is popularly known in Europe as Rhazes and also as the Arabic Galen. He served as a physician to the Samanid ruler of Persia. His authority in medicine is well-known and comes second to Abi Sina. According to the National Library of Medicine and *Saudi Aramco World*, Razi wrote on many different subjects. He was a great thinker and studied many sciences like theology, astronomy, and music. His book *Libber Pestilential* is famous for medical terminology, and his voluminous book *Al-Hawi* was the largest medical encyclopedia ever composed till that time. It had important information on every medical subject that was available in Greek and Arab sources. He was the first to distinguish between measles and smallpox, and his book *Al Kitab al Mansuri* was translated by a Jewish physician into Latin. Thousands of his case studies are preserved even today for reference. It was the first printed encyclopedia

used for medicinal purposes in Europe. "It is known that al-Razi encouraged cure through healthy and regulated food. This regiment was combined with his emphasis on the influence of psychological factors on health. Furthermore, Al-Razi was an expert surgeon, and was the first to use opium as anesthesia" (National Library of Medicine and *Saudi Aramco World*). (See also item no. 10 of part 2.)

9. Abu Abdullah Mohammad Ibn Jabir Ibn Sinan al-Raqqi al-Harrani al-Sabi **al-Battani** (850-929) was a great astronomer and mathematician born in Turkey. According to an article published on Battani by J. O'Connor and E. F. Robertson, he belonged to a Hellenist religion (Sabian). However, he is known to claim himself as a Muslim. He was known in the West as "Albategnius, Albategni, or Albatenius" (history. mcs). His writings on planetary motion were remarkably accurate, and he also made original contributions to mathematics, notably in spherical trigonometry. His book *Kitab Marifat* is a book on the science of the zodiac, which describes the quadrants of the celestial sphere and deals with the mathematical solution of the astrological problem. Al-Battani determined with accuracy true and mean orbit of the sun, the obliquity of the aplitic, and the length of the tropic year and of the seasons. He explored the Ptolemaic dogma of the immobility of the solar apogee by demonstrating that it is a subject to the precession of the equinoxes. Thus, he refuted the geocentric theory and propounded the heliocentric theory in which the earth is an spherical planet and not flat. His work provided solutions to the spherical trigonometry problems by through orthographic projections.

His best-known achievement was the determination of the solar year as being 365 days, five hours, forty-six minutes, and twenty-four seconds. He was able to correct some of Ptolemy's results that were long accepted as authoritative. He compiled new tables of the sun and moon, discovered the movement of the sun's apogee, treated the division of the celestial sphere, and introduced probably independently of the fifth-century Indian astronomer Aryabhatta the use of sine in calculation, and partially that of tangents, which formed the basis of modern trigonometry. (See also item no. 40 of part 2.)

10. Abu Zayd Ahmad bin Sahl **Al-Balkhi** (AH 236-322/850-934) was a famous scholar, known today for his contributions to geography. Balkhi was born in Shamistiyan, a village near Balkh in Khurasan. He traveled to Iraq and studied Islam, philosophy, astrology, astronomy, medicine, and natural sciences. He wrote *tafseer* (commentary) of the Holy Qur'an in a book called *Nazm Al-Qur'an*.

He also worked on creating maps and contributed to the classical school of Arabic geography. (See also item no. 36 of part 2.)

11. Abu Nasar Bin Mohammad bin Tarkhan **Al Farabi** (870-950) was born in Turkistan. He is referred as Al-Farabius or Avennasar in the Latin texts as an outstanding Muslim philosopher. He developed the terminology of Arab scholasticism by drawing upon the Qur'an. His work was adopted by Latin scholars and Saint Thomas Aquinas, a great Christian saint. Al Farasbi is known for his works on different subjects like logic, physics, metaphysics, ethics, philosophy, and politics. He adopted the theories of Plato's republic and was the first Muslim to classify the different branches of sciences. Due to his contributions, he was called Al Muallim Us Sani (the second teacher after Aristotle), who had accomplished the same task in ancient times. Al Farabi also founded logic in Islamic history. His works on mathematics, physics, ethics, and political philosophy left a concrete impression on his successors. Notable among them are Ibn Sina and Ibn Rushd. (See also item no. 37 of part 2.)

12. **Al Wahshiya** (900) was the alchemist of Egypt who had cracked the Rosetta stone, eight centuries earlier than Jean Francis. The achievement of cracking the code is famed as a critical moment in code-breaking history.

13. **Ma Yiez** (910-1005) was a Chinese astronomer and astrologist. He was the chief of the astronomical observatory of the Chinese Sang Dynasty and was the first Chinese Muslim to become an astronomer of repute in the Muslim world.

14. Abul Hasan Ali Ibn Abd Rerhman **Ibn Younus** (929-1009) was a prominent Muslim astronomer of his times. His astronomical tables and observations were published in Cairo before his death as Al Zidj al Kabir al Hakimi in 990. These observations were adopted by modern astronomers as their guide in formulating theories about the expanding universe. In his Zidjs he corrected many errors and discrepancies of his predecessors. His contributions on plane and spherical trigonometry continue to have a great impact on the field of mathematics. The observations reported by Ibn Yunus interested S. Newcomb for their possible usefulness in determining the value of the secular acceleration of the moon.

Furthermore, Ibn Yunus's original contributions to spherical trigonometry were so impressive that caught attention of Delambre, Von Braunmuhl, and Schoy who ventured to explore further and got fame in that branch of mathematics. (See also item no. 19 of part 2.)

15. **Al Zahrawi** (936-1013) was Islam's greatest medieval surgeon. His comprehensive medical texts, combined Middle Eastern and Greco-Roman classical teachings, shaped European surgical procedures until the Renaissance. He is considered "father

of surgery." His greatest contribution to medical history was *Al-Tasrif*, based on thirty-volume collection regarding medical practice.

16. **Ibn Sahl** (940-1000) was a great mathematician who wrote a treatise "On Burning Mirrors and Lenses." Ibn Sahl discovered the law of refraction, which was named after him: Sahl's law.

17. Mohammad **Abu Al Wafa** Al-Bazadjani (940-998), born in Iran. He is known for the development of trigonometry. Mathematicians owe him credit for his spherical trigonometry, right angle triangle, substitution, perfect quadrilateral with the proposition of Menelaus, the four magnitudes (sine a: Sin c = Sin A: 1), and the tangent theorem (Tan a: Tan A= Sine B : 1). The world of science is also indebted to him for the method of calculation of sine of 30', the result of which is agreed up to eight decimals with its real value. His geometrical constructions are of great interest to the scientists even today. (See also item no. 34 of part 2.)

18. **Ibn Hawaqul** (943-969): The great chronicler and geographer of the AD tenth century spent his last thirty years in traveling to remote parts of Asia and Africa. He simultaneously recorded his valuable ideas about these areas and their produce. He took detailed notes that gave a broad picture of that area in connection with items of cultivation and mineral wealth. For example, in his famous work is *Surat al-Ardh* (*Face of the Earth*), he gave a detailed description of Asia, Africa, Islamic Spain, and Italy (Byzantine Empire).

19. Abul Ali Ibn Hussain al Haytham or **Ibnal Haytham** (965-1039) was born in Basra but mostly lived in Egypt. In Egypt he tried to correct the flow of the Nile but utterly failed and left the job. He was the best physicist of his time and a great a mathematician. His work has been thoroughly studied in Europe. He was known as Alhazan and Avenetan in Europe. He wrote exhaustively hundreds of books on mathematics, physics philosophy, and medicine. He based his studies mainly on Ptolemy. He also edited and criticized Ptolemy's works. Some of his reputed works are *Maqalai Istikhraj samt al Qibla, Maqala fi Hayath al Alam, Kitab Fil Manazir, Maqala fil Darul Qamar, Fil Maraya lo Muharika Bikl Dawair* on mathematics, *Fi Suratl Kasoof,* and many more. He correctly explained the atmospheric refraction and the augmentation of the apparent diameter of the sun and moon when they are near the horizon. He established that the rays of light start from an object and travel toward the eyes and not the reverse as emphasized by Euclid, Ptolemy, and Al Kindi. He discovered spherical aberration and determined that the Milky Way was very remote from the earth and did not belong to the atmosphere. He made valuable contributions to the commercial mathematics used even today.

His work on optics was so impressive that it was used by Newton much later. Furthermore, he developed celestial mechanics, which explained the orbits of planets. His work on the planetary bodies laid foundations for future scientists such as Newton, Copernicus, Galileo, and Keppler. (See also item no. 20 of part 2.)

20. **Ibn Al Hahum** (965-1040) was a great physicist and mathematician whose writings on optics and the scientific method are outstanding. He is considered the father of optics, the pioneer of the scientific method, and the founder of psychophysics and experimental psychology. AD Tenth century stands out as an exploratory period in the Muslim history, and Ibn Al Hahum was a pioneer of such a scientific era.

21. **Al Mawardi** (972-1058) is well-known as Alboacen in Europe. He was a famous thinker in political science of AD tenth century, a great sociologist and jurist, and served as a chief justice in Baghdad, an ambassador of the Abbasid Caliph to several important and powerful Muslim states. His contributions in political science and sociology are famous. He formulated the principles of political science and elaborately discussed and enumerated the duties of the caliphs, the chief minister, the cabinet ministers, and gave guidelines about the responsibility of and the relationship between the government and citizens. He has discussed the affairs of state in both peace and war. He was the author and supporter of the doctrine of necessity. His works are still referred in legal and governing matters.

22. Abul Rehan Mohammad bin Ahmad **Al Biruni** (973-1050) was one of the greatest and much-acclaimed scholars. He was also a well-versed mathematician, astronomer, and master of physical and natural sciences. He was a distinguished philosopher, geographer, historian, linguist, and chronologist of his time. His parents were from Khwarizam, Iran. He completed his early education in Iran under the guidance of renowned masters like Abu Nasar Mansur and Abul Wafa, great mathematicians and scientists of their period. He traveled Iran, and when Mahmood of Ghazni conquered India, he joined his services and ventured to get firsthand information about India. His memoirs are well-known in annuls of history of India. He wrote exhaustively about renowned personalities of India.

His writings became classical and authentic record of those days. Apart from his writings on history, traditions, customs, and rituals of various communities in India, he also wrote books on subjects such as astronomy and astrology, which became standard texts for teaching Quadrivium for centuries. The scope of his writings was vast and profound, which made him a great luminary in the history of world sciences and made him a great teacher of Islam. As an astronomer, his contribution to refute the geocentric theory of the universe in favor of heliocentric one is commendable. (See also item no. 21 of part 2.)

23. Abu Ali Hussain Ibn Abdullah **Ibn Sina** (980-1037), popularly known in Europe as Avicenna, a contemporary of Al Bairuni. He was given the title of Shaik ul Raies. He was a great thinker-philosopher of Islam. He wrote many books on medicine; his voluminous treatises on medicine known as *Canon of Medicine* remained as textbooks for teaching medicine in Europe and elsewhere for many centuries, and another book called *Al Shifa* was known in Europe as *Sanatio*.

He was born in Bukhara to a Turkish mother and Persian father. He memorized Qur'an by heart at age ten. He studied propositions of Euclid on logic and philosophy. But his main study was medicine. Along with being a physician, Ibn Sina was also a teacher and guide for hundreds of students of medicine. He based his studies on the concepts of Greek physicians, particularly physician Galen. Ibn Sina was acknowledged in Europe as "the prince of physicians." He was also known as the expounder of philosophy." Ibn Sina is a legend whose work continues to influence the field of medicine, philosophy, and theology. Moreover, he left undeniable marks upon many important and renowned figures like Alburtis Magnus, Saint Thomas, Duns Scotus, and Roger Baker. Thus, he became the harbinger of the approach of the great event Renaissance. (See also item no. 11. of part 2.)

24. Abu Bakr Mohammad **Al Kardji** (died 1019) was born in Iran. He was a great mathematician and engineer. He composed *Al Kafi* and *Al Badi* in which he attempted to liberate algebra from geometry. In his book *Inbat al miyah Al-Khafiyya*, he introduced the manual of hydraulic water supplies. From Iran he migrated to Baghdad, where he held high positions in the administration and composed his works *Al-Fakhri*, *Al-Kafi*, and *Al-Badi*. In his book *Al-Fakhri*, Kardji revisited Diphonates's work *Arithmetica* and studied the successive powers of binomials and coefficient of algebraic equations. In *Al-Badi*, Kardji developed the fixed points treated by Euclid and Nicomachus, and in *Al-Kafi* Kardji demonstrated the use of functions. Kardji's another famous work, *Inbat almiyah\ al-khafiyya*, provides information on hydraulic water supplies and contains detailed instructions of constructing and servicing the subterranean tunnels, among many other subjects. (See also item 32 of part 2.)

25. **Al Zarqali** (1028-1087) was a great mathematician and astronomer of his times. He is known for constructing the precision instruments for astronomical use. He designed and constructed a flat astrolabe for universal use, which could be used at

any latitude. Most significant was his discovery of "water clock" for determining the hours of the day and night and the days of the lunar months.

He was the first to prove the motion of the aphelion relative to the fixed background of the stars. He measured its rate motion as 12.04 seconds per year, which is remarkably close to the modern calculation of 11.8 seconds. He also contributed to the famous tables of Toledo.

26. **Ibn Al Sawabi** (died 1033) was a great physician. He wrote the famous treatise under the title "Book of Water," the first known alphabetical encyclopedia of medicine enlisting names of diseases. He prescribed medicines and physiological process or a treatment for several diseases. He elaborated the functions of the human organs. For example, he explained the process of vision, similar to Ibn Al Haithum. His work also contains a course for the treatment of psychological symptoms. His main thesis regarding treatment through controlled food for certain ailments coupled with particular exercise is much appreciated as the textbook. He also suggested that n certain symptoms specific medicines must be prescribed.

27. **Omar Khayyam** (1048-1132) was a great mathematician, astronomer, and poet of his time. His poetry "Rubaiyyath-e-Umar Khayyam" was translated by Fitzgerald in nineteenth century. Although he is known to propagate the philosophy of "live, drink, and be merry," because of his poetry, he was a man of high standards and character. He was a Sufi and practiced theology, philosophy, and mathematics. Islamic scholars were few who mastered art and mathematics but none comparable to that of the caliber of the poet-philosopher-astronomer Khayyam.

It is said that Omar Khayyam also estimated and proved to an audience that included the then-prestigious and most respected scholar Imam Ghazali that the universe is not moving around Earth as was believed by all at that time. By constructing a revolving platform and simple arrangement of the star charts lit by candles around the circular walls of the room, he demonstrated that Earth revolves on its axis, bringing into view different constellations throughout the night and day (completing a one-day cycle of twenty-four hours). He also elaborated that stars are stationary objects in space that if moving around Earth would have been burnt to cinders due to their large mass. Some of these ideas may have been transmitted into the Christian science post Renaissance. (See also item 35 of part 2.)

28. Abul Marwan Abul Malikibn Zuhar or **Ibn Zuhar** (1091-1162) was another great physician of his time. In Europe he was known as Avenzoer whose works on medicine, particularly on anatomy, was translated in Hebrew and Latin and were adopted in universities. As a physician he devoted his life toward practicing

skills. His unique way of diagnosing through urine and pulse reading became the yardstick in Unani medicine, which is in use even today. He wrote on many subjects of medicine particularly on treatment of patients, their diet, purgatives, kidney diseases, and particularly for leprosy, which also included a particular section categorizing medical questions and their answers.

He was a prominent physician, clinician, and parapsychologist of the Middle Ages. He was the first to test different medicines on animals before using them with humans. He gave detailed description about a widespread "mite," which caused itching on the body. He was known for his practicality and never liked speculations in medical treatment. (See also item 22 of part 2.)

29. **Al Idrisi** (1099-1166) was a geographer and cartographer of the Middle Ages. Al-Idrisi constructed a world globe map of four-hundred-kilogram pure silver and precisely recorded on it the "seven in habituated regions," with trade routes, lakes and rivers, major cities, and plains and mountains. His world maps were used in Europe for many centuries. It is worth mentioning that Christopher Columbus used his world map. He also contributed to the science of medicinal plants.

30. Abu Bakr Mohammad bin Yahiya, **Ibn Bajjah** (1106-1138) was born in Spain. Ibn Bajjah was a great philosopher, astronomer, mathematician, and teacher of physical sciences. He was a scholar in political philosophy. He developed the theory of spiritual forms. His doctrine is of utmost importance in physics where he applied the force of gravity with results that had a far-reaching historic effect and helped Newton in formulating his dynamic theory of gravity.

Ibn Bajjah's work also had an influence on Galileo's writings. Ibn Bajjah's attempt to quantify projectile motion by considering the velocity as proportional to the differences between the force and resistance rather than to their ratio is of much significance in the light of the latter's attempt of Bradwardine and the Mertonian school to describe motion quantifiably. Ibn Bajjah made another significant attempt by criticizing Ptolemaic planetary system. Instead he proposed a system wholly based on eccentric circles in cosmology. Newton, Galileo, and others are indebted to him. (See also item 38 of part 2.)

31. **Ibn Rushd** (1126-1198) was born in Cordoba, Spain. He was a known as Averros in Spain. Ibn Rushd was a philosopher and an authority on Aristotle's philosophy. He was often referred to as the commentator (of Aristotle). In fifteenth century a school was established in Europe based on his commentaries on Aristotle. He is famous for the theory of unity of intellect corresponding to the theory of common soul, which elaborates and claims that the true knowledge consists in the identity of the knower

with the known. He is known to harmonize Qur'an with philosophy and logic. (See also item 9 of part 2.)

32. Abul Fatah Abdul Rehman or **Al Khazini** was born in Persia during the twelfth century. Originally a Greek slave, Al Khazini flourished in Merv and attended schools to study mechanics and hydro statistics. His writings on astronomy and physics (in AD 1130) became textbooks for Byzantine scholars. His book on hydrostatics contains a series of theorems deriving from the classic works of Archimedes, Euclid, and Menelaus. His outstanding writings on scientific matters made him an undisputed master in his subjects. Mieli, the Italian historian of science, has compared the determination of specific weights by Al-Biruni and Al-Khazini with modern results. Al Khazini's method was based on measuring the values of different substances by taking a particular substance with fixed value. His most significant work is seen when he after complete scrutiny and labor found out the comparative values of some precious metals like gold, mercury, emerald, and quartz showing in a separate table. (See also item no. 39 of part 2.)

33. **Ibn Al Baithar** (1197-1248): A great scientist of Spain, he was a great botanist and pharmacist whose works are still in use in the universities.

34. **Al Baturgi, Nur Ed-Din**: (died 1204) known in the West as Alpetraguis. He was a famous Arab astronomer and philosopher. He was born in Morocco, then settled in Seville, Spain. His astronomical disclosure was about a crater on the moon. It was verified by many astronomers. For his extraordinary discovery, he was honored by granting that crater his name: the Alpetraguis.

35. **Ibn Banna** (1256-1321): He was a great mathematician of his age and profusely studied Euclid, the Greek mathematician. He wrote a large number of works including an introduction to Euclid's elements. His books on algebra and astronomy are well-known even today.

36. **Ibn Shathir** (1304-1375) was a great astronomer well-known for his most famous work called "A Final Inquiry Concerning the Rectification of Planetary Theory." He discussed the motions of moon in detail in which he eliminated the need for an equant by introducing an extra epicycle, departing from the Ptolemaic system. This same method was adopted by Copernicus. He used it to elaborate his famous heliocentric theory of the universe. To prove his antigeocentric theory, Ibn Shathir demonstrated trigonometrically that the earth was not the exact center of the universe. Ibn Shathir's discoveries paralleled that of Keppler and Copernicus, yet the world only hears what the Europeans say. Ibn Shathir also challenged the notion that Earth is flat and static. Instead he asserted that Earth has an elongated

shape and that it is circling around the sun. He adopted the heliocentric theory of Imam Jafer-e-Sadique against the geocentric theory. The fact is that Ibn al Shatir's forgotten model was rediscovered in the late 1950s by E. S. Kennedy and his students at the American University of Beirut.

The discovery raised an intriguing question. It was quickly recognized that the Ibn Shatir and Margha inventions were the same type of mechanism used by Copernicus a few centuries later to eliminate the equant and to generate the intricate changes in position of the earth's orbit.

Copernicus, of course, adopted a heliocentric arrangement as modeled by Ibn al Shatir, and the problem of accounting for the slow but regular changes in a planet's orbital speed remained exactly the same as mentioned by Ibnal Shatir (excerpts from Owen Gangerich from his Islamic astronomy, *Scientific American*, April 1986).

Further to this Copernicus had referred twenty-three times in his book *DE Revolutionibus* about Al Batani, another Muslim astronomer who also refuted the geocentric theory of Ptolemy. That suggests that Copernicus was also influenced by many more Muslim astronomers who had rejected the geocentric theory of the universe and struggled to emphasize that Earth was not flat but a spherical planet as others.

37. Abd Rehman Ibn Muhammad **Ibn Khaldun** (1332-1406) was a great personality of the declining days of Islamic empires. He was a great philosopher, historian, and sociologist, father of historiography and sociology. He was a great scholar, teacher, and a principled magistrate who was responsible to maintain law and order in a lawless society. He studied Qur'an, hadiths (sayings of the Prophet), and fiqh (Islamic jurisprudence) under the guidance of the famous teachers of Tunis of the North Africa.

His great work *Muqaddama* is well-known in the Islamic literature and a much-referred book by scholars and historians. It is an introduction to his book *Kitab al Ibar*, a collection of origins of history of the Arabs and Berbers of North Africa. It is a historian's craft. It presents an encyclopedic synthesis of the methodological and cultural knowledge necessary to enable the historians to produce scientific works on annuls of world history.

He created a new science by recording the basis of the changes in the human behavior in a particular society at different times. According to Khaldun historical facts need motives, and they cannot be recorded in vacuum but need to be recorded according to the political structure, historical background, sociology, and economic factors of that particular time. His work contemplates the study of the whole of the human past based on its social, economical, and cultural aspects, thereby setting out rules of constructive criticism, based essentially of the criterion of conformity with reality of the nature of things. He remarks that at certain exceptional moments in history, one feels as if he/she is a part a changing world, a new order. In these circumstances he emphasizes the need to record the situation of the humanity and of the world is crucial. Ibn Khaldun felt that the civilization he belonged to would soon vanish. He knew that he or any other power could not avert the coming end of the Islamic empires, but he made sure to keep record the crucial changes.

Finally, his *Muqaddamah* became a source to a number of disciplines, which became independent sciences after the Renaissance. He laid down rules to describe the fundamentals of history. Ibn Khaldun saw history as a real science and not a mere historical record of events. He beautifully demonstrated this point by denominating the causes of occurrences of certain events. He said that events occur as a result of social and economic structures of a given time. Furthermore, he divided his study of society into different social and psychological elements, which become the foundations of not only political psychology, general psychology, ethical psychology but also the economic psychology. (See also item 30 of part 2.)

38. Ahmad **Ibn Majid** (1432-1500) was one of the famous Arab navigators. He became famous in the West as the navigator associated with helping Vasco da Gama who found his way from Africa to India. He was the author of nearly forty works of poetry and prose. His most important work was *Kitab al Fatwa Fil Usul ilm al Bahar* (*Book of Useful Information on the Principles and Rules of Navigation*), written in 1490.

39. Aamir Jalal **Al Mosawi** (1450): One of the most distinguished Iraqi physician. He was the head of Copernicus scientist's international panel in Iraq. He demonstrated a new model for the management of end-stage renal failure. He also described the first case of Coffin-Siris syndrome in Arabs.

Note: There are thousands of Muslim scientists, philosophers, thinkers, astronomers, etc., who transformed the Middle Ages and helped to keep the torch of knowledge alive. The author does not wish to list them all here as it is beyond the scope of this book. However, the abovementioned list is to just give the reader an idea about the many great thinkers of Islam who busied themselves in learning and teaching while the West was stagnating in superstition. More information on any of the abovementioned scholars can be easily found online or in libraries. Some of sources used for providing information about them are *Islamic Encyclopedia* and *Encyclopedia Britannica*. Wikipedia was also a big help in finding some reliable sources for the above information. Others are Glick, Thomas; Eds (2005), Medieval science, technology, and medicine : an encyclopedia. ""Abu Musa Jabir ibn Hayyan"". Encyclopædia Britannica Online and History of Analytical Chemistry By Ferenc Szabadváry.

Impact of Translation of Muslim Masterpieces: Foundation for the European Renaissance

In order to translate the scientific works of the eminent Muslim scholars, which were in Arabic language, many Europeans first learned the Arabic language; then they translated the following important books from the Muslim world, especially Islamic Spain into Greek and Latin. One of the most prominent translators in Spain was Gerard of Cremona, who translated ninety books from Arabic to Latin.

Some of the many works of various translators are the following:

1. Mohammad Ibn Moosa Khwarizmi's "Algebra wal Muqabila"
2. Jabi Ibn Aflah's "Elementa Astronomica"
3. Al Kindi's "On Optics"
4. Ahmad Ibn Muhammad Farghani's" On Elements of Astronomy on the Celestial Motions"
5. Al Farabi's" On the Classification of the Sciences"
6. Al Razi's "The Chemical and Medical Works"
7. The Books of Swabith Ibn Qurra
8. The Books of Arzakhel, Jabir Ibn Aflah, Abul Qasim, and Ibn Haythum (including "The Book on Optics")
9. The Books of Mohammad Ibn Jaber and Al Khwarizmi
10. The Books of Abul Qasim (including the al Tasrif, Mohammad al Farazi's Great Sindhanta based on the Surya Sidhanta and the works of Barhamgupta)
11. The Books of Al Razi and Avicina (including "The Book of Healing" and *The Canon of Medicine*)
12. "The Books of Averroes"
13. The Books of Tyhabit al Qurra, Al Farabi, Ahmad Ibn Mohammad ibn Khathir, Humayan Ibn Ishaque, and his nephew Hubaysh ibn al-Hasan

14. The Books of al Kindi, Abraham Baer Hayya's Liber Embadorum, Ibn Sarabi's (Serapion Junior)

15. The Books of Qusta Ibn Luca

16. The Books of Maslamah Ibn Ahmad al Majriti, Jafer Ibn Mohaqmmad, Abu Mash'ir, and al Ghazali

17. The Books of Nooruddin al Betrugi, including "On the Motions of the Heavens"

18. Ali Ibn Abbas al Majusi's medical encyclopedia "The Complete Book of the Medical Art"

19. Abul Mashar's "Introduction to Astrology"

20. The Books of Maimonides

21. The Books of Ibn Zezla (Byngezla)

22. The Books of Mesawaiyh, Serapion, al-Qifti

23. Albe'thar. Abu Kamel Shuja's Algebra

24. The Books on Chemical practices of Geber

25. The De Proprietatibus Elementorum, an "Arabic work on geology written by a pseudo-Aristotle." By the beginning of the thirteenth century

26. Mark of Toledo translation of the Qur'an and various medical works

27. Fibonacci presented the first complete "European account of the Hindu-Arabic numerals" from Arabic source in his" Liber fe Abaci (1202).

28. http://en.wikipedia.org/wiki/Islamic_science—_note-Bieber#_note-Bieber Al Khazini's "Zij as-Sanjari" was translated into Greek by Gregory Choniades in the thirteenth century and was studied in the Byzantine Empire.

29. "The astronomical corrections to the Ptolomeic Models" made by Al Battani and Averroes

30. "The non-Ptolemaic models" produced by Mohiuddin Urdi (Urdi lemma), Naseruddin Tusi (Tusi Couple)

31. Ibnul Shatir was later adapted into the Copernicus model

32. Al Kindi's (Alkindus) law of Terrestrial Gravity influenced Robert Hookes's law of celestial gravity, which in turn inspired Newton's law of gravitation

33. Abul Rayhan al Bairuni's Ta'rikh al-Hind and Kitab al-qanun al-Mas'udi were translated into Latin as Indica and Canon Mas'udicus respectively

34. Ibnul Nafis's "Commentary on Compound Drugs" was translated into Latin by Andrea Alpago (d. 1522), who may have also translated Ibn al-Nafis's "Commentary on Anatomy in the Canon of Avicenna," which first described pulmonary circulation and coronary circulation, and which may have had an influence on Michael Servetus, Realdo Columbus

35. William Harvey's Translations of "the algebraic and geometrical works of Ibn al Haythum," Omar Khyyam and Nasiruddin al Tusi were later influential in the development of non-Eucledean geometry in Europe from the seventeenth century

36. Ibn Tul bin Tufil's Havy Ibn Yaqdhan's was translated into Latin by Edward Pockoke in 1671 and into English by Simon Ockley in 1708 and became "one of the most important books that heralded the Scientific Revolution.

37. Ibnul Baitar's Kitab al-Jami fi al-Adwiya al-Mufrada also had an influence on European botany after it was translated into Latin in 1758.

Furthermore, an eminent European scholar Will Durant states about the Muslims and their innovations in science and philosophy in these befitting words:

> Chemistry as a science was almost created by the Muslims; for in this field, where the Greeks(so far as we know) were confined to industrial experience and vague hypothesis, the Saracens Muslims introduced precise observations, controlled Experiments, and careful records. They invented and named the composed lapidaries, distinguished alkali and acids and investigated their affinities, studied and manufactured hundreds of drugs. Alchemy, which the Moslems inherited from Egypt, contributed to chemistry by a thousand incidental discoveries, and by its method, which was the most scientific of all medieval operations.

Another scholar, George Sarton, wrote in the *Introduction to History of Science*:

We find in his (Jabir, Gaber) writings remarkably sound views on methods of chemical research, a theory on the geologic formation of metals (the six metals differ essentially because of different proportions of *sulfur* and mercury in them) preparations of various substances (e.g. basic lead, carbonates, arsenic and antimony from the solo hides).

He further states, "The main, as well as the least obvious, achievements of the Middle Ages was the creation of the experimental spirit and this was primarily due to the Muslims down to the twelfth century."

A prominent scholar, Oliver Joseph Lodge, wrote in the *Pioneers of Science* that "the only effective link between the old and the new science is affordable by the Arabs. The dark ages come an utter gap in the scientific history of Europe, and for more than a thousand

156

years there was not a scientific man of repute except in Arabia." Thus, the experimental method, reason, and observation introduced by the Arabs were responsible for the rapid advancement of science Allama Iqbal wrote in his *The Reconstruction of Religious Thought in Islam Medieval Times.*

Thus, these and many more books that were translated into Latin, Greek, and English languages helped the European scientists to study and formulate their theories and formulas, which became the foundation stones for the European Renaissance.

European Renaissance and Afterward

The European Renaissance based on the Muslim Renaissance really started from a period when human consciousness had attained enough maturity and confidence to challenge the already established doctrines of the churchdom. There was a bitter rivalry among the religious authorities and the torchbearers of scientific understanding. For those confrontations, many had to pay heavily with torture and even by death. Among these challengers, there came the brilliant Polish astronomer Copernicus (1473-1543) who after careful and detailed observations of the Muslim astronomers' heliocentric theory declared that Earth and other planets of the universe are revolving around the sun. He also declared that Earth is not flat but spherical in shape. He thus propagated the heliocentric theory based on Muslim astronomers' findings. This was a great challenge indeed, which nullified the centuries-old doctrine of the universe and gave a new understanding of the universe. The astronomers were puzzled by this new doctrine and started gazing at the universe through their telescopes to find out the real truth.

Galileo (1564-1642), the Italian astronomer, took great pains in constructing a big telescope hitherto inbuilt and glimpsed the universe under the new concept and found what Copernicus had told was utterly correct. This revolutionized entire ideology of the universe and foundations of modern astronomy were laid down during the sixteenth century, bringing a significant change and challenge to the supremacy of the Roman Catholic ideologies.

This all happened because the Middle Ages were ruled primarily by the three powerful Eastern Muslim kingdoms: the Ottomans, Safavids, and Mughals. It was under them that much of the knowledge was passed from the Greek and Latin sources to Arabic and English while the West was still struggling to get out of its dark period. The fall of the

Constantinople (1453) to the Ottoman Empire drove many Italian and Greek scholars from the East to the West. The most significant and revolutionary discovery was that of printing press in 1440, which gave a real advancement to knowledge. This brought a new interest in the world of learning by translating manuscripts originally written in Latin, Greek, and Arabic languages.

"Of all the translations," Hoyt says, "who helped bring fruits of Muslim Civilization to Europe, probably the most important was that of the Italian Scholar, Gerard of Cremona, who learned Arabic language first and spent most of his life in translating the scholastic works of the Muslim Scientists and had taken the trouble for translating at least ninety voluminous books almost in all sciences including the *Almagest* of Ptolemy. The books on medicine written by Bu Ali Sena itself consisted of more than a million words, and they were all translated by him bit by bit.

The period when the West began to open its doors to knowledge and changed its way of thinking in many different aspects of life is called the European Renaissance. This all happened because certain prominent and pioneering Muslim intellectuals invested their skills in the study of important sciences, such as mathematics, mechanics, astronomy, astrology, alchemy, chemistry, medicines, geography, cartography, music, etc. They hoped to transform scientific data from metaphysical speculations to experimental and operational realities. They put their intellectual abilities to identify and verify observations and accurate descriptions based on correct measurements. They developed the objective scientific attitude in all their pursuits. In this adventure they were rightly and promptly guided by the Holy Qur'an, which directed them to postulate minutely on each and every object of the universe. Thus, with their intellectual curiosity they explored and transmitted the science of bygone days into a reality. With this new method of understanding, they established the foundation of that scientific knowledge, which was hitherto unknown to the Western world.

Thus, it can be said that the knowledge that was hidden so far in the custody of the prejudiced few, now spread like fire in many languages. This uprising for learning paved the way for establishing grounds for research and experimentations.

Many scholars from the West and East came together to participate in the new changes that were occurring in the West based on the Islamic Renaissance. Apart from Copernicus of Poland and Galileo of Italy, a contingent of scholars, philosophers, scientists, astronomers, artists, and literates emerged on the learning front. Among them are famous Leonardo da

Vinci of Rome; Harvey, Bacon, Newton, and Darwin of England; Mendel and Freud from Austria; Linnaeus and Arrhenius from Sweden; Descartes, Pascal, Curvier, and Pasteur from France; Von Humboldt, Liebig, Whorf, and Einstein from Germany; Lyle Maxwell from Scotland; Kelvin from Ireland; Marie Curie from Poland; Mendeleyev from Russia; Bohr from Denmark; Maeterlinck from Belgium; Rutherford from New Zealand ; Osler from Canada; and Franklin, Henry, and Langley from USA. Many scholars from the Middle East, India, Crete, Persia, China, Japan, and from various parts of the world brought fragments of knowledge, which gave birth to the twentieth-century technology of which the mankind is proud of having inherited from those scholars.

While knowledge grew on one hand, so did the desire to explore. Thus, the seeds that were sown by the Islamic Renaissance sprouted and took root in the European Renaissance. As knowledge spread from the East to the West, scholars rushed to discover the world around Europe. Fundamental change in the outlook and behavior of the individual coupled with the awakened and powerful nation states opened up new horizons for exploration. Along with the spread of knowledge, the Middle Ages also saw a rise in oceanic voyages, and discovery of new lands was encouraged by governments that established trading corporations. East India Company of England and another like company in Netherlands explored their trade zones into the Eastern Hemisphere as far as India and Indonesia for spices, silk, cotton fabrics, tin, etc. The American continent was discovered by Columbus in 1498. However, it was during this time that England saw the golden age of Henry VIII and Queen Elizabeth, Spain was being governed by Ferdinand II of Aragon, and France was ruled by Francis II. Many city states of Ferrara, Florence, Montana, Milan, Venice, and papal Rome were established. Europe saw many advancements and progress toward the end of the Middle Ages. However, they were accomplished by the spread of knowledge and voyages that were inspired by Islamic Renaissance based on the Holy Quran and the sayings of the prophet Muhammad (pbuh). Thus, we Muslims are proud to inherit the legacy of the Muslim pioneers of the medieval period and later on transferred to the European intelligentsia to crop the fruits for the betterment of mankind. Jazakallashu Khairun. Amen!

*   *   *   **PART ONE ENDS**   *   *   *

GO TO PART TWO

PART TWO

AL-QUR'AN AND ISLAMIC SCIENCE
PRACTICAL APPLICABILITY FOR THE BENEFIT OF SOCIETY
BY PROFESSOR SYED AKHEEL AHMED

TABLE OF CONTENTS

PART TWO

I

Introduction

Faded was a glory that was Greece; gone was the grandeur that was Rome. Ahead lay the "golden period," the five-hundred-odd years (AD seventh to twelfth centuries) during which learning was held in high esteem, experiment was encouraged, and originality was a sacred asset. Science entered a period of liberation from bondage and slavish convention, which continued until it was broken by those bad spirits of crusades.

History forms the basis of all knowledge and is a convenient avenue of approach to any subject of study. It is therefore only natural to regard the evolution and progress of Islamic science from bygone times as an essential background to modern scientific education. Unfortunately, however, the rapid advances and new discoveries of recent years have tended to eclipse the work of the early pioneers; and although reverence is still accorded to the memory of such great figures of Islamic history as Ar-Razi (Rhazes), Jabir-ibn-Hayyan (Geber), Omar Khayyam, the history of Islamic science in general has not received the recognition, which the importance of the subject would appear to demand.

There is at present no systematic effort to study Islamic science in any country, including Islamic states Iraq, Iran, and Saudi Arabia, to mention just a few. Nor are there enough periodicals devoted to the cause of Islamic sciences. Nevertheless, there are few publications that have kept interest alive. A too-often early contribution to science by a Muslim scientist has been regarded as merely quaint and sometimes amusing—alchemy, for example—now obsolete and of little value to the modern world. On the other hand, it is encouraging to note, especially in the younger generation, a growing appreciation of the true purport of history of Islamic science and its bearing upon the science and technology of today. The need for a historical background to Islamic science is securing recognition among those who regard the truth and facts of history as something more than a mere information accomplishment. Since no Indian author has produced in recent years to meet this need, an attempt has been made in the following pages to construct an outline of the progress of Islamic science from the days of Prophet Mohamed to the end of fifteenth century. An outline does not aim at finality, and many worthy contributions might have been omitted due to its vast subject matter and the loss of original manuscripts.

A history of Islamic science should not be simply a chaplet of biographies or yet a maze of dates and events but rather a consecutive narrative, showing the progress of the human and material development from the earliest times to the present day. The work of the leading scientists and philosophers, the fashions and thoughts in Islamic science through the ages, the geographical mark of science from Greece to Jundishapur and Baghdad and Thence by way of Cairo to Cordoba, the epoch-making researches of Ar-Razi (Rhazes) and Ibn Sina (Avicenna) and Ibn al-Haytham (Alhazen) and many other—these are but a few topics that the historian must fit into his mosaic of Islamic history, each detail as it falls into a place, revealing a steady and natural sequence. It is a noble theme, and it is hoped that the story, however imperfectly told, may stimulate interest in those achievements of the past, which help us to solve the problems of the present and which must constitute the foundation of all future progress of the present generation.

II

*Islamic Science—
An Overview*

As the world moves toward the twenty-first century—an era of high technology and innovation change—the attitude of Muslims toward science and technology will undergo a phenomenal change. The effectiveness of this change will depend upon sociotechnical changes in Islamic society and on its adoption to the new thinking and new challenges.

> There is no question, but, today, of all civilizations on this planet, science is the weakest in the lands of Islam. The dangers of this weakness cannot be over-emphasized, since honorable survival of a society depends directly on its strength in science and technology in the condition of the present age.

The spread of ideas demands a new impulse. The coming of Islam six hundred years after Christ was the new powerful impulse. It started as a local event, but once Prophet Mohamed conquered Mecca in AD 630, it took the southern world by storm. In a hundred years, Islam captured Alexandria, established a fabulous city of learning in Baghdad, and thrust its frontier to the east beyond Isfahan in Persia. By AD 730 the Muslim empire reached from Spain and Southern France to the borders of China and India—an empire of spectacular strength and grace—while Europe lapsed into the Dark Ages.

In this proselytizing religion, the science of the conquered nation was gathered with a kleptomaniac zest. At the same time, there was liberation of simple local skills that had been despised. For instance, the first domed mosques were built with no more sophisticated apparatus than the ancient builders' set square that is still used. The Masjid-i-Jomi (the

Friday Mosque) in Isfahan (Iran) is one of the statuesque monuments of early Islam. In centers like these, the knowledge of Greece and of the East was treasured, absorbed, and diversified.

Prophet Mohamed had been firm that Islam was not to be a religion of miracles: it became in intellectual content, a pattern of contemplation and analysis.

> Allah is the light of the heavens and the earth. His light may be compared to a niche that enshrines a lamp, the lamp within a crystal of star like brilliance, light upon light. In temples which Allah has sanctioned to be built for the remembrance of his name do men praise him morning and evening, men whom neither trade nor profit can divert from remembering him. (Al-Quran 24:35-37)

Islam has been a live participant in the dynamic science and technology transformation of the mediaeval period to the extent the prevailing socioeconomic political capabilities permitted. It adopted a variety of strategies that globalize the influence of science on society, such as import of knowledge from far-off countries like China and India and adoption and transformation of the knowledge into technology. This tradition of learning and practice led to impressive contribution to the then-world's science and society.

One of the remarkable achievements of Muslim scientists of the mediaeval period is that they turned science from metaphysical speculation into experimental and operational paths. Their concerns with identification and verification—and hence with observation, accurate description, and measurements—did much to develop an objective scientific attitude. Joining great intellectual curiosity to a love of knowledge, they not only preserved and transmitted the science of antiquity but also gave it a new foundation.

Islamic science2 may be said to have flourished between the eighth and twelfth centuries (of our era), during which time it was, in fact, the almost-exclusive repository of Greek learning. Latin translations of Arabic texts sparked off great Western intellectual rebirth, and it is from them that Christian philosophers and scholars took their cue.

Islamic science took some time to reach its apogee. Lacking means of exchanging information with scholars from other countries, Muslim scientists were at first left to their resources. At the time there was no such thing as "Islamic science" but only Greek, Persian,

Indian, and Chinese sciences. Loath to adopt any one to the exclusion of the others, the Arab conquerors were the first to give science the international character, which I consider one of its fundamental characteristics. Neither Alexander nor the Romans made as profound an impression on their subject races as did the Arabs, who taught them the sacred language of Koran as a profound religious duty. Arabic became the international scientific language; any scientific text of importance was written in Arabic and read all over the cultured world.

The rise of Islamic science should be considered at two levels. First, it is essentially a cosmopolitan endeavor crossing ethnic and religious boundaries. Those who participated were Arabs as well as Iranians, Turks, and others in addition to Muslims, Jews, Christians, and Sabians3. It was heir not only to Alexandria for the Greek and Hellenistic traditions but also to Persia, India, Central Asia, and China. Thus, drawing on a rich and varied heritage, and sustained by many peoples, science in Islamic civilization became, for the first time in history, an international enterprise.

Second, it is a vital and intimate part of European history of science, appropriately termed the "intermediate civilization." Islam makes an essential transition from the civilizations of antiquity, both Middle Eastern and Hellenistic, to the dawn of the modern era. Islamic science enriched the classical legacy. At the same time, it prepared the ground for the rise of empiricism by intellectually discrediting that legacy and thereby contributing to the gradual dissolution of the classical world picture. The process of intensive translations from Greek, Syrian, Pahlavi4, and Sanskrit into Arabic between the eight and the tenth centuries led initially to an unprecedented accumulation of scientific and medical learning and later to its synthesis through the alembic of Islamic civilization.

The rise of Islamic science is usually explained on the basis of the obvious stimulus provided by the Quran. According to Dr. Mohamed Aijaz-ul-Khatib of Damascus University, for Muslim societies science is not a luxury but a necessity. "Some 750 verses, almost one-eighth of the Quran, exhort the believers to study nature, reflect, make the best use of reason, and make scientific enterprise an integral part of the community life. In contrast, the legislative verses are only 250"5. Thus, a special concern with knowledge ("ilm") is deeply rooted in the Islamic tradition. It derives from the central belief that Allah is unknowable. To know of Allah, one must study his "signs," i.e., the natural world. Perception of nature is regarded as a necessary prelude to the awareness of God. Thus, the pursuit of knowledge is equated with faith and religious duty.

Another fact in the rise of Islamic science is the practical requirements of the then-wealthy mercantile society. For example, mathematics was needed for accounting and banking purposes, standard weights and measures for international trade, celestial navigation for travel on both land and sea, and Muslims needed a calendar with astronomically defined times of prayer as well as the direction of Mecca from every city in the lands of Islam (daral-islam).

The combined influences of religious and social conditions and patronage extended by the then caliphs gave a great impetus to science. Thus, science became part and parcel of the life of every Muslim city. Every caliph took a personal interest in its progress. Among the best known of these patrons were Al-Mansur6 (136-158/754-775), the founder of Baghdad, Harun ar-Rashid7 (147-194/764-809), an Al-Mamun8 (198-218/813-833) who sent his emissaries in search of manuscripts worth translating into Arabic. Doubtless, there were many who, in the name of religion, objected to all foreign ideas, but the love of science triumphed over their objections. In their search for truth, Muslim scientists were primarily interested in gathering knowledge that had stood the test of time, possibly on the assumption that nothing new could be discovered. But this very search gave them a taste for methodical investigation and opened up unsuspected avenues.

Their classification of previous results, for instance, led them to revise the very concept of science. While the Greeks, under the influence of Plato and Aristotle, had divided the sciences according to their essential character and method of investigation, the Muslims even when they adopted the Greek labels used classification not only as an inventory but also as a program. They held that scientific methods could not be defined from a priori intelligibility of their objects but that the appropriate methods emerged in the course of scientific research. This change of view marked an important step toward a truly experimental approach; only by investigation we discover what methods lead to truth. While Aristotle distinguished between theoretical, practical, and "poetic" science and though Ibn Rushd9 (520-595/1126-1198) (also known as Averroes) maintained this classification, most other Muslim scientists attempted to synthesize the three. This effort led to a complete reversal of the prevailing views; science was no longer held to be a synonym for contemplation. It became an active effort.

As mentioned earlier, a special concern with knowledge or "ilm" is deeply rooted in the Islamic tradition. A case in point is the following verses from Holy Quran: "Thou seest not, in the creation of all-merciful any imperfection. Return thy gaze, seest thou any flaw? They return thy gaze, again and again. Thy gaze comes back to thee dazzled, a weary" (Al-Quran 67:3-4).

Perception of nature is prelude to an awareness of God. Therefore, the pursuit of knowledge is regarded as a religious duty. For this reason, epistemology had a central position in Islamic philosophy in terms of a concern with the question of the source of knowledge, whether in reason or revelation, and the manner of its acquisition.

It was also realized that both the extent and the quality of knowledge was determined by the means through which it was attained—that is, all knowledge was relative to man's nature. Complete knowledge could only be attained when its instrument was fully understood. For this reason, psychology and medicine took a uniquely privileged position in the Islamic pantheon of sciences. This is further reflected in the leading role of the physician-philosopher (hakim) in intellectual activity, as exemplified by Ar-Razi (236-313/850-920) (Rhazes)10, Ibn Sina (370-429/980-1037) (Avicenna)11, Inb Tufayl12 (d. 581/1185), Ibn Rushd (520-595/1126-1198) (Averroes), and many others.

As an important instrument, man could only approximate perfect knowledge by acquiring and amassing information as a corporate endeavor. This can be achieved not only through books but also through a systematic observation of the world around him.

To systematize such knowledge, enormous encyclopedias of science and medicine were prepared. For example, in Al-Hawi (the continents), Ar-Razi (Rhazes) gaves the previous Greek, Syrian, Indian, Persian, and Arabic views each disease. He compared them with his own clinical observations and then expressed a final opinion.

Another physician-philosopher-scientist Ibn Sina (Avicenna) 11 prepared not one but two encyclopedias. His *Kitab ash-shifa* (*The Book of Healing*) covered philosophy and the sciences. His monumental *Kitab al Qanun fi't tibb* (*The Canon of Medicine*) was such a definitive work that it dominated the teaching of medicine in Europe until the seventeenth century.

In Islam all knowledge "ilm" was regarded as science, and no branch of science was left untouched or unexplored. The sciences were generally classified into two branches. The first was the revealed science (al-ulumal naqliyyah), the sources of which were found in the Quran. They were attainable through a tradition (Sunna) deriving from the prophets who transmitted them. These included theology (katam), Jurisprudence (fiqh), mysticism (tasawwuf), and philology for the correct reading and understanding of the Quran.

The second branch was the rational or the intellectual sciences (al-ulm al-aqliyyah), which consists of knowledge distilled by reason, reflection, and observation. This was further subdivided into the mathematical and the physical sciences. The former included such subjects like arithmetic, geometry, optics, astronomy and astrology, music, science of weights, mechanical devices, etc. The latter included the natural sciences, medicine, chemistry and alchemy, and the science of minerals, plants, animals, to mention a few.

The development of the physical as well as the mathematical or the "exact sciences" was not centralized around a single institution such as "madrasa." The role of three other institutions—the libraries, the hospitals, and the observatories—needs to be mentioned:

The libraries started as repositories for collections and became "institutes of science" as exemplified by the famous Bayt al Hikmah (215/830) (House of Wisdom) in Baghdad founded by the caliph al-Mamun (d. 218/833). The Fatimid Caliph al-Hakim (d. 411/1021) founded an academy in Egypt with a similar name, Dar al-Hikmah (Abode of Wisdom). These institutes were responsible for the preservation and transmission of ancient classical texts through translation, communication of contemporary learning through teaching and stimulation of intellectual activity through extensive collection of scientific works.

The hospitals known by the Persian term "bimaristan" were designed for the purpose of both the practice and the teaching of medicine. They enabled the medical sciences to develop experimentally. On the staff of these hospitals were physicians, surgeons, ophthalmologists, and pharmacists. At the end of their theoretical and practical training, students were examined and issued with a diploma (ijaza), listing their skills and their teachers, which was then accepted throughout the Islamic countries as a license to practice medicine.

The observatories developed into centers for astronomical research as well as for the teaching of mathematical sciences. It was here that the notion of testing—which was implicit in Claudius Ptolemy's (AD 100-170) 13 *Almagest*14, for example—gave rise to the concept of observational and computational science.

The effect of the Islamic achievements began to be felt in Europe by the end of the tenth century. The real impact, however, occurred with the translations from Arabic to Latin in the twelfth century. The transmission of cultural and scientific ideas from Islam to medieval Europe was a complex process. This was mainly due to the inherent difficulty that an emerging European society had in assimilating the ideas of a more advanced civilization. At this time Islamic civilization was in its "golden age." Culturally and economically it had reached its apogee. And scientifically it had made a decisive departure from the classical tradition. Islamic scientists preserved Greek science, but importantly, they added to it their own contribution of observational knowledge: the forerunner of empiricism and ancestor of modern experimental science. As a result, there came into the common pool a new series of inventions quite unknown and inaccessible to Greek and Roman technology. These included steel, silk, paper, and porcelain. These, in turn, provided the basis for further advances, which were later to stimulate the West to its great technical and scientific revolution in the seventeenth and eighteenth centuries.

On the intellectual side also there was little break in continuity. As J. D. Bernal15 observed in his *Science in History*, after the turbulent century of conquest, even the leaders of Islam sought avidly for the knowledge of the Greeks and as much of their culture as the Quran would allow. On reading Islamic scientific works, one is struck by a rationality of treatment that we associate with modern science.

The history of Islamic science can be divided geographically and chronologically. In the beginning, the East was the main center of learning, scholars from Persia, Egypt, Syria, and India flocking to Baghdad. Then with the conquest of Spain by the Omayyad's, Cordoba began to supplant Baghdad, so that it is mainly through Spain that Arabic learning spread all over the world, and this despite the fact that the Crusades brought the West into close contact with eastern Arabia.

Soon after Baghdad was founded in the year AD 762 by Abbasid Caliph Abu Jafar al-Mansur, it began to eclipse Jundishapur16. Baghdad also absorbed the Alexandrian tradition via Harran (the Sabian capital, famous for its astronomers, mathematicians, and translators). Al-Mamun, the founder of Baghdad academy of science (Bayt al Hikma), was especially interested in biology and encouraged cultural exchanges with India. Yahya ibn Khalid invited Indian physicians and philosophers to teach in Baghdad, which had become the greatest scientific center of the East and which continued to flourish until the final disappearance of the Abassid Caliphate.

In the history of Islamic science, it is impossible to distinguish sharply between an era of translation and an era of original research. The greatest of all translators, including Hunayn ibn Ishaq17 (194-259/809-873) during ninth century wrote original treatise as well. The eighth and ninth centuries may well be described as an era of learning and research, which gave an impetus to set up the Cairo academy of science (Dar al Hikmah) in Egypt while in Spain based on Baghdad model al-Hakam II18 set up an immense library.

The tenth century was an era of stabilization of mature scientific activity and publication in the Muslim world, as well as a time of reflection, assessment, and categorization of the extraordinary intellectual enterprise, which had sprouted in the Islamic empire during the eighth century, flourished in the ninth, and then settled into a productive era of equilibrium. During the second half of the tenth century, the achievements of Arabic civilization were chronicled in three encyclopedic works:

The *Fihrist al uluum* (*Index of the Sciences*) of Abu al Faraj Muhammad Ibn Ishaq Ibn Abi Yaqub al-Nadim (d. 995)

The extensive neo-Platonic encyclopedia (Rasaa-il-Epistles) compiled collectively by the ikhwaan al-safaa (the brethen of purity)

The mafaatiill al-uluum, the keys to the sciences.

Of these three, the keys to the sciences most closely resemble a practical handbook, being a catalogue and taxonomy intended to classify and explain the technical terms and procedures used in the sciences of the time. As such, it is a rich source of unadulterated information about the practice of these premodern disciplines and of considerable importance for the study of medieval Islamic culture.

The eleventh century was the most brilliant of all, for in it flourished some of the greatest Arabic scientists: the astronomer Ibn Yunus19 (d. 399/1009), the physicist Ibn al-Haytham20 (354-430/965-1039) known in the West as Alhazen is famous particularly, for his work in optics; and the two most famous men of them all: Ibn Sina (Avicenna) 11 and Al-Biruni21 (362-442/973-1048). During the twelfth century, Islamic science continued to flourish especially in the West under the leadership of Ibn Rushd9 (Averroes) and Ibn Zuhr22 (d. 557/1162) (Avenzoar). The period after the twelfth century is commonly regarded as one of decline. The Islamic world rapidly slides into intellectual bankruptcy to remain frozen in a medieval phase of evolution. This, however, is not quite the case. What happened between the twelfth and fifteenth centuries was that the power moved farther East and passed from the Arabs to the Turks and Iranians. During the time the cultural and intellectual activities flourished, and the science continued to progress, particularly in mathematics and astronomy.

The observatories at Moraga (Maragah) started in 1259 under Mongol patronage, at Samarkand, built by Ulugh Beg in 1420, and Taqi ad-Din's at Istanbul (1575) not only attracted the best minds but also provided the finest equipment and instruments from astrolabes to giant mural quadrants and armillary spheres. At Samarkand, Al-Kashi (d. 1429) invented the decimal fraction and made a remarkably accurate calculation of tangent, among others. In Damascus, Ibn Ash Shatir (1304-75) produced non-Ptolemaic theories of planetary motion, which later on was found to have remarkable influence on Copernicus (1473-1543). Many of the astronomical instruments used by Tycho Brahe (1546-1601) have been found to be very similar to those used at the Istanbul observatories.

The period of decline came in the post-Columbian era with the European conquest of the new world. Islamic powers lost their control of world trade. Economic decline was accompanied by a process of cultural stagnation and increasing intellectual isolation. What is remarkable is the fact that the influence of Islamic scientific ideas did not decline and disappeared completely.

In the sixteenth and seventeenth centuries, when its scientific and intellectual creativity was dead, the Islamic impact on Europe was greater than at any other time since the Middle Ages. This was chiefly due to the fact that Europe was now intellectually ready to assimilate the earlier Islamic achievements in optics, mathematics, astronomy, etc., which had failed fully to appreciate before.

The article attempts to justify a relationship between science and society and the role of Islam in shaping the lives of millions of Muslims for a more meaningful life. Further, it tries to prove that the relationship between science and Islam is more complementary than contradictory. An effort is made to correct as far as possible the erroneous impressions about Islam and its attitudes toward science and to underscore the dynamic role played by Muslims for the development of science and technology through the ages, in general, and medieval period, in particular.

III

Science, Scientist, and Society: Some Issues

What is science? This question has been asked many times and answered in many different variations. But it seems the basic things over which there seems to be general agreement is that science is a study of nature, animate as well as inanimate. This seems deceptively simple but in reality calls for qualities on the part of the person pursuing science of a high order and, incidentally, have contributed to the scientist being regarded by the layman as someone quite out of the ordinary. Since science is a study of nature and an accumulation of natural knowledge, it calls for a set of altitudes on the part of the students of science.

First, it demands the total rejection of authority of dogma and unproven doctrines. It calls for a capacity and a disposition to deal with facts as the scientist sees them. It seeks the application of methods where honesty and integrity are supreme and are of unquestioned importance. It is a search for order, for a coherent relation between facts as well as events in nature. It is a faculty by which studies of isolated phenomena are woven into general laws, for science not only collects facts and accumulates information but based on these facts and information makes general statements and enunciates laws. Based on these laws, science predicts and then goes on to control phenomena. There are other factors too of science. Science rests on a system of values. Science demands a passionate concern for truth for its own sake. Science is characterized by emphasis on objectivity and impartiality. In short, science is the greatest social activity of disciplined inquiry into the natural world.

It will be seen from the above that while acquisition and accumulation of knowledge of the physical and biological world around us are important, the qualities and attributes called for in men for these pursuits are even more so. That is what makes science and the scientific attitude so distinctive and uniquely human.

J. D. Bernal, a historian of science and technology, has written "a most comprehensive and readable analysis of the evolution of science and technology in human history called *Science in History*." He states:

> Science has so changed its nature over the whole range of human history that no definition could be made of it. Although, I have aimed at including everything called science, the centre of interest . . . lies in natural science and technology because . . . the science and society were at first embodied in tradition and ritual and only took shape under the influence and the model of the natural sciences . . . . Science stands as a middle term between the established and transmitted practice of men who work for their living and the pattern of ideas and traditions which assume continuity of society and the rights and privileges of the classes that make it up.

Science is the organization of the knowledge in such a way that it commands move of the hidden potential in nature. It admits no sharp boundary between knowledge and use. Its theories have often been made by men whose imagination was directed by the uses to which their age looked. Newton turned naturally to astronomy because it was the subject of his day, and it was so because finding one's way at sea had long been a practical preoccupation of the society into which he was born. Astronomy also had some standing because it was used very practically to cast horoscopes. Michael Faraday worked all his life to link electricity and magnetism because this was the glittering problem of his day, and it was so because his society, like ours, was on the lookout for new sources of power. Consider a more modest example of today: the new mathematical methods of automatic control, a subject sometimes called cybernetics, have been developed now because this is a time when communication and control have in effect become forms of power. These inventions have been directed by social needs, and they are useful inventions; yet it was not their usefulness that dominated and set light to the minds of those who make them.

Science today seems to stand at the crossroads. The phenomenal growth of science and its handmaiden technology have placed in the hands of man enormous powers and possibilities. Their almost continual and uninterrupted growth since the middle of the seventeenth century, and more especially during this century, has provided man with means to make his life easier, healthier, and more productive. They have pulled him out of a slave culture and provided hi' satisfaction that he is able not only to understand nature but to an extent influence nature too. However, more recently, doubts have entered the minds of men if all the benefits conferred by science and technology have brought him real happiness! Questions are asked if, with all the material and consumer goods that man has surrounded himself, there has been a real improvement in the nature of man if his dreams of a better civilization have been realized. Wars, aggression, uneven development, coexistence of poverty, and plenty deep schisms among peoples of the world all have led to a profound suspicion and doubt in regard to efficacy of science as the redeemer of human life and happiness. The charge that while science has provided man with material goods it has left his spiritual needs unmet has come as a recent but rude realization. Uneven, unbalanced technological development has left man unprepared to meet the rapid advances in industry and technology. Technologically advanced countries are slowly but reluctantly led to discover that science has surrounded man with many useful things, all of which are external to him, leaving his inside empty. A great amount of knowledge but little wisdom!

Science today is a property, and therefore like all property, it is used for the benefit of those who own it. In the present-day context, the major part of scientific effort is dedicated to the twin purpose: extraction of profits and maintenance of the control that permits extraction. It is therefore not surprising that there is a fervent plea that science be abandoned and that man turn his attention to other more important issues that concern him—art, literature, philosophy, religion—in general, issues that have a bearing on man's relation with other men. A very valid plea!

But on account of that, can we abandon science? Can we set even a temporary moratorium on scientific learning and discovery? No, it is impossible. Man cannot assume a position of "not knowing"1. Such a position is unnatural to him. No, we must continue all that we have been doing. We have to do some more things, some newer things. We must continue to learn more of and from nature. But we must turn attention to man to human affairs. Science has come of age; and instead of, or perhaps in addition to, seizing upon the easier problems concerning nature, we must now meet the serious social problems that confront man. A science of nature is useful rewarding, but it's only when it becomes a science of human nature can science be truly ennobling.

This is not easy. Man is a difficult animal, and there are no rules to go by. Human affairs are not conducted to order and are governed by much ignorance and prejudice. The methods of science often are found to be inadequate and inapplicable to man. There are few guidelines and fewer methods. We need to develop more methods and some criteria to know man. For without knowledge of man all knowledge is sterile.

A scientist has two interests: the interest of his time and his own interest. In this his behavior is no different from any other man's. The need of the age gives its shape to scientific progress as a whole. But it is not the need of the age that gives the individual scientist his sense of pleasure and of adventure and the excitement that keeps him working late into the night when all his supporting staff have gone home at five o'clock. He is personally involved in his work. The sense of personal exploration is as urgent and as delightful to the practical scientist as to the theoretical. As the world's interest has shifted since the Industrial Revolution to the tapping of new springs of power, the theoretical scientist has shifted his interests too.

His speculations about energy have been abstract as once they were about astronomy, and they have been profound now as they were then because the man loved to think. The Carnot cycle and the dynamo grew equally from this love, and so did nuclear physics and Kelvin's interest in low temperatures. A scientist masters nature not by force but by understanding, which is why science has succeeded where magic failed.

Scientists are sometimes deeply religious and struck by the purpose, order, and precision of the universe. The founders of modern science, Galileo and Newton, were generally very religious subscribers to the beliefs and practices of Christian church. Nevertheless, science and religion went their separate ways after the great divide was heralded by the Copernican revolution in the seventeenth century. Here is an example from modern times that vividly illustrate the above point.

In 1979, the Nobel Prize for Physics was awarded to Abdus Salam, Steven Weinberg, and Sheldon Glashow for having discovered the fundamental theory uniting two basic forces of nature: the "weak" and the "electromagnetic." Known as the Salam-Weinberg theory, it represents one of the most profound discoveries of this century, but look at the beliefs of its discoverers! Salam quotes profusely from the Quran, prays regularly, and even makes some of his well-wishers uncomfortable by his zealousness and devotion to the Ahmedi sect to which he belongs (this sect was ex-communicated from Islam in 1974, and Salam is legally not considered a Muslim in Pakistan). But this appears to have only strengthened his resolve. On the other hand, Weinberg is Jewish by birth. But he is an avowed atheist for whom the universe is an existentialist reality devoid of sense and purpose. An enormous ideological gulf separated these two brilliant physicists. And yet they both arrived at precisely the same theory of physics more or less simultaneously!

The impact of scientific advances on society will take a long time and much space, but a reference to some of the more important areas would probably be appropriate. The most striking example is the work in atomic physics and technology. The discovery of nuclear fission and later, of fusion, has placed before humanity possibilities of almost limitless power not only for the good of man but also for his total annulation. Other areas, such as electronics, photonics, polymers, advanced materials, and their applications in automation, computers, radars, communication equipment, rubbers, plastics, fibers, composites, which even as recently as fifty years ago were unimagined. In biology, recent discoveries in genetic engineering, immunology, biotechnology, antibiotics, and the functioning of living systems, of plants and animals, and of man have led to a greater understanding of the life of man and made it more comfortable. Recent advances in agricultural sciences have helped produce not only higher yields of food crops but also newer strains and varieties. Many originally hazardous surgical operations have now been rendered relatively free from danger consequent on newer techniques and a better understanding of the body functions. While heart transplants continue to be a disputed adventure, there has been greater success with other organ transplants, notably the kidney and the liver. Cancer is still a troublesome and AIDS a great challenge. We are now nearer a solution than we were, and it should be possible before the end of the present century for this dreaded situation to be met fully.

The present century also witnessed, in its first quarter, an ever-growing insight into the structure of the atom by means of quantum mechanics. In parallel we observe the development of electronic industries based upon a better understanding of the interactions between electrons of one atom with the other. When the nature of the chemical bond was revealed by further applications of quantum mechanics to atomic and molecular dynamics, a deeper understanding of the structure of metals, crystals, and other materials was achieved. This led to an expansion of chemical industries and to the production of new materials. It finally brought about the invention of transistors and semiconductors on which the computer industry thrives.

The next scientific step into the deeper layers of matter was penetration into the structure of the atomic nucleus. Nuclear physics has brought about the exploration of nuclear power and the application of artificial radioactivity to medical purposes and materials testing. Biology, with its revelations of the chemical nature of the life process and deciphering of the genetic code, has found many fruitful applications in medicine and in the chemical industry.

On the other hand, none of these scientific steps could have been taken without the help of technology. This is most obvious in more recent developments that would' have been impossible without the help of the latest achievements of electronics and other precision technology. One has only to recall the complicated and sophisticated technology that goes into the construction of a modern accelerator.

Of course science has been misused in many ways, most tragically in providing the means to wage war and causing destruction. The classic examples are the fission and fusion bombs, the many kinds of missiles, and the means for waging chemical and biological warfare. The use of some of these agents in Vietnam and the most recent exhibition of the technological muscle power in Iraq has made many scientist cynical about scientific research. But perhaps in no other way have science and technology demonstrated their destructive abilities than on the environment unchecked and often unnecessary industrial development, production, and promotion of needless consumer goods, unplanned and reckless exploitation of scarce and certainly nonrenewable natural resources, specially fossil fuels, and accumulation of nondegradable waste products have all created environmental problems never before encountered on Earth.

As one historian of science Jerome R. Ravetz has observed, much of the blame lies with what he calls "the tragedy of modern physics," the appalling historical accident that transformed the most aristocratic, pure, and philosophical branch of science into a new technology of mass destruction and so brought hatred and ignominy not only on physics but the whole profession as well. "I am as dead, the destroyer of worlds," observed Robert Oppenheimer as he watched the first test explosion of the H-bomb. Ravetz compares this as a disgrace of physics, which led the aged Einstein to wish he had spent his life as a watchmaker to the pitiful men of the Galileo affair.

One consequence of these developments is that the eminent publicist Paul Johnson was provoked in 1977 to write a book titled *Enemies of Society*. Paul Johnson's list of enemies is wide ranging from undermines of linguistic truth, priests, witch doctors, inane philosophers, scientists and their doppelgangers, ivory tower dwellers, and managers of knowledge factories. Johnson believes that "philosophy is inclined to abdicate intellectual leadership to science, and it is handing over to men [scientists] who feel themselves increasingly unpopular, misunderstood and travestied." F. Bacon thought an ideal scientist should be "sober, chaste arid severe," also humble and innocent. But his definition of the ideal scientist's aim to establish and extend the power and dominion of the human race itself over the universe is neither humble nor innocent, and the awesome image of the modern scientist is projected back by public opinion from his aims and achievements.

The hostile image of scientist is not merely confined to fiction. It has embraced real-life scientist as well because those who campaigned against nuclear science joined the environmental lobby in insisting that science is too destructive to be allowed total freedom in its pursuits. To quote the historian Ravetz again, this unpopularity of real and fictional scientists coincides with a crisis in its internal development*. Nuclear physics, asserted Ravetz, now finds itself at a dinosaur stage; unable to evolve further, it awaits its extinction unless some happy accident rescues it. It is a view endorsed even by the physicist Dr. H. S. Lipson of Manchester, who thinks that physics, having exhausted its obvious lines of inquiry and deprived of innovatory talent, may share the fate of Latin becoming obsolete!

In retrospect, the part played by science in the development of the man's society cannot be underrated. Science has not only provided almost limitless power to man, but it has been the very instrument of change and the great link between man and his environment. In the broadest sense, society is nothing other than the result of adjustment of man to his environment and his ability to change the environment to his needs, and science has been the most profound agent of this change. In that sense, science is the vital link between man and his environment, which man has used not only to fashion his environment to meet his needs but also to adapt himself to the changed environment he has thus created. In this process, it is not only the physical and biological environment that has figured, but it is also the man's relationship with the finer aspects of life, viz, music, art, and religion. Human society in that sense is highly dynamic and has shown adaptability, and change is quite striking in contrast with animal societies.

IV

Science Versus Religion: Intellectual Dimensions

N o discussion on science and human society can be complete without reference to religion, for in addition to science, religion is the one great enduring force that has played a dominant role in the life of man and his society. And like science it is a peculiarly human institution. The relationship between the religion and science has been intimate, if often conflicting, for both have entered man's life and both seem to be inescapable components of human existence. Many philosophers and scientists who have dealt with this relationship indeed wondered what this relationship is or what it should be.

Science is nothing else than the search to discover unity in the wild variety of our experience. A religion, in general, and Islam, in particular, does exactly the same. The approaches of science and religion are different: that science accepts no perforce creeds, is free from orthodoxies and heresies, that evidence and reason are the cornerstones of scientific thinking and that it rejects things it cannot verify are all true. It is also true that, in contrast, religion enjoins man to accept certain rigid creeds and subscribe to them—that in many traditional religions there prevails an authoritarian, demanding orthodoxy and unquestioning faith is also true. In fact, it is this diversity of approach and method that has resulted in conflict. As science advances, knowledge accumulates, and the areas of man's life governed solely by belief and myth would diminish and in certain cases may vanish. But it is doubtful that faith will disappear altogether. If faith and belief disappear altogether, only knowledge remains.

Religion, regardless of its age, its structure or content, its injunctions and tenets, its creed and rituals—every religions basic core manifests a tendency for the establishment of a correct relationship between man and the universe. Its cultural theme is to provide a useful guide to life and living. Primitive religions were merely meant to emphasize the existence of supernatural beings capable of influencing natural events and even to infuse fear and ensure submission. They encouraged the development of a dualist theory recognizing two realms, the natural and supernatural, and stressed the historical reality of supernatural events, reincarnation, resurrection, miracles, etc. Prayers and propitiatory practices were woven into this scheme (incense, bequeathing rich gifts, asceticism, penitence, sacrifices). The awesome mysteries of life and death were used to create in man not only a reverence for life but also fear. In the primitive mind they inculcate ways of the conduct of affairs of men and problems of life.

Developed religions, on the other hand, stressed more on the moral code of men than on the dire consequences of infringement of these codes. Islam, for example, emphasizes man's role in the universe, his mission, his relations with fellowmen, and his actions and aspirations in the context of the totality of his development. In fact, religion's supreme role lies in a reconciliation of the existence of man as a rational questioning being somewhat in the way of mediating between the unknown and inexplicable on the one hand and the mundane and seeing world on the other. Many contemporary thinkers believe that religion is conceived as the realm of ultimate values while science is said to be that of preliminary ones. But recent advances in the sciences have so broadened the concern of science that it now includes many of these ultimate questions, especially of man. Most men of science are now coming to believe that within the sciences themselves there are factors that bring a new faith to our consideration of nature and of man, factors that provide a new understanding of human values, the acceptance of order, and the predictability in nature.

Religion is concerned with human aspirations, not human achievements, while science is concerned with what men do and how. Religion's realm is what man ought to do and why. Man should be careful not to decry knowledge or science but, having accepted it, should go beyond knowledge. In fact, he should be continually engaged in the pursuit of creating a new human being. He should be the supreme instrument in the interpretation of knowledge and faith. For man cannot do without either. Without knowledge he is primitive; without faith he will be no more than an animal.

V

Science and Quran: A Few Arguments

There has been an impressive collection of false notions about Holy Quran and its scientific temper, mostly among the majority of Western intellectuals. One must, on this point, allow him one or two excuses.

First, apart from the newly adopted attitudes prevailing among the highest Christian authorities, Islam has always been subject in the West to a so-called secular slander. Anyone in the West who has acquired a deep knowledge of Islam knows just to what extent its history, dogma, and aims have been distorted. One must also take into account the fact that documents published in European languages on this subject (leaving aside highly specialized studies) do not make the work of a person willing to learn any easier.

Second, the passages from the Holy Quran especially those relating to scientific data are badly translated and interpreted; consequently, scientists have every right to make criticisms—with apparent justification—that the holy book does not actually deserve at all. For example, the chapter 23 of Holy Quran, which addresses the subject of human reproduction, is a typical example of this kind of error (which will be discussed later). Another blatant example is R. Blucher's well-known translation, inserting a title that does not figure in the Holy Quran: duties of the holy war (obligation de guerre sainte). This is at the beginning of the passage that is indisputably a call to arms but does not have the character that has been ascribed to it. After reading this, how can the reader who only has the access to the Holy Quran via translations fail to think that a Muslim's duty is to wage a holy war?

Why do such errors in translation exist? They may be explained by the fact that modern translators often resume, rather uncritically, the interpretations given by older commentators. In their day, the latter had an excuse for having given an inappropriate definition to an Arabic work containing several possible meanings; they could not possibly have understood the real sense of the word or phrase that has only become clear in the present day—thanks to scientific knowledge. These problems of translations are not present for the texts of the Judeo-Christian revelation: the case described here is absolutely unique to the Quran.

For example, the human ovum was first described by Graff in 1672, and five years later the sperm was discovered by Antonie van Leeuwenhoek in 1677. It is an amazing fact that the Quran referred to these cells in the human body almost a thousand years before they were confirmed by human eyes. In a series of verses (Al-Quran 22:5, 23:12-14, 49:13, 53:45-46, and 76:2), the Holy Quran depicts their subsequent behavior leading to fertilization and implantation in the uterus followed by stages of development that have established precisely in the same sequence by modern science.

It is easy to see therefore how for centuries commentators of the Holy Quran, including those writing at the height of Islamic culture, have inevitably made errors of interpretation in the case of certain verses whose exact meaning could not possibly have been grasped. It was not until recent past that it was possible to translate and interpret them correctly. This implies that a thorough linguistic knowledge is not in itself sufficient to understand these verses from the Holy Quran. What is needed along with this is a highly diversified knowledge of science, which is essential to the understanding of certain verses of the holy book.

The scientific consideration, which is very specific to the Holy Quran, greatly surprised the West. It is difficult for the Christian world to believe the text compiled more than fourteen centuries ago referring to extremely diverse subjects such as creation, astronomy, explanation of certain matters concerning the earth and the animal and vegetable kingdom, human reproduction, etc.—all of them totally in keeping with modern scientific knowledge! A careful study of the Quran reveals the highly accurate nature of certain details referred in the holy book, which commensurate with the present-day scientific ideas.

The question is whether the Quranic verses can be interpreted in the light of modern scientific discoveries and innovations.

In this connection there are two groups of people: one who approves of it and the other who denies. The first group do not subscribe to the opinion that Quranic verses related to nature can be justifiably explained scientifically. Their arguments are precisely based on the following points.

The revelation of the Quran in the language of Arabs of the early Islamic period makes it obligatory to follow the meaning of the verses (related to nature) in line with the vocabulary used by them. They knew their language and understood its implication well.

The Holy Quran, as a matter of fact, is a book of guidance and deals precisely with the commandments and also provides education for mankind for the betterment of their lives in the material world as well as in the world hereafter.

3. Scientific creativity and discoveries about nature are based on theories and hypothesis not consistent at all. And now many of these theories stand rejected, the fact that the scientists themselves have for long considered them correct notwithstanding.

Any attempt, therefore, to explicate the verses related to nature by modest Muslims taking recourse to sciences, which are they liable to change, lacks propriety and justification. In fact, what is considered to be scientifically correct today may not remain the same tomorrow with the addition of new instruments and improved methodology. Obviously science, which is ever dynamic, cannot be justifiably used for the explication of the verses of Quran, which are considered to be true for all the time and cannot be even slightly altered.

The second group subscribes to the opinion that modern science may justifiably be used for Quranic interpretation. The basis of their stand is clearly revealed by their arguments against the first group.

The first argument is refuted on the basis of two points.

The Quran has been revealed for the entire mankind and that it must last till the doomsday. In fact, it addresses to persons of all standards notwithstanding the fact of their civilizational differences, ever-changing nature of sciences, advancements, and their abilities and thoughts. People of all standards will be benefited according to their capacity. And if some people fail to understand the meaning of the verses, they should, in fact, for their own benefit refer the matter to great researchers and the *ulama*. As it stated in the Quran itself, ask for those who possess the message (Al-Quran 16:43).

Innumerable layers of meanings in the passages are also one of the miracles of the Holy Quran. These layers of meaning operate in two ways:

(i) A passage gives a particular meaning on the surface but simultaneously on a deeper level one more meaning that is different and contradicts the first.

(ii) Certain verses have different meanings. They are revealed at different times as a result of the development of the art, sciences, and continuous scientific discoveries and inventions. Now it becomes the responsibility of the contemporary Muslim scholars to decipher the meaning with the contemporary knowledge and sciences.

The second argument presented by those who oppose the scientific approach to the interpretation of the verses of the Quran consider the holy book as a book of guidance. It has nothing to do with physical sciences. Nor has it anything to do with discoveries and researches of the natural world. This argument is only partially true. The Quran is, in fact, a book of guidance.

Commandments apart, it also invites contemplation on his wonderful skill of creation. But how? As a matter of fact, the wisdom of God is to provide innumerable sources of guidance. Sometimes, therefore, he addresses gently and, in pleasing manner, sometimes warns in a strongly worded vocabulary. He adopts strong methods to open up the eyes and provides insight and thereby forces people into contemplating on his wonderful creation, his great skill, and its manifestations. Perhaps that was the only reason behind the description of the signs of nature in the Quran.

The third argument of those who oppose scientific exegesis of the Quran (mentioned by the first group) is indicative of the fact that scientific truths are no more substantial than mere hypotheses and theories. For some time, the scientists consider it true but soon after reject it. Their understanding has been purely transitory and cannot be relied upon in the matter of Quranic exegesis. But this statement is commonly refuted. What is liable to continuous change cannot, in fact, constitute the core of the principle of science. It is only the hypothesis that is very much in argument and research and may justifiably be changed. As a matter of fact, a hypothesis is finally concluded taking recourse to well-established scientific facts and theories. The more the valid information about nature is made available through analogy and comprehension, the more the opportunity is provided for accommodation, alteration, and even for validation of the hypothesis.

But it is important to note that the scholars of natural science, like all other scholars, may differ in point of their awareness, study, and expertise. While talking about the Quran, one may take recourse to scientific facts and their reliance on hypotheses and theories. The two scientific facts and reliance on hypotheses and theories are different entities. This is illustrated by the following examples:

(i) The fact that the living body is made up of cells and that these cells are complete in themselves and help the functioning of life by their mutual cooperation was discovered about one and a half centuries ago. This has not been refuted even after wonderful discoveries by a number of developed versions of microscopes and sophisticated instruments of investigations. The theory of cell discovered one and a half centuries ago is still valid despite the invention of electronic microscopes, which revealed the presence of chromosomes and lysosomes. Biochemistry, biophysics, and molecular biology do reveal genes and molecules. But do they refute the theory of cells?

(ii) Mankind has known atomic theory for long time. The atomic theory is based on the assumption that matter is made up of atoms. Do modern research and its inferences (that revealed the presence of proton, electron, neutron, and even more subtle and wonderful particles) refute the atomic theory?

Ghaneem27 offers a proposal that for a viable interpretation of the verses pertaining to nature, the experts of ulum-e-shariah (experts in Islamic jurisprudence—Muftis) and modern science should sit together at the level of academy and frame basic rules and guidelines. Also, it is essential to stop using ambiguous terms like "scientific interpretation," "contemporary interpretation," and "interpretation through contemporary point of view."

The relationship between the Quran and science is a priori, a surprise, especially since it is going to be one of harmony and not of discord. A confrontation between scientific temper of Quran and the secular ideas proclaimed by science is perhaps, in the eyes of many people today, something of a paradox. The majority of today's scientists, with a small number of exceptions, of course, are indeed bound up in materialist theories and have only in difference or contempt for religious questions, which they often consider to be founded on legend. In the West, moreover, when science and holy books are discussed, people are quite willing to mention Torah and Bible among the books referred to but they hardly ever think of Quran. So many false judgments based on inaccurate ideas have indeed been made about it that today it is very difficult to form an exact notion of the reality of Quran, Islam, and Muslims.

In the words of Maurice Bucaille, "the totally erroneous statements made about Quran and Islam in the west are sometimes of systematic denigration. The most serious of all the untruths told about it are however, those dealing with facts; for a while, mistaken opinions are excusable, the presentation of facts running contrary to the reality is not."

VI

Influence of the Holy Quran on Muslim Scientists:

SOME REFLECTIONS

The Quran holds a unique place among the books of revelation. It is not a book of science, but it is a book of guidance for intellectual and moral emancipation of humanity at large. And yet it contains several passages that are of scientific importance.

> And verily in cattle (too) will ye find an instructive sign,
> From what is within their bodies.
> Between excretion and blood,
> We produce for your drink, milk pure and agreeable
> To those who drink it. (Al—Quran 16:66-67)

The Quran through hundreds of its verses tends to cultivate a reflective personality, which may enable man to probe nature for secrets that are sought to ensure his material and spiritual prosperity and progress. The beautiful world man is living in has been created with incredible precision and dexterity. Its enormous canvas is sprinkled with innumerable "signs" each unique in its own right. They stand out as mute witnesses in praise of an intelligent being at work. Nature, in short, is an open book of wonders for those who have eyes to read and a vast laboratory to test their skills. For men of intellect and wisdom who as per Quran are "men who remember Allah standing, sitting, and lying down on their sides

191

and contemplate the [wonders of] creation in the heavens and the earth, [with the saying]: 'Our Lord not for naught hast thou created [all] this! Glory to thee give us salvation from the chastisement of the fire" (Al-Quran 3:191), the message that emanates from these signs is loud and clear. The holy Quran reminds:

> Soon we shall show them our signs in the (farthest) regions (of the earth) and in their own souls, until it becomes manifest to them that this is the truth. (Al-Quran 41:53)

"Do they not look at the camels how they are made? And at the sky, How it is raised high?

And at the Mountains; how they are fixed firm? And at the earth, how it is spread out" (Al-Quran 88:17-20) and again "Behold! In the creation of the heavens and the earth, and the alternation of night and day, there are indeed signs for men of understanding" (Al-Quran 3: 90).

Thus, the Quran continually speaks of cosmos and of what it contains in a way directing the mankind toward acquisition of knowledge. It speaks about the new moons, about the sun and the moon, day and night, the earth and the creatures that roam over it, the sky and stars that adorn it, the sea whose surface is criss-crossed with ships sailing in pursuit of God's bounty, of the animals we take as beasts of burden and others as ornaments, and of all that the earth contains for knowledge and art. In speaking about all these, the Quran asks man not only to look into them and study them but also to enjoy their effects and to feel grateful to God for his bounty. With such discipline as the Quran has enjoined, and by following its insistent call to seek cosmic knowledge, man may fulfill his destiny. If he responds to the call of the Quran and fulfills its requisite rational contemplation of the cosmos with scientific temper, then it would be possible to achieve happiness and to put an end to human suffering on Earth.

The revelation of the Quran commenced in AD 610 when the Prophet Mohamed (peace be upon him) who could neither read nor write was about 40 years old. The Muslim calendar is dated form the time Muslim community life began with the migration (hijrath) of the Prophet (peace be upon him) from Makkah to Medina on 15/16 July 622.

It is an established fact that at the time of the Quranic revelation, scientific knowledge had not progressed for centuries; and the period of activity in Islamic civilization, with its accompanying scientific upsurge, came after the close of Quranic revelation. Anyone who knows anything about Islamic history is aware that the period of the Middle Ages, which saw the cultural and scientific upsurge in the Arab world, came after Prophet Mohamed (peace be upon him). Majority of scientific facts that are either suggested or very clearly recorded in the Quran and hadith have only been confirmed in modern times.

The Quran is not, however, a book that has the object explaining certain laws governing the universe; it has an absolutely basic religious objective. The descriptions of divine omnipotence are what principally incite man to reflect on the works of creation. They are accompanied by references to facts accessible to human observation or to laws defined by God who presides over the organization of the universe both in the sciences of nature and as regards man. One part of the assertions is easily understood, but the meaning of the other can only be grasped if one has the essential scientific knowledge it requires. This means that in former times, man could only distinguish an apparent meaning, which led him to draw the wrong conclusions on account of the inadequacy of his knowledge at the time in question.

The AD seventh century (first hijri) was a period of the most intense intellectual activity among the Muslims whose numbers as well as the problems of their "Islamic acculturation" were increasing exponentially. This activity was centered on the most concentrated study of the Quran, the sayings and exemplary traditions (hadith or sunnah) of the Prophet as well as his biography (sirah) and the Arabic language.

While studying the Holy Quran from the point of view of science and literature, many of its verses, particularly the similes, allegories, metaphors, and imageries, drew from the natural phenomena around us and stated as such for the purpose of strengthening its religious objectives attract the attention. It appears that besides their religious objectives, if some of these statements from different verses be pulled together and are correlated in sequence, we can have a message for the material benefits of humanity as a whole. It is interesting to note that the statements relating to natural phenomena around us in the verses of the Holy Book are in perfect keeping with the scientific information accumulated in the concerned disciplines.

The Holy Prophet of Islam (peace be upon him) emphasized that the quest for knowledge and sciences is obligatory upon every Muslim, man and woman. The Prophet himself had besought his disciples to seek knowledge from the cradle to grave no matter if their search took them as far afield as China for "he who travels in search of knowledge, travels along Allah's path to paradise." True, the knowledge of Quran preached (ilm) was above all knowledge of the religious laws, but Islam never made a clear-cut distinction between the sacred and the profane. Hence, for instance, there are many hadiths (sayings attributed to Prophet Mohamed) concerning medicine, in general, and remedies, in particular, on which Muslim scientists and philosophers based many of their dicta and actions. Thus, when Ibn Rushd (Averroes) wrote that Quran invites men to observe nature and to seek rational knowledge, he expressed the opinion of all Muslim scholars that the earth was given to man for constant reverent study. Thus, Prophet spoke, "The ink of the scholar is more holy than the blood of the martyr."

The injunctions in Holy Quran and the sayings of Holy Prophet were so intense that barely a hundred years after the prophet's demise, the Muslims had made in their task to master the then-known sciences. Besides establishing institutes of advanced study (Bait ul Hikmah), they acquired an absolute ascendency in the sciences that lasted for the next 350 years.

It would nevertheless be wrong to imagine that, in the history of Islam, certain believers had never harbored a different attitude toward science. It is a fact that, at certain periods, the obligation to educate oneself and others was neglected. It is equally true that in the Muslim world, as elsewhere, an attempt was sometimes made to stop scientific development. All the same, it will be remembered that at the height of Islam, between the AD eighth and twelfth centuries, i.e., at a time when restrictions on science and scientific pursuits were in force in the Christian world, a very large number of studies and discoveries were being made at Islamic universities. It was there that the remarkable cultural resources of the time were to be found. The Caliph's library at Cordoba (Spain) contained more than four hundred thousand volumes. This is why scholars from all over Europe went to study at Cordoba just as today people go to the United States to perfect their studies. The present-day science is greatly indebted to Arabic culture for mathematics, astronomy, physics, chemistry, geology, botany, medicine, etc.

For the first time, science took on an international character in the Islamic universities and advanced centers of the Middle Ages. At this time, men were more steeped in the religious spirit than they are today; but in the Islamic world, this did not prevent them from being both believers and scientists. A phenomenon very strange in the Christian world!

An aspect of reverence for the sciences in Islam was the patronage they enjoyed in the then-Islamic world. To paraphrase what H. A. R. Gibb has written in the context of literature:

To a greater extent than elsewhere the flowering of sciences in Islam was conditional on the liberality and patronage of those in high positions. So long as, in one capital or another, princes and ministers found pleasure, profit or reputation in patronizing the sciences, the torch was kept burning.

There is no question that Western science is a Greco-Islamic legacy. However, it is commonly alleged Islamic science was a derived science, that Muslim scientists followed the Greek theoretical tradition blindly and added nothing to the scientific method. This statement is false. The assessment of Aristotle by Al-Biruni clarifies the apprehension:

> The trouble with most people is their extravagance in respect of Aristotle's opinions, they believe that there is no possibility of mistakes in his views, though they know that he was only theorizing to the best of his capacity.

In Briffaults29 words:

> The Greeks systematized, generalized and theorized, but the patient ways of detailed and prolonged observation and experimental inquiry were altogether alien to Greek temperament what we call science arose as a result of new methods of experiment, observation, and measurement, which were introduced into Europe by the Arabs. (Modern) science is the most momentous contribution of the Islamic civilization.

These thoughts are echoed by George Sarton, the great historian of science:

> The main, as well as the least obvious, achievement of the middle ages was creation of the experimental spirit and this was primarily due to the Muslims down to the 12th century.

One of the tragedies of history is that the tempo of the modern spirit in sciences was interrupted: it did not lead to a permanent change of direction in scientific methodology. Barely a hundred years after Al-Biruni and Ibn-al-Haytham worked, creation of high science in Islam effectively came to a halt. Mankind had to wait five hundred years before the same level of maturity and the same insistence on observation and experimentation was reached, with Galileo, Tycho Brahe, and their contemporaries.

VII

The Concept of Exact Sciences: Role of the Arabic Language

The vitality, complexity, and depth of intellectual activity in the medieval Islamic world during the AD eighth, ninth, and tenth centuries are well-known. Within that world, although many scholars were not ethnic Arabs, most were Muslims and all wrote in Arabic, which was an international mode of scientific communication and a vehicle for synthesis of many cultural traditions.

The concept of "exact science" was first given by the Muslims. The exact sciences that made up the medieval quadrivium were astronomy, arithmetic, geometry, and music. Together with the tritium (grammar, dialectics, and rhetoric), they constituted the "seven liberal arts." The characteristic structure of the Arabic language had profound influence on Muslim scholars; for example, all Arabic words are trilateral—that is to say, they are made up from 3,726 "immortal" root words of three consonants each. Inflection is by internal vowel changes, and since vowels are not written down, reading calls for prior thought and selection. Names, verbs, and prepositions alike are subject to trifocal flexional endings (i'rab—vowels).

Because of these structural properties, Arabic favors the expression of analytic, atomistic, occasionalistic, and apophthegmatic thought. A recent technical study on the semantic involution of concepts (tadmin) has shown how many Semitic languages tends toward shortened and abstract formulations—how they "algebraize" while Aryan languages

196

"geometrize." In fact, just as thought may be projected into space as in Pythagorean figured numbers, so it can be turned back on itself at appropriate times to construct its object.

Arabic, which facilitates this "interiorization" of thought, is particularly suited to expressing exact scientific concepts and to developing them, in much the same way as mathematical concepts have evolved historically. These began with the initiative and almost contemplative arithmetic and geometry, which, with Plato, proceeded to the science of algebraic constructions in which arithmetic and geometry are fused together.

The Arabic language had profound influence on the algebriazation of the alphabet. The twenty-eight letters of the Arabic alphabet represent not only all the numerals but also the twenty-eight classes of ideas of Muslim philosophers. Thus, Ibn Sina's arguments in the Nayruziya are based on a philosophic alphabet; and forty years before him, the philosopher Abul-Hasan Deilemi asserted that there were two classes of irrefutable arguments: the series of twenty-eight letter of the alphabet and the series of integral numbers. By that he meant that it was legitimate to fit the twenty-eight alphabetical symbols into some kind of mechanical scheme, which would reflect any series of real events.

In this way, Arabic science managed to produce abstract "arguments" based on alphabetical numbers; every word can "release" a number of objects designated by letters adding up to the same total. For example, "Ayn," "the 'essence," originally meant "seventy" and is equivalent to Ya + sad = 10 + 60 = 70. In this connection, it is interesting to note that Muslim astrologers constructed a "thinking machine," the *zairja*, which was discussed by Ibn Khaldun.

In brief, the Muslim scholars' contribution to exact science is considerable. In fact, they did a great deal to turn science from metaphysical speculation into experimental and operational paths. Their concern with identification and verification—and hence with observation, accurate descriptions, and measurements—did much to develop the objective scientific attitude. Joining great intellectual curiosity to a love of knowledge, they not only preserved and transmitted the science of antiquity but also gave it a new foundation.

VIII

Innovations in Mathematics

Muslims regarded mathematics as the gateway leading from the sensible to the intelligible world, the ladder between the world of change and the heaven of archetypes. Unity, the central idea of Islam, is an abstraction from the point of view, even though in itself it is concrete. With respect to the world of the senses, mathematics is simply an abstraction; but considered from the standpoint of the intelligible world—the "world of ideas" of Plato—it is a guide to the eternal essences, which are themselves concrete. Just as all figures are generated from the point and all numbers from unity, so do all multiplicities come from the Creator, who is one. Number and figures, if considered in the Pythagorean sense—that is, as ontological aspects of unity and not merely as pure quantity—become vehicles for the expression of unity in multiplicity. The Muslim mind has therefore always been drawn toward mathematics, as may be seen in the great activity of the Muslims not only in the mathematical sciences but in Islamic art as well.

Islamic world inherited three different systems of numerical calculations of different origins, viz, finger reckoning, Indian system, and Babylonian system and were in usage simultaneously for many centuries.

Finger reckoning is of unknown origin, which performs its operation by retaining the results of intermediate steps by holding one's fingers in certain positions. It was also called arithmetic of the scribes (or secretaries) where numbers were written in works. The little of a handbook of this type of arithmetic written in Baghdad about AH 370/ AD 980 by Abu'1-wafa al-Buzjani indicates that it was intended for the use of government bureaucracy. The system, in fact, continued to be used by members of the secretarial class despite the existence of the much superior type of reckoning, which had come from India in the II/VIII century or earlier and on which many handbooks were available.

The Indian system of reckoning is based on the place-value idea, which is able to express any number, however large, with the help of only ten figures, including a sign for zero (sifr), which indicated an empty place. Medieval Muslim authors referred to those figures as "Indian1 or "dust" numerals, thereby indicating their origin and the fact that the operations effected by their means were performed on a dust board. In the Islamic world, Indian numerals existed in two forms—one in the East, the other in the West—it was from the latter that medieval Europe derived its Arabic numerals. It is unfortunate that the astronomers then simply ignored the advantage of the Indian system of numeration.

The Babylonian system is more complex than Indian system. Here letters of the alphabet stood for numbers. It was, in fact, a mixed system in which a non-place-value decimal notation was used for integers and a place-value sexagesimal system for fractions. This meant that in Islam the most sophisticated computations were performed in sexagesimals indicated by alphabetical symbols. Despite the apparent analogy between the decimal and sexagesimal systems, and although decimal fractions had already appeared in the fourth or tenth, it was not until al-Kashi's time that a unified place-value system was formulated for both fractions and integers.

The development of arithmetic by the Muslim scholars was more for the practical utility than for academic curiosity. The Muslims had to solve a number of concrete problems, such as the division of taxes, the calculation of lithe and the division of estates according to the Koranic law. Most of their practical rules were therefore based on proportions. Furthermore, practical problems also brought them face-to-face with such progressions as the sum of even or odd numbers, though they failed to prove their generality. Many arithmetical texts written by Muslim mathematicians refer to weights and measures to the purity of coins and to the methods of counting.

Arithmetical texts usually classify their subject matter into integers, fractions, and other numbers. The Muslims adopted the Greek definitions of arithmetical operations but used methods of their own. Some of their procedures, which strike us as unnecessarily complicated and rather unnatural, are so only because they were based on the prior analysis of number construction. For instance, al-Ajuli's division by 2 of a number:

Dividend   1,365
Intermediate Quotient   0,132 -1

Add   55
Final quotient   682 (682 x2) + 1 = 1,365

The figure 5 is written below and to the right of the intermediate quotient of every odd number of the dividend, and the two are added on the implicit assumption that $1/2 = 0.5$ (though decimal fractions were unknown to Muslims).

Muslim mathematicians extracted square and cube roots by successive approximations and even constructed root tables. They also used the abacus for the same purpose and were not slow in observing that numbers ending in 2, 3, 7, 8 or in odd number of zeros could not be perfect squares. In particular, they developed practical rules of arithmetic and demonstrated the existence of numerous identities, though they failed to bring out the general commutative, associative, and other laws involved, i.e.:

$$am + bm = (a + b) m$$
$$a-b = ab$$

It must be emphasized how much arithmetic problems were originally tied to linguistic problems. Arabic language has no special terms for unit fractions smaller than one-tenth. Hence, fractions, in general, were expressed by m parts of n. Moreover, the Arabs regarded fractions either as unit parts or else as ratios between the several itself. Only the first of these views corresponds to a mathematical extension of the concept of number, and its general acceptance was impeded by the metaphysical belief in an indivisible and absolute unit that was not a number, the monad of certain Pythogorean doctrines. Hence, the Muslim mathematicians never adopted the modern way of writing fractions, except when the numerator and denominator consist of only one digit each. Moreover, whenever the denominator could be broken down into aliquot parts lower than ten, they expressed each fraction by a series of fractions and of fractions whose successive denominators were the aliquot parts, thus:

$$\frac{19}{35} \text{ became } \frac{43}{57} \text{ that is to say: } \frac{3}{7} + \left(\frac{4}{5} \text{ of } \frac{1}{7}\right) \text{ or}$$

$$\frac{3}{7} + \frac{4}{5x7} = \frac{15+4}{35}$$

When the denominator was a prime number or when its aliquot parts contained prime number higher than ten, it was looked upon as an ordinary divisor. This complex approach was one of the main reasons why the Arabs failed to develop a general theory of fractions.

Muhamed ibn Musa al-Khwarizmi31 (d. 226/840) is a great Muslim mathematician (born in Khwarizm, Persia) after whom the algorithm is named. The word "algebra" is derived from his use of word "al Jabr" ("coercion," "restoration"), which first appeared in his book on mathematics *al-Muqalah fi hisab al-Jabr wal-Muqabilah*. It was the Latin translation of this work that introduced the algebraic concept into Europe.

The word "Jabr" means "restoration." It is the adding something to a given sum or multiplying it so that it becomes equal to another. The word "Muqabalah" means "comparison." This term is applied for the comparison of the two sides of an equation as $a + b = 5$. It seems that the word "al Jabr" was originally used for these simple operations, i.e., addition and multiplication, but later on it came to mean the whole subject.

Al Khwarizmi used two operations in the process of solving linear and quadratic equations, namely, those of eliminating negative qualities and reducing positive quantities of the same power on both sides of the equation. He deals with the problems of second-degree equations, describes multiplication and division, and discusses the measurement of surfaces. The treatise also discusses first-degree equations illustrated by numerical examples and makes distinction among six cases of the equation pertaining to the second degree. For example:

Squares equal to roots	$ax2 = bx$
Squares equal to numbers	$ax2 = c$
Roots equal to numbers	$ax = c$
Squares and roots equal to numbers	$ax2 = bx = c$
Squares and numbers equal to roots	$ax2 + C = bx$
Roots and numbers equal to squares	$bx + C = ax$

Besides, the author gives solution to the linear and quadratic equations, which ultimately results the idea of positive and negative signs. The author also gives geometrical solution, illustrated with figures of quadratic equations such as $Y + 10X = 30$. His systematic approach is said to have impressed on subsequent algebraic works contributed by al-Kar, adji32, al-Amuli, Abu Kamil$_{33}$, Abu I'Wafa34, and Umar al-Khayyam$_{35}$. The latter's classifications have justly remained famous both in the Islamic world and the West.

Geometry

The contribution of Muslims to the field of geometry may be classified into two branches: constructional and arithmetical. In case of the former, the Muslims expressed the elements of geometrical figures in terms of one another, i.e., by the methods of Greek geometry, and investigated the same problems, which their Alexandrian predecessors had studied such as mean proportionals and the trisection of an angle.

The contribution of the Muslim scholars to the arithmetical or numerical approach has been very impressive. In the words of Suter:

> In the application of arithmetic and algebra to geometry and conversely in
> the solution of algebraic problems by geometrical means, the Muslims far
> surpassed the Greeks and the Indians.

The most famous contributions to this field were Ibrahim ibn Strain's writings on the quadrature of the parabola, Abu'l Wafa's writings on the construction of regular polygons involving cubic equations, and Abu Kamil's writings on the pentagon and the decagon.

In cartography, Muslim scholars used the Persian method of the six Kishwars. In this, a central region was represented by a circle, surrounded by six circles of equal radius that touch the central circle and their neighbors. The resulting honeycomb pattern has a far less distorting effect on the peripheral regions of a map than have other methods of projection (Ptolemy, Peutinger, Mercator). Al-Balkhi's36 atlas was constructed on this principle. Finally, the geometrical concepts as the point, the line, and space were the subjects of many arguments between Muslim scholars who looked upon space as a cover or support (Aristotelian space) and those who considered it as a container (the platonic space of Abu'l-Baraqat).

IX

Mechanics

The idea of mechanics as applied mathematics was not foreign to Islamic civilization, being clearly implied in the works of Greek philosophers and mechanicians. The Greek concept of mechanical technology was often expressed in Arabic by the phrase "ilm al-hiyal" or "science of devices." Abu Nasr Muhamed ibn Tarkhan al-Farabi37 (257-339/870-950) (in Europe he was called al-Farabius and also Avenasser; among the Muslims he was called al-mu'allim ath-thani, "the second teacher," after Aristotle) in his catalogue of the sciences declares that the aim of this science is to determine the means by which those things whose existence is demonstrated in the various mathematical sciences can be applied to physical bodies. Elaborating this important idea, he explains that in order to produce the truths of mathematics artificially in material objects, the latter may have to be subtly altered and adopted. In this sense, the "science of devices" is a general art that includes algebra (on this account a kind of applied arithmetic that seeks to determine unknown numerical qualities) as well as building and surveying the manufacture of astronomical, musical, and optical instruments, and the design of wondrous devices. All these and similar arts, says al-Farabi, are principles of the practical crafts of civilization.

It is therefore worthy of note that many of the writers on mechanics such as Banu Musa, al-Biruni21, al-Karadji32, Umar Khayyam 20, Ibn al-Haythara were not entirely armchair mechanicians. The Banu Musa (is the popular name for the three sons, Ahmad, Hasan and Muhammed of Musa Shakir who acquired renown as scientists at the court of Baghdad in the III/IX century. They were mathematicians, astronomers, and engineers who designed the mechanical creations of the time. They participated in the labor of translating Hellenistic writings into Arabic at the famous Bayt al-Hikmah, whose work on mechanical devices is largely concerned with trick vessels. They supervised various engineering projects for their patrons, the caliphs at Baghdad.

An important document on Islamic mechanical technology is the treatise entitled "The Book of knowledge of Ingenious Mechanical devices" written in the beginning of VII/XIII century by Ibn ar-Razzaz al-Jazari. The treatise describes in great detail the construction of a large number of devices of a wide range, which the author divided into five categories: clocks of various kinds, vessels, measuring basins, fountains, and water-raising machines.

A series of noteworthy physicists followed Ibn al-Haytham (Alhazen20) and al-Biruni[21] and continued their study especially in mechanics, hydrostatics, and related branches of physics. Also the criticism of the theory of projectile motion of Aristotle was followed along lines established by Ibn-Sina (Avicenna) leading to the important studies of Ibn Bajjah (Avempace)38 and other later Muslim philosophers and scientists who exercised much influence upon Latin medieval mechanics. In this domain the Muslim scientists developed the theory of "inclination" and founded the basis of the impetus theory and the concept of momentum, which were further elaborated by late medieval scientists in the West. Moreover, Ibn Bajjah's (Avempace) attempt to qualify projectile motion by considering the velocity as proportional to the difference between the force and the resistance rather than to their ratio is of much significance in the light of the later attempt of Bradwardine and the Mertonian school to describe motion qualitatively.

Of the later Muslim physicists, one of the most important is Abu'l Fath, Abd al-Rahman al-Khazini 39, originally a Greek slave who flourished in Merv at the beginning of the VI/XII century and who continued the study of mechanics and hydrostatics in the tradition of al-Biruni and the earlier scientists. He also wrote several works on astronomy and physics, among which is *The Book of the Balance of Wisdom*, which is perhaps the most essential Muslim work on mechanics and hydrostatics, and especially the study of centers of gravity.

Al-Khazini1's works mark a further development to the earlier works of Banu Musa, al-Biruni, and Umar Khayyam. He combined an interest in hydrostatics with mechanics and concentrated especially on the concept of the center of gravity as applied to balance. In his efforts, he was followed a century later by Abu'l-v Izz al-Jazari, whose *Book of Knowledge of Ingenious Geometrical Contrivances* is the definitive work on mechanics in the Islamic world. He was in turn followed by Qaysar al-Hanafi who was especially expert on the mechanics of the water wheel. It was he who constructed the famous celestial globe that survives today in the national museum of Naples, Italy.

Just as the Muslims made the study of the rainbow into a separate science, so did they create a separate science of the balance in which al-Khazini was the undisputed master. His *Book of the Balance of Wisdom* is the outstanding work in this science in which he also discussed the view of earlier scholars including ar-Razi (Rhazes), Khayyam, and al-Biruni. It is particularly of interest that al-Khazini describes an instrument that, according to him, al-Biruni used in his famous measurements of specific weights of different substances.

In brief, Al-Khazini gives a detailed statement of the theory of the balance, of centers of gravity, and of the general way of applying the balance in order to measure the specific weight of bodies made of either one or two substances. The selections presented below from *The Book of the Balance of Wisdom*—whose very title is reminiscent of the cosmic balance of Jabirian alchemy but is here applied specifically to physical problems—demonstrate the delicacy that the use of the balance had reached among Muslim physicists. More specifically, they afford an indication of the method employed y al-khazini in making his measurements of specific weights. (See table in reference 39).

X

Astronomy

Behold! In the creation of the heavens and the earth,
And the alternation
Of Night and Day,
There are indeed sings
For men of understanding.
—Al-Quran 3:190

The first science in the modern sense that grew after the advent of Islam was astronomy (ilm an-anjum; also lim al-hay'ah, iim al-falak). It is natural to come to astronomy straight from mathematics; after all, astronomy was developed first and became a model for all the other sciences just because it could be turned into exact numbers.

The rudiments of astronomy exist in all cultures and were evidently important in the concerns of early peoples all over the world. One reason for this is clear. Astronomy is the knowledge that guides us through the cycle of the seasons—for example, by the apparent movement of the sun. In this way there can be fixed a time when to harvest, move their herds, and so on. Therefore, all settled cultures have a calendar to guide their plans, and this was true in the then-Islamic world as it was in the river basin of Babylon and Egypt.

The point is that astronomy does not stop at the calendar. There is another use among early peoples, which, however, was not universal. The movements of the stars in the night sky can also serve to guide the traveler, particularly the traveler at sea who has no other landmarks. The Arabs were good navigators. For Muslims of the medieval period, astronomy was not the apex of science or of invention. But it was a test of the cast of temperament and mind that underlies a culture. A culture from the injunction and inspiration from Quran that emphasizes the need for observation of physical phenomenon and natural processes and reflecting on whatever is observed. The frequent references to the natural phenomena of the universe in the Quranic verses such as the different stages of the moon (Al-Quran 36:39) and the revolution of the sun and the moon at a certain speed and according to a system (Al-Quran 55:5) are by implication incentives for scientific investigations. The Arab astronomers had a peculiar inquisitiveness that combined adventure with logic the empirical with the rational into a single mode of inquiry.

It is pertinent to reflect here why astronomy was developed so early and so elaborately and in effect because the archetype for the physical sciences. In themselves, the stars must be quite the most improbable natural objects to rouse human curiosity. The human body ought to have been a much better candidate for early systematic interest. Then why did astronomy advance as a first science ahead of medicine? Why did medicine itself turn to stars for omens, to predict favorable and the adverse influences competing for the life of the patient? Surely the appeal to astrology is an abdication of medicine as a science. A major reason is that the observed motions of the stars turned out to be calculable and from an early time (perhaps 3000 BC in Babylon) lent themselves to mathematics. The preeminence of astronomy rests on the peculiarity that it can be treated mathematically; and the progress of physics and most recently of biology has hinged equally on finding formulations of their laws that can be displayed as mathematical modes. The Muslims looked upon astronomy as the noblest, the most exalted, and the most beautiful of sciences, only because the study of stars was an indispensable religion observance.

One of the Greek inventions that Muslim astronomers, notably Irabhim ibn Habib al Fazari, elaborated and spread was the astrolabe. For a long time the astrolabe was the pocket watch and the slide rule of the world. As an observational device, it was primitive. It only measured the elevation of the sun or a star, and that too crudely. But by coupling that single observation with one or more star maps, the astrolabe also carried out an elaborate scheme of computations that could determine latitude, sunrise and sunset, the time for prayer, and the direction of Mecca for the traveler. And over the star map, the astrolabe was embellished with astrological religious details, of course, for mystic comfort. Later this instrument made a vital contribution to the voyages of the age of European exploration. The preeminence of Muslims in astronomy gave them a lead in navigation, and for this reason the school founded by Prince Henry the Navigator in Algarve in Portugal contained Arab astronomers, and it was Arab navigators who guided the Portuguese in many of their voyages. Ahmad ibn Majid al-Najdi, who wrote treatises on navigation in verse (10 aid memorization) and prose was the pilot in the voyage of Vasco da Gama to India.

A regular study of astronomy and mathematics began at Baghdad in the second half of the eight century during the reign of the second Abbasi Caliph al-Mansur (136-158/754-775). After that the patronage and generosity of other Muslim rulers particularly the seventh Abbasi Caliph al-Mamun (169-218/786-833) provided stimulation to the astronomical and mathematical researchers of every kind. A great incentive for the study of astronomy came from an Indian astronomical work called *siddhanta*, which was brought to the court of Yaqub ibn Tariq in AD 767 who was one of the great astronomers of his time. Yaqub ibn Tariq introduced him to the caliph al Mansur. Kanka showed the book to the caliph who ordered to translate into Arabic. He also ordered that the work based on siddhanta should be composed, which could serve as a reference book for the Arabs. Mohamed ibn Ibrahim took this responsibility and prepared a book, which was called by the astronomers as *Sind Hind al-Kabir* (*The Great Siddhanta* or *Maha Siddhanta*). It was used until the time of the caliph al-Mamun. Then Al-Khwarizmi, Muhamed ibn musa (d. 226/840), who was one of the greatest scientists, prepared a summary of this book. He also compiled astronomical and trigonometric tables according to the combined methods of Indians, Persians, and Greeks. These tables were revised by Maslamah al-Majriti during the second half of the tenth century. The tables gained so much popularity that they were used even in China. In the twelfth century the translation of these tables was made into Latin.

Translations in astronomy were also made from a variety of languages, besides Sanskrit, from Pahlavi, from Syriac, as well as from Greek. The result was an eclecticism that marked the early productions of Islamic astronomy and that also made a later appearance in Muslim Spain. After the translation of the Ptolemy's *Almagest* from Greek to Arabic during the reign of Caliph al-Ma'mun, the system was quickly recognized, and from then on, Islamic astronomy remained predominantly Ptolemaic in conception and method.

"Almagest" is the Latinized form of the Arabic "al-Majisti," which itself was the Arabization from the Greek Megale syntax. This is Ptolemy's second-century work on astronomy, which explained the apparent motion of the planets through the theory of epicycles and deferments.

In departing from the purely mystical theories of Pythagoras concerning the motion of the planets, the Megale syntaxes represented an important step toward the empiricism of modern science. Yet its empirical tendency was not a divorce from the perception that the heavens were above all a symbol of a higher reality; the physical world was still contained in an ideal or spiritual world. Ptolemy, like other Greek philosophers, may have known that the earth went around the sun (it is now known that some peoples of antiquity used both geocentric and heliocentric systems for calculation); but he knew above all that the world came from the spirit, and his planetary model reflected that knowledge, accommodating the data of observed motion as facts of secondary importance.

Islamic astronomy was based upon the theories of Ptolemy as expounded in the *Almagest*, and it was through the Arabic translation that the Ptolemaic theory was reintroduced as medieval Europe resumed the study of ancient sciences.

The Arabs inherited from Ptolemy a concept of testing, which they constantly kept before their minds and frequently put into practice. In the beginning of the IV/X century, the Harranian astronomer Abu Abd Allah Mohamed al-Battani40 (244-317/858-929), whose az-Zij as Sabi was modeled after the Almagest, ascribed to Ptolemy the injunction' that observations be made after him for the purpose of testing his own observations just as he himself has made tests of the observations of his predecessors. This exhortation—which is, in fact, implicit in Ptolemy's book—was taken quite seriously by Islamic astronomers, and the words "mihna" and "itibar" used by the translators of *Almagest* to render the Greek concept of testing can be seen almost everywhere in the medieval Arabic literature on astronomy. The lesson learned from the example set by Ptolemy was assiduously applied. Throughout the history of Islamic astronomy, observations were made at various places and at various centers of astronomical research. Thus, a group of Muslim astronomers created accurate tables (*zij*) of planetary motion: the zij as-Sabi of Al-Battani (called Albategnius in Europe), the zij of Al-khwarizmi, the zij al-Hakimi of the Fatimids made by the astronomer Ibn Yunus from his observatory on the Muquattam hills outside Cairo, the zij-il-Khanid of Maragha, and many others. These often served for the creation of special calendars such as the Jalali, which were noted for their accuracy. Also, under the Abbasids, Habash al Hasib made observations of solar and lunar eclipses and of planetary position at Baghdad, Samarra, and Damascus. Ibn Yunus conducted observations at Cairo in the IV/X century. At shiraz, beginning in the year 359/969, the famous as-sufi made a series of observations to determine the lengths of seasons. Toward the end of the IV/X century, the great al-Biruni was engaged in observation of lunar eclipses in Khwarazm. In the VII/XIII century, astronomical observations were carried out for a continuous period of about twenty years at Moraga where Hulegu had built in 685/1259 an observatory in which a group of astronomers worked, headed by Nasirad-Din at-Tusi. This may have been first observatory in the full sense of the word. It had a staff of about twenty astronomers drawn from various parts of the Islamic world including one from China; it was equipped with a library, and in it instruments (quadrants, armillary, astrolabes) were designed and constructed. In the first half of the IX/XV century Sultan Ulugh Beg founded an imposing observatory at Samarkand whose remains can still be seen.

Most of these observations yielded, for example, new values for the inclination of the ecliptic; the rate of equinoctial precision; and the mean motions of the sun, the moon, and the planets and so on. This limitation cannot be ascribed to the instruments used, some of which (like those constructed by al-Urdi at Maragha) were sophisticated and capable of producing more significant results than those in fact obtained by their means. The astronomers at Maragha and later ibn ash-Shatir at Damascus produced non-Ptolemaic planetary models, which have recently been compared with their counter parts in Copernicus.

Islamic astronomy drew inspiration from Greek knowledge and Ptolemaic astronomy, the sciences of Harranians and Nestorians of Jundishapur, later through Persia, it drew upon Indian Science, notably the works of Brahmagupta and Aryabhata and the Maha Siddhanta.

The influences of Islamic astronomy upon Europe were very considerable. It made its first impact through the work of Arab astronomers in Spain, such as az-Zarqali (Azarquiel in Europe) who edited the Toledan Tables and then showed a direct reflection in the first European books on astronomy such as the *Libros del Saber de Astronomia* of King Alfonso X el Sabio ("the wise"). Islamic observatories must also have influenced the work of the later European astronomers Tycho Brahe and Keppler.

The early dominance of Islamic astronomy on Europe is indicated by the preponderance of words of Arabic derivation in the technical vocabulary of modern astronomy. The table shows a few Arabic words adopted in the European vocabulary:

English Word	Arabic	Vocabulary Meaning
albedo	al-baida	The index of the reflection of a celestial body
Zenith	samt ar-ras	the direction of the head
Nadir	an-nazir	the opposite
the star vega	an-nasr al-waqi	the falling eagle the star

the star	bayt-al-Jawzah	armpit of the center Betelgeuse
The star Algol	Al ghul	"the ghoul"
the star Rigel	Ar rijl	"the foot" of Orion
the star Deneb	adh-dhanb	"the tail"
the star	ad-dabaran	"the follower" of the Al debaran Pleiads

As is true of all traditional astronomy as, for example, the Jyotividya of Hinduism, the science of Islam was inseparable from an interpretation of celestial phenomenon as a symbolic cosmology or what is now called astrology.

XI

Astrology

Astrology is usually condemned in Islam, as in the most religions, because it is a science potentially misleading to the soul. The danger inherent in astrology, despite the insights it offers as a cosmological and symbolic science, is that it may trap the soul in some existential illusion or error—that is to say, divination can throw up some illusion, which is actually the projection of a subjective flaw. If what is foreseen by divination then appears to be confirmed by events, the soul is snared in an unreality of its own making. As the hadith says, "even when the soothsayers tell the truth, they lie" and "Let no one malign fate for God says, 'I am destiny.'"

Moreover, Islam commends surrender to fate and the importance of the attitude precludes from the outset recourse to predictions. Nevertheless, astrology for the purposes of divination has been widely practiced. In antiquity virtually all mathematicians were astronomers and all astronomers were astrologers. Such men as Nasir ad-Din at-Tusi and al-Biruni were famous astrologers. The latter attacked astrologers for poor calculations rather than for their science.

Arab astrology is derived from the Greco-Egyptian tradition and the Tetrabiblos of Claudius Ptolemy*. The Arabs added the points on the individual horoscope known as the Arabian parts. These are derived by taking the arcs, which separate planets such as the sun and moon; adding or subtracting other arcs; and mapping the resulting arc on a horoscope starting from the horizon in order to determine sensitive points, such as the "part of fortune," the "point of spirit," etc. This system may indeed have given rise, or at least be related to, a traditional Arab system of fortune telling, still practiced in the marketplace, which involves measuring distances on the body of an individual—the arm, head, leg, and so forth—and adding and subtracting the measures to produce a divination.

The Arabs assigned to the moon twenty-eight houses (manazil), one for each day of its cycle. In Arabic the signs are called buruj, "towers" or "mansions." Individual stars played a greater role in interpretation than they do in the West, especially the pairs of naw'i stars, which at a given moment are observed on the rising and sinking horizons, corresponding to the ascendant and the descendant. This defined the horizontal axis or the individual nature. The nonindividual or ontological axis was the vertical between the Samt ar-ras ("the highest point" from which zenith" is desired, also called the Media Coeli) and samt an-nazir (whence "nadir," Imum Coeli).

Naw'i is derived from "naw" "the appearance of the first light," and it refers also to the entrance of the moon into each of its twenty-eight mansions, the manzil al-qamar. The study of the progressions of the moon is called the "ilm al-anwa" and constitutes traditional Arab agricultural meteorology. The best-known book on this science is the *Kitab al-Anwa of Ibn Qutaybah al-Dinawari*.

Other systems of divination existed among the Arabs, such as the mandalah, the "ilm ar-rami" (drawing figures on sand"), magic squares (al-waf z) combined with interpretations derived from the ilm al-huruf ("science of letters").

In addition to predictions, or perhaps above all, astrology was used as basis for cosmological theory to understand the secrets of creation in the sense that "the heavens declare the glory of God." The cycles of events, or of lives, were made intelligible by sacred symbolism in the cycles of the planets.

In traditional astrological or astronomical diagrams, the divisions of the zodiac, and even each degree (which represents one revolution of the earth) are assigned to an angel; the identity of the angel is the link or the correspondence, between a celestial mechanism and a higher supra-individual order of reality. Such diagrams of traditional Arab astrology as are available to us today are not easily comprehensible; some aspects may appear to be arbitrary because they are inadequately conceptualized. Nevertheless, they cannot be dismissed for while they are not systematic, they were intended to be guideposts to an individual contemplation, which would yield up an understanding within the scope of a personal experience.

The cycles of the planets were applied to manifestations on the human plane—that is, events and history. These cycles (Ar. akwar or adwar) range from the precession of the equinoxes, a cycle of slightly less than 25,700 years (a number known to most traditional cosmologies, not from measurements, an impossibility that gives rise to fantastical suppositions, but by induction from ideal proportions in mathematics, or as among the Pythagoreans and al-Farabi, from music) to the cycles of the moon, and the daily turning of the earth.

XII

Music

The question whether music is permissible at all began to be debated in the first century of Islam, and the debate has continued to this day, filling may thousand pages. Apart from the theological arguments, opposition to music on the part of certain early religious authorities seems to have arisen from the role it had begun to play in society. The "new music" was associated more and more with a life of pleasure and a taste for luxury. It acquired connotations of frivolity and sensuality, reinforced by the participation of women in music making and by the dancing and the drinking of intoxicating beverages that went with it.

There is no clear line of demarcation between sacred and secular music, and sacred music itself has throughout its long history oscillated between art and folk music. According to some of the traditions adduced in the controversy, the Prophet would have approved of the latter but not of the former, and art music was consequently completely banished. Nevertheless, the interpretation of the two genres has meant that the emphasis has continually fluctuated.

But what exactly were the uses of music in religious contexts, which gave rise to such passionate disagreements? There were three that were particularly important: the chanting of the Quran, the call to prayer and a few hymns for special occasions and holy days.

The musical setting of the Quran goes back to the second half of the I/VTI century, but it is not related to either Jewish or Christian musical traditions and according to literary sources drives from ancient to incantations and chants of pre-Islamic poetry. Its purpose is to enhance the meaning of the text and convey it in an effective way. Treatises on the subject codified rules (*tajwid* ["embellishment of the reading"]), whose aim was to teach the reader how to present the sacred text to the faithful in a comprehensible and moving way while avoiding any heresy that might result from a misreading. Accentuation, prolongation, and assimilation of certain letters, pauses, and correct pronunciation were all covered, as well as the three possible speeds: slow and solemn, rapid, and intermediate. It is often stressed that such chanting has nothing to do with the art music and is actually in theory not counted as music at all. Nevertheless in practice it has always absorbed elements from art music. In some countries it is even performed in different modes. But the basic traits are always kept and ornate style, and instrumental accompaniments are avoided.

Theory and Practice

Islamic society during medieval period was eager for knowledge of all kinds, and music was no exception. The study of music became a necessary part of every cultured man's education. The intellectual flowering reached a climax in the IV/X century, and music has played a significant role. But as the greatest of Arabic theorists al Farabi (d. 339/950) wrote in his *Kitab al-Musiqi al-Kabir*, "theory did not appear until practice had already achieved its highest development." This was certainly the case by his own time.

Musical theory took its deep roots during second half of the II/VTI century. Many Greek manuscripts were acquired by the enlightened caliph al-Mamun and were translated. The first to take advantage of these newly discovered treasures was al-Kindi, "philosopher of the Arabs." He wrote thirteen musical treatises and is considered the first distinguished representative of the Arab musica speculativa, a category of writing that presented two major trends, one emphasizing the ethical and cosmological aspects of music, the other mainly its mathematical and acoustic side. Al-kindi's writings belong predominantly to the first.

The second trend, which studies music scientifically as an activity that is strictly mathematical and almost independent of the human ear, is mainly represented by the great philosophers and theorists al-Farabi (257-339/870-950), Ibn Sina (Avicena) (370-429/980-1037), Ibn Zayla (d.440/1048), and Safi ad-Din al-Urmawi (d. 693/1294) who deal with the theory of sound, intervals and their ratio, harmonies and dissonances, genres, systems, modes, rhythms and rhythmical modes, as well as with the theory of composition and the construction of musical instruments. Both kinds of writing rely heavily on Greek sources but do not reproduce them mechanically. The Arab theorists expanded and improved their modes to correspond with the living music of their own time.

Books on the theory of the practice of music were written mainly for educational purposes to provide a comprehensive groundwork in actual music, making for both amateur and professional, though the theoretical aspects are not entirely neglected. Ahmad al-Katib's perfection of musical knowledge, for instance, ranges over a wide field of subjects with observations and advice from problems of phonetics to breathing and pronunciation, the arranging of musical concerts, audience reactions, plagiarism, classification of voices, and treatment of voice, while on a more theoretical level he explains current terminology and problems relating to modality. To some extent the Tajwid al-Quran (embellishment of the reading) should be included in this category since it deals with actual performance and aims to educate the reader.

XIII

Alchemy

Alchemy is the story of man's observation and reflection on the nature and cause of what we know as chemistry. Like all history, it records not only man's grouping for the truth and for the enrichment of his experiences but at the same time the widening of the human mind and the accompanying evolution of thought.

Alchemy deals with physical, psychological, and spiritual domain of existence. Physical alchemy deals with various substances, especially metals, and is employed by artisans and members of craft guilds while the spiritual alchemy is the transformation of the soul. Keeping in mind the overall distinction between alchemy as a prelude to chemistry, we must remember that ancient and medieval man did not separate the material order from the psychological and spiritual in the categorical manner that has become customary today. There was a naiveness in the mentality of the physical and psychological domains, seeing a deeper significance in physical phenomena than just plain facts. It is this belief in the multiple states of being, their interrelationships, and the possibility of moving from one level to another that comprises the general matrix of the long tradition of alchemy whose origins extend back to prehistoric times.

The term "al-kimiya1" is found in a text belonging to the earliest period of scientific prose writing in Arabic; and as "alkimia," it was in turn introduced to Latin readers in a translation of the text made before AD 1151. Hermes Trismegistus (or Idris), renowned philosopher, defined "alchemy as a corporeal substance composed from the one and through the one, joining the most precious things together through relationship and effect, and naturally converting the same things by a natural commixture and by the best-artifices."

Today alchemy is understood not as an obscure precursor of chemistry and even less as an aberration of science but as a living branch of the tree of human evolution, influenced and pervaded by all the forces shaping life.

The source of alchemy might have been derived from a number of earlier civilization, from ancient technical skills of the Egyptians to the recipes originating in Babylonia and Assyria, the alchemist prescriptions of pseudo Democritus, and to the sophist synopsis, from Chinese knowledge transmitted by the Mongols. Pliny and Plutarch call chemistry an Egyptian art. This would support the assumption that Egypt, especially Alexandria, was the determining influence in the shaping of Arab alchemy.

Muslim alchemists speculated regarding the origins of alchemy as an art and an entity. They went back as far as Adam. They considered Hermes Trismegistus or Idris (Enoch of the book of Genesis, V: 18-24; and The Epistle of Jude, V: 14-15) as a pioneer. After him many names of the Old Testament prophets and sages are listed, including the patriarchs Abraham, Isaac and Jacob, and prophets and kings such as Joseph, Moses, David, Solomon, Ezekiel and Daniel (Gen. 26:2-5,26-33; 30:25-43; 37:5-10; Ex. 7:10-21). According to some Arabic writers, Indians and Persians took over where the Hebrew prophets left off. There were no clear or direct references or mention of impact from other sources such as the paranoiac Egyptian, Babylonian, or Chinese, although such interactions evidently existed. Thereafter, through the conquest of the East by Alexander the Great (356-323 BC), alchemy and vital sciences were revived among the Greek philosophers. Reading figures included Aristotle, Democritus, Zosi'mos of Panopolis (upper Egypt, end of third century), and Olympiodoros (flourished about AD 400). Muslim alchemists considered Jesus Christ as a resourceful alchemist with great ability and an advocate of the "honorable" art.

Muslim alchemists boldly listed Mohammed, the prophet of Islam, as a supporter who bestowed favor on their activities. They insisted that the Holy Quran testified to the need and importance of alchemy by mentioning repeatedly such words and phrases as "al-mizan" ("balance"), "al-Sirr al-maknun" ("the hidden secret"), "al-tadbir" ("the preparation"), "al-tasrif" ("the management") and "the hajar" (stone)—expressions often referred to and used by alchemists in everyday life.

The salient features of Islamic scientific, philosophical, and alchemical expositions are classified under three phases.

In the first phase, alchemy passed through a period of a primitive practical approach supported by rational observations of natural phenomena and laboratory experiments. Many workers were meticulous alchemists, although there were charlatans and impostors among them. Apparently, the major aim of the Muslim alchemist was to make silver and gold from lesser metals by the use of the elixir or the philosopher's "honored" stone.

In the second phase, there was a period of ascetic and mystical alchemists whose writings and practices were with allegories, symbolisms, occultisms, mysteries, and theosophies. They used astrological and cosmological interpretations in their search and vocabulary. They relied heavily on poetry for their expressions and imaginative methodology. Through their impact, occultism, theology, and alchemy became strongly integrated.

The third phase was a period that saw the application of iatro-chemistry (medicinal chemistry) and the propagation of the idea that alchemy's foremost aim was the preservation of good health and the cure of diseases not necessarily the making of gold and silver. In medical treatment, therefore, Muslim alchemists relied on the use of drugs and chemicals for cures.

First Phase: In the chronological list of Muslim alchemists, Khalid bin Yazid (died in Damascus in AD 704) ranks first. He was a great Arab patron of learning and promoted many disciplines, including alchemy. In fact, he is first in Islam to order the translation of many texts from the Greek, Coptic, and other languages into Arabic and wrote several epistles on alchemy. One pertaining to the assessment of Arabic-Islamic alchemical activities was made by the historian-sociologist Ibn Khaldun (733-808/21332-1406):

> Alchemists searching after an elixir that transforms lesser metals into gold, studied the properties, virtues and temperaments of the elements used for its preparation—Besides, minerals animal refuse and excretions : urea, manure, bones, feathers, blood, hairs, eggs and nails were also used. They employed distillation, sublimation, calcination and other techniques to separate extracts that lead to the preparation of the elixir. If the elixir obtained is added to concocted lead, copper or tin over fire, then they turn into pure gold.

According to Ibn Khaldun the procedures adopted by Muslim alchemists are summarized as follows:

They take the prepared material in a mortar, or over a smooth stone slab and treat it with water until the substance is fully integrated. It is dried either under the sun or over fire. Sublimation and calcination are used' to extract an earthy powder or liquid essence, which often when treated according to the rules, results in a solid or liquid (the elixir). If added to heated copper it turns to silver, or added to heated silver it converts to genuine gold. This elixir is composed of the four elements; water, earth, air and fire with qualified faculties resembling the leaven in the dough. Frankly no alchemist ever got anything out of it, no matter how hard were his labours . . . . There are, nevertheless many sincere people who dabble with alchemy, but we know of none among the learned sages who actually achieved any results to report. Most of them spent their entire lives carrying on experimentations to no avail.

Historically speaking, the quest of Muslim alchemists to convert lesser metals to gold has been a failure. Nevertheless, during the process many new elements were discovered, new compounds synthesized, and new concepts introduced. The succeeding paragraphs justify the statement.

According to Ibn Khaldun, seven known metals—gold, silver, lead, tin, copper, iron, and zinc—differ either in their origins or in their properties and qualities. Adherents to the first assumption belong to Ibn Sina's school of thought, who insisted that each kind of metal is created separate from the other independently. There is no way that alchemy can change what God had created. The second assumption, emphasized by al-Farabi's school followed mainly in al-Andalus (Moorish Spain), taught that the differences are only in the apparent qualities (dry, wet, soft, or hard) and in the colors. Basically, however, all the elements are of the same kind. Therefore, these substances can be converted from one state to another. Followers of this latter school believed that transmutation could be achieved in shorter intervals than the normal course through alchemical processes and by increasing the effective powers on metals. Matter formed naturally in a specific time changes by necessity during the period of its formation from state to state till it reaches the end of its development and maturity. In alchemy, it is assumed the work of nature can be perfected more swiftly by mechanical and technical processes and procedures than if nature takes its own course.

In effect, what interested the alchemists was the intensity of chemical reactions. Thus, they realized that certain substances reacted vigorously while others were inert. They looked upon color changes as signs of the utmost importance but failed to appreciate their true significance, which as we know now rests on complicated ionic processes. Color changes were chosen simply because they were the most obvious, although they are of less importance and are beyond the capabilities of the investigators. In other words, Arabic alchemists adopted concepts that failed to describe any real phenomenon. Thus, Jabir ibn Hayyan (103-160/721-776) (Geber) introduced the concept of "potency" of substances, by which he referred to the respective "distances" of gold, silver, copper, tin, lead, iron, and other substances from the elixir governing the transmutation of metals. Now since no elixir exists, the distances were obtained by arithmological manipulations, and it is this sort of approach that turned alchemy into an esoteric science.

Second Phase: Failing to obtain satisfactory results in pursuing the acquiring of the "philosopher's stone," even with the aid of qualitative analyses and laboratory experimentations, many alchemists turned to metaphor, mystical symbolism, and occultism. Others resorted to talismans and sorcery following cosmo-psychological routines. Under the Fatimids (909-1171) this stage of alchemical practice enjoyed a peaceful time. One of its many adherents was Arfa Ras, the eloquent preacher-teacher of Fez in Morocco (d. 1198). He was praised as "the poet of philosophers and the sage of the poets." In his book and short epics, he portrayed alchemy in mystical love, religious asceticism, and anecdotes. Intellectually, the second phase in considered to be a dark period for alchemists.

Third Phase: A breath of fresh air swept over the arts of Arabic alchemy and medicine as a result of the works of the physician Ibn Sallum of Aleppo. In his book *Ghayal al-Itqan*, he explains the relationship of alchemy with medicine and revived interest in iatrochemistry (medical chemistry). Further, he discusses with precision the relationship between diseases on the one hand and astrology, planets, and drugs on the other. He prescribed mercury and antimony salts and potassium nitrate in therapy. He devoted a section to pharmaceutical preparations, and the distillation of aromatic water, spirits, and minerals. Like al-Zahrawi and many other Muslim physicians before him, he used extractions (adhan, essences, and liniments from plant origins) in the cure of diseases. According to Ibn Sallum alchemy is a branch of medicine having two functions: internal and external. First, the alchemy liquefies and purifies metals from impurities and corrupted elements and scoria that cause decay, separating or joining them at will. Second, the lesser metals such as lead and copper can be converted from the lowest degree of perfection into the noblest and highest state.

Intron chemistry, which flourished in the golden age of the Islamic civilization, found its fullest expression in the works of Ibn Sallum. He helped usher the modern era of medical chemistry in the region. This was a down-to-earth approach to the problem of health and disease. In the same vein, alchemy and technology served as subordinates to medicine. It viewed both fields working like a team to alleviate sickness and secure good health. Longevity and care of elderly were a part of the interest in preventive medicine and the preservation of health. For alchemists health was for this life to enjoy, but the "afterlife" is a religion and belief subscribed by Islam. Money, riches, prestige, and better living were fundamental in Arabic-Islamic alchemy. Believing in life after death was a matter of religious conviction.

In conclusion. alchemy, as a cosmological science of Alexandrian origin, is like a crystal that, when brought into the light of the living esotericism of Islam, begins to glow with great brilliance. Its integration into Islam like that of its sister art, astrology, is to result in certain transformation of its formulations. Alchemy, in its highest meaning, is a spiritual technique for liberating the soul from its material bonds by making it realize that the world is not a series of images and dreams of the individual psyche but the dream of the universal or world soul in which the human soul must participate. Alchemy was thus a way of awakening man from that illusion, which the Alchemist calls the world by means of the contemplation of the primordial beauty of nature and participation in the dream of the world soul through the removal of the limitative barriers of the individual psyche.

XIV

Chemistry

Alexander von Humbolt in his *Kosmos* expresses the view "that the most important contribution by the Arabs to the natural sciences was their work in chemistry." The accomplishments of the Arabs are, in his opinion, of significance that he feels justified to say that they opened up a new branch of the natural sciences.

The subject of chemistry has been a fascination from the time immemorial. The remarkable and unexpected changes in appearance, such as the phenomena of the disappearance and reappearance of an efflorescence in a puddle, the combustion of a heavy branch of tree to a handful of white ashes, and the conversion of metals into dust and their reconversion to metal, have aroused man's interest from the earliest ages. His first tendency was to attribute all such phenomena to direct human or superhuman agencies.

Science Is "Understanding" and Technology Is "Utilization"

Alchemy in its totality is not a prelude to chemistry. The origins of chemistry are found in the physical alchemy whose subject matter is the mineral world. However, between the alchemy of the medieval period and modern chemistry, there is a continuity of subject matter and perhaps some similarity of certain techniques as to their point of view and ultimate objective; however, there is an abyss between them. In alchemy, nature is sacred; all the operations performed upon it therefore have an effect upon the soul of the alchemist himself by virtue of the analogy between the microcosm and macrocosm. Chemistry, on the contrary, could come into the foreground only after the substances with which alchemy dealt were deprived of their sacred character so that operations upon them affected only the substances.

In Islamic history it is difficult to make a distinction between alchemy and chemistry. Among the famous alchemical writers, we find some who deal essentially with inner transformations, others with chemical ones, and a third group uses external operation as a support for the inner transformations of the soul. For example, among Islamic alchemical works, al-Iraqi's writings belong for the most part to the first category, Ar-Razi's to the second, and Jabir's mostly to the third, as will be seen in the selections presented from Jabir's, Ar-Razi's, and al-Iraqi's works later. Jabir ibn Hayyan (103-160/721-776) (Latinized as Geber) is a celebrated chemist whose contributions are very great. His works may be broadly classified into three categories: (1) modification of the Aristotelian doctrine of the four elements, (2) development of methodologies, and (3) synthesis of new substances.

Sulphur-Mercury Theory

In the modification of the Aristotelian doctrine Jabir proposes the sulfur-mercury theory, which explains that all the metals are, in essence, composed of mercury and coagulated with sulphur. They differ from one another only because of the difference of their accidental qualities, and this difference is due to the difference of their varieties of sulphur, which, in turn, is caused by variation in the earth, and in their exposition with respect to the heat of the sun in its circular motion. This theory explains the constitution of minerals, which if considered only from the physical point of view is the origin of the modern acid-based theory. The sulfur-mercury principles, which in each domain of manifestation correspond to the active (or masculine) and passive (or feminine) principles, became from a chemical point of view, the acid and base through whose union a salt is formed. Alchemically, this theory explains the masculine-feminine duality upon which all cosmic existence depends and in terms of which all the medieval cosmological sciences sought to explain the phenomena of nature. Further Jabir divided the materials with which alchemy deals into three classes, each having certain specific qualities, based on the predominance of one of the natures: (1) the "spirits," which become completely volatized into fire; (2) the "metallic bodies," which may be hammered, possess a luster, produce a sound, and are not "mute" like "spirits" and "bodies"; and (3) the "bodies" (mineral substances), which cannot be hammered but can be pulverized. Moreover, the "spirits" are five in number—sulphur, arsenic, mercury, ammonia, and camphor. The metals include lead, tin, gold, silver, copper, iron, and *kharsini* ("Chinese iron").

Development of Methodologies

Unlike the Greek predecessors, Jabir did not merely speculate but performed experiments to reach certain conclusions. He recognized and stated the importance of experimentation in chemistry. He combined the theoretical knowledge of the Greeks and practical knowledge of the craftsmen and himself made noteworthy advances both in the theory and practice of chemistry. It is impossible to reach definite conclusion regarding the extent of his contributions until all the Arabic writings ascribed to him have been properly edited and studied.

Jabir gave a scientific description of two principal operations of chemistry. One of them is calcination, which is employed in the extraction of metals from their ores. The other is reduction, which is employed in numerous chemical treatments. He improved upon the methods of evaporation, distillation, sublimation, crystallization, and melting. These are the fundamental methods employed for the purification of chemical substances, enabling the chemist to study their properties and uses and to prepare them. The process of distillation is particularly applied for taking extract of plant material and concentrate acetic acid from vinegar. ("Alembic" is the general term used for distillation vessel and often referred to as one of the apparatuses used in distilling rose water. The complete distilling apparatus consists of three parts: the "cucurbit" [*kara*], the "head" or "cap" [*anbik*], and the "receiver" [*kabila*]).

Synthesis of New Substances

In the opinion of Jabir the cultivation of gold was not the only object of a chemist. The preparation of new chemical substances was also regarded by him as the chief object of chemistry. The world of chemistry owes him the first preparation to isolate arsenic and antimony in their elemental state from their sulphides. Besides, the most important discovery made by Jabir was the preparation of sulphuric acid, nitric acid, and aqua regia. The importance of sulphuric acid can be realized by the fact that in this modern age the extent of the industrial progress of a country is mostly judged by the amount of sulphuric acid consumed in that country. Jabir prepared nitric acid by distilling a mixture of alum (of Yemen) and copper sulfate (of Cyprus). Then by dissolving ammonium chloride into this acid, he prepared aqua regia, which, unlike acids, could dissolve gold in it. In technology, Jabir's contribution is significant; he deals with such application as the use of manganese dioxide in glass making, varnishes, waterproof cloth and protect iron, as well as use of iron pyrites for writing in gold and distillation of vinegar to concentrate acetic acid.

Jabir is the author of a large number of books on chemistry and a book on astrolabe. About one hundred chemical works ascribed to him are extant. His fame chiefly rests on his chemical books preserved in Arabic. Some of the chemical writings to which Jabir's name is attached were translated into Latin. The first such version, the *Book of the Composition of Alchemy*, was made by Robert of Chester in AD 1144. The Kitab al-Sabin (the *Book of the Seventy*) was translated by Gerard of Cremona in the twelfth century. The translation of the *Sum of Perfection* was made by Richard Russell.

In the history of Islamic science, Al-Razi's position stands top in the list of clinical physicians (which will be discussed later). He enjoyed fame in medieval and Renaissance Europe matched only by that of Ibn Sina (Avicenna). Before turning to medicine, however, Ar-Razi was an alchemist. In fact, it has been said that, as a result of too-strenuous experimentation with alchemical processes, his eyesight began to give way, and it was in desperation that he gave up the practice of alchemy.

Ar-Razi's alchemical works are the first treatise of chemistry. His careful classification of substances is an important achievement from the point of view of chemistry, not alchemy. His secret of secrets the *Latin Liber Secretorum Bubacaris*, which is the most famous of his alchemical works, is a text of chemistry that has preserved the alchemical language. It describes the chemical processes and experiments, which Ar-Razi himself performed and which can be identified in their modern equivalents form of distillation, calcination, crystallization, etc. Ar-Razi in this and other works gives also a description of a large number of chemical apparatuses, such as beakers, flasks, phials, casseroles, naphtha lamps, smelting furnaces, shears, tongues, alembics, pestles, mortars, and many others that have in part survived to the present day.

Ar-Razi considered himself a disciple of Jabir, and even the titles of most of his alchemical works are either identical with or resemble closely those of the Jabirian corpus. But Jabiriatt alchemy was based on the principle of the esoteric interpretation—"hermeneutic exegesis"—of nature as the cosmic text (ta'wil). Through the application of this method of interpreting the inner meaning of things, every Jabirian science, and especially alchemy, was concerned with both the external and symbolic or inward meaning of phenomena. Ar-Razi, by denying prophecy and therefore the possibility of this spiritual exegesis that is inseparable from it, also negated the symbolic dimension of alchemy and transformed it into chemistry.

Ar-Razi departed from symbolic and metaphysical dimensions of Jabir's alchemical worldview. He described the chemical and medical properties of substances, and he is, in fact, credited with major discoveries in the domain including that of alcohol and of certain acids. In denying prophecy and the possibility of an esoteric interpretation of things, Ar-Razi also eliminated the symbolic dimension of alchemy having a science that was concerned with external properties alone, namely, chemistry.

Al-Iraqi regarded alchemy as the divine origin unlike ar-Razi, who confined himself to chemical properties of things. Al-Iraqi remained faithful to the teachings of Jabir studying the external and physical properties of materials in conjunction with their symbolic significance and in relation to the psychological and spiritual domains. He is the author of one of the best-known Islamic alchemical tracts: the *Cultivation of Gold*. In this book he aims not to invite but to continue faithfully the doctrines of the masters of the art. For example, al-Iraqi follows Jabir in regarding metals as a single species, differencing only in accidents, a species that he readily compares with plant and animal species. He expresses these ideas, however, in a manner that reveals his own mastery of alchemy rather than by the simple repetition of Jabir's ideas. Likewise, he has a similar conception of the all-embracing prime matter, which he however describes in his own novel way.

XV

Medicine

Islamic medicine is one of the most famous and best-known facets of Islamic civilization, being one of the branches of science in which the Muslims most excelled. Not only during the Middle Ages were the Muslims physicians studied seriously in the West, but even during the Renaissance and the XI/XVII century, their teachings continued to carry weight in Western medical circles. It was, in fact, only a century ago that the study of Islamic medicine was completely omitted from the curriculum of medical schools throughout the Western world. In the East, despite the rapid spread of Western medical education, Islamic medicine continues to be studied and practiced, and is far from being merely of historical interest.

Islamic medicine came into being as a result of the integration of Hippocratic and Galentic traditions of Greek medicine with the theories and practices of the Persians and Indians, within the general context of Islam. It is therefore synthetic in nature, combining the observational and concrete approach of the Hippocratic school with the theoretical and philosophical method of Galen, adding to the already vast storehouse of Greek medical knowledge the theories and experiences of the Persian and Indian physicians, especially in pharmacology. Furthermore, Islamic medicine remained for the most part closely allied to alchemy, seeking as did Hermetic and stoic physics the concrete causes for individual phenomena rather than the general causes sought by the peripatetic "natural philosophy." In this manner, it also retained its ties with numerical and astrological symbolism, which had already become an important element of Alexandrian hermeticism before the rise of Islam.

Islamic world produced most distinguished medical theoreticians and practitioners in history at the time when the state of medicine if| Europe was very poor. The Muslims who came in touch with Frank physicians during the Crusades expressed much scorn for their ignorance and barbaric practices. Thabit, a Christian physician of the Syrian prince Usamah, served two cases, ending fatally on account of the barbaric surgery of a Frank. The study of Islamic medicine was made for centuries in all the Western countries, particularly in France. The Arabic medical writings formed the core of the European medical literature and were included in the syllabi of the European universities. The medical curriculum was largely based on Ibn Sina's *Qanun* and the ninth book of al-Razi's al-Mansuri. The introduction of the Islamic medicine into Europe is an interesting chapter of history.

According to Dr. Robert Briffault, an eminent Western scholar, the allopathic system of medicine is the outcome of Arabic medicine. He remarks:

> The pharmacopoeia created by the Arabs is virtually that which but for the recent synthetic and organotherapic preparations, is in use at the present day; our common drugs, such as nux vomica, senna, rhubarb, aconite, gentian, myrrh, calomel, and the structure of our prescriptions belong to Arabic medicine.

He also disclosed that the medical school of Montpellier (France) Padua, and Pisa (both in Italy) were founded on the pattern of that of Cordoba (Spain) under Jew doctors trained in Arab schools. The Qanun of Ibn Sina and the surgery of Abu'l-Qasim al-Zahrawi remained the textbooks of medical science throughout Europe until the seventieth century.

History of Islamic Medicine

The Arabs who, under the banner of Islam, conquered both Alexandria and Jundishapur and thus gained mastery over the main centers of science and medicine, also had a simple medicine of their own, which did not undergo any immediate change with the coming of Islam, but had to wait until the II/VIII century to become transformed by Greek medicine. The first Arab physician whose name is recorded by later chronicles is al-Harith ibn Kaladah, who was a contemporary of the Prophet and had studied medicine at Jundishapur. The Arabs of his day, however, remained for the most part skeptical about this form of medicine. Of much greater significance to them were the sayings of the Prophet with regard to medicine, hygiene, diet, etc., with all the ardent faith that characterized the early Muslim generations.

Islam, as a guide for all facts of human life, had also to concern itself with the more general principles of medicine and hygiene. There are several verses of the Quran in which medical questions of a very general order are discussed; there are also many sayings of the Prophet dealing with health, sickness, hygiene, and other questions pertaining to the field of medicine. Such diseases as leprosy, pleurisy and opthalmia are mentioned; remedies such as cupping, cautery, and the use of honey were proposed. This body of sayings on medical questions was systematized by later Muslim writers and became known as *Medicine of the Prophet* (Tibb al-Nabi). The beginning of the fourth volume of the collection of prophetic traditions of al-Bukhari, which is one of the most authoritative sources of its kind, consists of two books in which are collected, in eighty chapters the sayings about illness, its treatment, the sick, etc.

All the sayings of the Prophet are guide posts for the life of the devout Muslim and thus played a major role in determining the general atmosphere in which Islamic medicine has come to be practiced. The medicine of the Prophet became the first book to be studied by a medical student before he undertook the task of mastering the usual compendia of medical science. It has thus always played an important role in creating the frame of mind with which the future physician has undertaken the study of medicine.

The Beginning of Islamic Medicine

With medical texts of Greek, Pahlavi, and Sanskrit origin translated into Arabic and a sound technical vocabulary firmly established, the ground was prepared for the appearance of those few giants whose works have dominated Islamic medicine ever since. The author of the first major work of Islamic medicine was Ali ibn Rabban al-Tabari, a convert to Islam, who wrote his *Paradise of Wisdom* (Firdaus al-hikmah) in 236/850. The author, who was also the teacher of Ar-Razi drew mainly upon the ibn Masawaih and Hunain. In 360 chapters, he summarized the various branches of medicine, devoting the last discourse, which consists of thirty-six chapters, to a study of Indian medicine. The work, the first large compendium of its kind in Islam, is of particular value in the fields of pathology, pharmacology, and diet, and clearly displays the synthetic nature of this new school of medicine, now coming into being.

The two towering personalities who have left concrete impressions in the pages of history of Islamic medicine are Ar-Razi, a student of Al-Tabari who was without doubt the greatest clinical and observational physician of Islam and Ibn Sina, the most influential, both in the East and the West.

The skills of Ar-Razi in prognosis and his analysis of the symptoms of a disease its manner of treatment and cure have made his case studies celebrated among later physicians. Ar-Razi himself recorded some of the more unusual cases he encountered during his medical practice. To quote, the attacks of mixed fever, sometimes, quotidian, sometimes tertian, sometimes quatrain and sometimes recurring once in six days. These attacks were preceded by a slight rigor, and micturition was very frequent. In an another case, in which Ar-Razi's mastery of treatment by means of psychological shock is well displayed, is described in the "Four Discourses" of Nizami-i Arudi, and has become famous among later students of medicine. Besides, Ar-Razi was also well versed in anatomy in which he like other Muslim physicians continued the tradition of Galen. The passages from *Book of al-Mansur* give a fair picture of anatomical knowledge among Muslim physicians. The work of Ar-Razi best known in the Western world is his treatise on measles and smallpox, which was published in Europe many times, as late as the eighteenth century. Besides, he composed several large medical works, including his compendium and short treatises on various diseases. Nevertheless, his *Book of al-Mansur* and *Kitab al-Hawi* are his two great masterpieces.

The *Kitab al-Hawi* (continents) is the most voluminous medical work ever written in Arabic. It must be regarded as the most basic source for the study of the clinical aspects of Islamic medicine. It was studied avidly in the western world from the VI/XII to the XI/XVII century. When Ar-Razi and Ibn Sina were held in higher esteem than even Hippocrates and Galen, and it constitutes one of the mainstays of the traditional curriculum of medicine in the Islamic world. As a master of psychosomatic medicine and psychology, Ar-Razi treated the maladies of the soul along with those of the body and never separated the two completely. He, in fact, composed a work on the medicine of the soul in which he sought to demonstrate the way to overcome those moral and psychological illnesses, which ruin the mind and the body and upset that total state of health that the physician seeks to preserve. In this book named *Spiritual Physick* in its English translation, Ar-Razi devotes twenty chapters to the various ailments that beset the soul and body of man. The contributions of Ar-Razi to medicine and pharmacology as contained in his many medical writings—of which al-Biruni mentions fifty-six—are numerous. He was the first to isolate and use alcohol as an antiseptic and mercury as a purgative, which became known in the Middle Ages as "Album Rhasis." After Ar-Razi, the most outstanding physician whose writings have been of universal import was Ali ibn-al-Abbas al-Majusi (the Latin "Haly Abbas") who is best known for his *Kamil al-Sinaah* (*The Perfection of the Art*) or *Kitab al-Maliki* (*The Royal Book* or *Liber Regius*), which is one of the best-written medical works in Arabic and remained standard text until the works of Ibn Sina appeared. The *Liber Regius* is of particular interest in that in it al-Majusi discusses the Greek and Islamic physicians who preceded him, making a frank judgment of their virtues and shortcomings. The works of al-Majusi, as well as those of most of the other early physicians in Islam, were overshadowed by those of Ibn Sina, the most influential of all Muslim.

XVI

Geography

The Muslims did not conceive of geography as a well defined and delimited science with a specific connotation and subject matter in the modern sense. The Islamic geographical literature was distributed over a number of disciplines and separate monographs on various aspects of geography were produced under the titles as Kitabul Baldan, Suratul Arz ul Masalikl wal mamalik, Ilmul Turuk, etc.; Al Bairuni considered "ASl Masalik," the science that dealt with fixing the geographical position of places. Al Mukaddsi came nearest to dealing with most aspects of geography in his work Ahsan al-takasim fi marifat al-akalim.

The term "jughrafiya," the title of the works of merinos of Tyre (c. AD 70-130) and Claudius Ptolemy (c. AD 90-168), was translated into Arabic as Surat al-ard, which was used by some Arab geographers as the title of their work. Al-Masudi (d. 345/956) explained the term as Kat al-ard Surve off the Earth. However, it was used for the first time in the Rasail Ikhwan al-Safa in the sense of "map of the world and the climes." The present use of the term "jughrafiya: for geography in Arabic is a comparatively modern practice.

Geographical Concepts and Quranic Verses

In pre-Islamic times the Arab's knowledge of geography was confined to certain traditional and ancient geographical nations or to place-names of Arabia and the adjacent lands. The three main sources where these are preserved are the Quran, the prophetic tradition (hadith), and the ancient Arabic poetry. Many of these notions must have originated from Babylonia in ancient times or were based on Jewish and Christian traditions and indigenous Arab sources.

The geographical concepts or information contained in ancient Arabic poetry reflect the level of understanding of the pre-Islamic Arabs of their knowledge. The Quran preserves traces of some geographical and cosmographical ideas, which resemble ancient Babylonian, Iranian, and Greek concepts and the Jewish and Christian biblical traditions. The Quranic verses

"Do not the unbelievers see that the heavens and the earth were joined together, before we clove them as under" (Al-Quran 21:30)

Allah is he who

"Created seven firmaments and of the earth, a similar number, through the midst of them [all] descends. He commands : that 'ye may'" (Al-Quran 65:12)

"Allah is he who raised, the heavens without any pillars, that ye can see, then he established himself, on the throne, he has subjected the sun and the moon! Each one runs (its course), For a term appointed. He doth regulate all affairs explaining the signs in detail" (Al-Quran 13:2)

"And we have made, the heavens as a canopy, well-guarded" (Al-Quran 21:32)

"He withholds the sky from falling on the earth except, by his leave" (Al-Quran 22:65) and verses that describe the earth as being spread out and the mountains set thereon firm so that it may not shake, all form a picture which resembles the ancient Babylonian concept of the universe in which the earth was a disc-shaped body surrounded by water and then by another belt of mountains upon which the Firmament rested. There was water under the earth as well as above it. Again, the concept like that of "the sun setting in a spring of murky water" (Al-Quran 18:86) referring to the Atlantic, the concept of the two seas, one of sweet water and the other saline (Al-Quran 25:53,), referring to the Mediterranean and the Arabian Sea, and that of al-barzakh, 'the barrier' in the Quran, e.g. burud], baladun or baladatun indicate the non-Arab origin of the concepts with which these terms are associated in the Quran.

There are some traditions attributed to Ali ibn Abi Talib (d. 40/660), Ibn Abbas (d. 66-9/686-8), Abd Allah bin Amr bin al-Aas, and others, which deal with cosmogony, geography, and other related questions; but it seems that these traditions, which reflect the ancient geographical notions of the Arabs, were connected in a later period to counteract the scientific geographical knowledge that was becoming popular among the Arabs of the period although they were presented as authentic knowledge by some geographers in their works. Though scientific knowledge advanced, some of the traditions exercised deep influence on Arab geographical thought and cartography.

Influence of India, Iran, and Greek Geographical Knowledge

Indian geographical knowledge passed on to the Arabs through the first translation into Arabic of the Sanskrit treatise Sur/a-Siddhanta, which mainly belonged to the Gupta period. Among other Sanskrit works translated into Arabic were *Aryabhatiya* by Arabhatiya of Kusumapura (b. AD 476) who wrote in AD 499 and Khandakhad, also known as Brahmagupta, son of Vishnu of Bhillamala (near Multan). He was born in AD 598 and wrote this work in AD 665. It was a practical treatise-giving material in a convenient form for astronomical calculations.

The concept of the seven kishwars is the Iranian influence on Islamic geography. In this system the world was divided into seven equal geometric circles, each representing a kishwar, in such a manner that the fourth circle was drawn in the center with the remaining six around it, and included Iranshahr of which the most central district was al-sawad. The Arab geographers continued to be influenced by this system for a long time, and in spite of the view of al-Biruni that it had no scientific or physical basis and that the Greek division of the times was more scientific, the Greek division of the world into three or four continents never appealed to them. The concept of the two main seas, namely, the Bahr al Rum and Bahr Fars (the Mediterranean and the Indian Ocean), which entered the land from the Bahr al-Muhit (the Encircling Ocean), one from the north-west, i.e., the Atlantic and the other from the east, i.e., the Pacific, but were separated by al-Barzakh ('the Barrier1, i.e., the Isthmus of Suez), also dominated Arab geography and cartography for several centuries.

The Iranian traditions deeply influenced Arab maritime literature and navigations, as is evident from the use of words of Persian origin in the nautical vocabulary of the Arabs, e.g., *bandar* ("port"), *naakhuda* ("shipmaster"), *rahmani* ("book of nautical instructions"), and *daftar* ("sailing instructions"). Certain Persian influences are apparent in Arab cartography as well, an indication of which is found in the use of terms of Persian origin, e.g., taylasan, shabura, kuwara, etc., to describe certain formations of coasts.

The Greek influence on the Arab geographers was more than Indian and Iranian influence. Moreover, authentic data are available on how Greek geographical and astronomical knowledge passed on to the Arabs in the medieval period. The process began with the translations of the works of Claudius Ptolemy and other Greek astronomers and philosophers into Arabic either directly or through the medium of Syria.

In brief, the works of Indian, Iranian, and Greek astronomers, geographers, and philosophers, when translated into Arabic, provided material in the form of concepts, theories, and results of astronomical observations, which ultimately helped geography to evolve on a scientific basis.

Over half a century of Arab familiarity with and study of Indian, Iranian, and Greek geographical science, from the time of the caliph al-Mansur up to the time of al-Mamun resulted in completely revolutionizing Arab geographical thought. Concepts such as the earth was round and not flat and that it occupied the central position in the universe were introduced to them for the first time properly and systematically. Thus, by the beginning of the III/IX century the real basis was laid for the production of geographical literature in Arabic, and the first positive step in this regard was taken by Caliph al-Mamun, who successfully surrounded himself with a band of scientists and scholars and patronized their academic activities. During his reign, some very important contributions were made toward the advancement of geography: the measurement of an arc of a meridian. The mean result gave 562/3 Arabic miles as the length of a degree of longitude, a remarkably accurate value; al-zidj al-mumtahan (the verified Tables) were prepared by the collective efforts of the astronomers. Lastly, a world map called al-sura al-Mamuriyya was prepared, which was considered superior to the maps of Ptolemy and Marinos of Tyre by al-Masudi.

The Arab astronomers and philosophers made equally important contribution to mathematical and physical geography through their observations and theoritical discussions. From the time of the introduction of Greek philosophy and astronomy in the second half of the II/VIII century up to the first half of the V/XI century, a galaxy of philosophers and astronomers worked on various problems of mathematical, astronomical, and physical geography. The works of the Greek scientists had already provided enough basis and material for this. Thus, the results of the experiments, observations, and theoretical discussions of the Arab scientists were recorded in their more general works on astronomy and philosophy or in monographs on special subjects like tides, mountains, etc. The contemporary and later writers on general geography in Arabic often, though not always, reproduced these results in their works and sometimes discussed them. Thus, a tradition was established of writing on mathematical, physical, and human geography in the beginning and of any work dealing with geography. This is noticeable, for example, in the works of Ibn Rusta, al-Yakubi, al-Masudi, Ibn Hawkal, etc.

By the III/IX century a considerable amount of geographical literature had been produced in various forms in the Arabic language, which were given the generic title al-Masalik wa'1-mamalik. In all probability the first work bearing this title was that of Ibn Khurradabhbih. The first draft of this work was prepared in 231/846 and the second in 272/885; it became the basis and model for writers on general geography and was highly praised by almost all geographers.

The geographical works produced during the III/IX and IV/X centuries may be divided into two broad categories. First is the works dealing with the world as a whole but treating the Abbasid Empire (mamlakat al-Islam) in greater detail. They attempted to give all such secular information as they could not find a place in the general Islamic literature, and hence, this category is called the secular geographical literature of the period. The second category of works belongs to the writings of al-Istakhri, Ibn Hawkal, and al-Mukadassi, for whom the term "Balkhi school" has been used, as they followed Abu Zayd al-Balkhi. They confined their works to the world of Islam, describing each province as a separate entity and hardly touching on non-Islamic lands except the frontier regions.

An important aspect of the development of Arabic geographical literature of this period was the production of the maritime literature and travel accounts, which enriched the Arab's knowledge of regional and descriptive geography. This became possible firstly because of the political expansion of the Muslims and the religious affinity felt by them toward one another irrespective of the nationality or race and, secondly, because of the phenomenal increase in the commercial activities of the Arab merchants. Incentive to travel and exploration was provided by several factors, viz, pilgrimage to Mecca, missionary zeal, deputation as envoys, official expeditions, trade and commerce, and mariners' profession. The Arabs' urge to explore new lands was mainly prompted by desire for trade and rarely for the sake of exploration. In brief, the Arabs of this period did not make any substantial contribution to or improve upon the knowledge acquired from the Greeks.

The V/XI century may be taken as the apogee of the progress of Arab geography. The geographical knowledge of the Arabs, both as derived from the Greeks and others and as advanced by themselves through research, observation, and travel, and by this period, reached a very high level of development. Besides, geographical literature had acquired a special place in Arabic literature, and various forms and methods of presenting geographical material had been standardized and adopted. The importance of al-Biruni's contribution to Arab geography is twofold. First, he presented a critical summary of the total geographical knowledge upto his own time; and since he was well versed in Greek, Indian, and Iranian contributors to geography and in that of the Arabs, he made a comparative study of the subject. He pointed out that Greeks were more accomplished than the Indians, thereby implying that the methods and techniques of the former should be adopted. But he was not dogmatic and held some important views that were not in conformity with Greek ideas. Second, as an astronomer he not only calculated the geographical position of several towns but measured the length of a degree of latitude, thus performing one of the three important geogetic operations in the history of Arab astronomy. He made some remarkable theoretical advances in general, physical, and human geography.

Among the astronomers and geographers of V/XI century who deserves mention is Ibn Yunus and al-Bakri. The former made valuable observation in the observatory on the Mount al-Mukattam in Egypt while the latter is the best representative of lexicography of the period in as far as place-names were concerned. Al-Bakri's geographical dictionary of Mu'dJam ma stadJam min asma al-bilad wa 1-mawadi is an excellent literary-cum-geographical work. It discusses the orthography of place-names of the Arabian peninsula, mainly, furnishing literary evidence from Arabic literature, ancient Arabic poetry, Hadit, ancient traditions, etc. His second geographical treatise *Kitab al-masalik wa' t mamalik* has not survived in its entirety.

From VI/XII to the X/XVI century Arab geography displayed continuous signs of decline. The process was chequered, and with some exceptions like the works of al-Idrisi and Aba'1-Fida, the general standards of works produced were low compared to those of earlier periods. The scientific and critical attitude toward the subject and emphasis on authencity of information that was the mark of the earlier writers and gave place to mere recapitulations and resumes of the traditional and theoretical knowledge found in the works of earlier writers. This was in a way the period of consolidation of geographical knowledge, and the literature may be divided into eight broad categories.

World Geographical Accounts

The tradition of describing the world as a whole as practiced by the geographers of the classical period continued to be followed by some geographers of this period, but works dealing exclusively with the world of Islam had become rare, for the Abbasid Empire had itself disintegrated.

Cosmological Works

Several works were produced that dealt not only with geography but also with cosmology, cosmogony, astrology, and such other topics. The main purpose of these works seems to have been to present in a consolidated and systematic from world knowledge for the benefit of the average reader.

The Ziyarat Literature

A special feature of this work is that it deals with the towns and places of religious significance and. In short, these works were meant to be religious guides for pilgrims and devotees and represent the period of religious reaction in Islam.

Geographical Dictionaries

Yakut al-Hamawi (d.626/1229) produced one of the most useful works in Arabic geographical literature, namely, Mud jam al-buldan. Computed in 621/1224, this geographical dictionary of place-names, which includes other historical and sociological data, was in keeping with the literature and scientific traditions of the earlier period and represented the consummation of geographical knowledge of the time. The work also represented that period of Arab geographical development when scholars thought in terms of compiling geographical dictionaries, which would not have been possible without the vast amount of geographical literature that had already come into existence. Another important work of Yakut is the Kitab al-Mushtarik wa5fan wa'1-mukhtalif sakan composed in 623/1226.

Travel Accounts

The Arabs' knowledge of regional and descriptive geography was considerably enriched by the production of travel literature in Arabic on a large scale. Besides the usual incentives for travel like the pilgrimage to Mecca or missionary zeal, the extension of Muslim political and religious influences, especially in the east, had opened up for Muslims new vistas of travel and more opportunities for earning a livelihood.

Among the outstanding travel accounts may be included the work of al-Mazini (d. 564/1169), the Rihla of Ibn Jubayr (d. 614/1217), Tarikh al-Mustansir (written in c. 627/1230) by Ibn Mudjawir, then the Rihlas of al-Abdari (d.588/1289), al-Tayyibi (698/1299), and al-Tidjani (708/1308), among others, whereas these accounts are of great importance for the Middle East, North Africa, and parts of Europe. They furnished contemporary and often-important information the work of Ibn Battuta (d.779/1377) entitled *Tuhfat al-nuzzar*. It remained the most important medieval travel account in Arabic for the lands of India, Southeast Asia, and other countries of Asia and North Africa.

Maritime Literature

Arab maritime activities were confined to the Mediterranean and the Arabian seas. However, the works of Ibn Madjid of Sulayman al-Mahri represent the height of the Arabs' knowledge of nautical geography. These navigators used excellent sea charts, which are supposed to have had the lines of the meridian and parallels drawn on them. They also used many fine instruments and made full use of astronomical knowledge for navigation. There is little doubt that their knowledge of the seas was considerably advanced, especially of the Indian Ocean, for in their works they describe in details the coastlines, routes, etc., of the countries they visited. They were familiar with the numerous islands of the East Indies.

Astronomical Literature

Much of the contributions by Muslims in this field is already discussed in chapter 10.

Regional Geographical Literature

Between the VII/XIII and the X/XVII centuries, a large amount of geographical literature both in Arabic and Persian came into existence on a regional basis. But outstanding contributions were made toward originality in thought or practice. The production of literature on regional geography was closely connected with the extension of Islam and Muslim political power in the East.

In summary, geography was most cultivated by the Muslims. In it, they left behind a very large writing, mainly in Arabic but also in Persian and Turkish. The possibility of traveling from the Atlantic to the Pacific without having to cross any real frontiers as well as the annual pilgrimage to Mecca in which an opportunity was provided both for a long journey and for the exchange of ideas with scholars from nearly every part of the known world of that time—both these helped to enrich geography beyond what was known to the Greeks and Romans or to the medieval Latin authors. Al-Biruni, after discussing the difficulty of gaining geographic knowledge in ancient times, writes in the *Book of the Demarcation of the Limits of Areas*:

To obtain information concerning places of the earth has now become incomparably easier and safer (than it was before). Now we find a crowd of places, which in the (Ptolemic) "Geography" are indicated as lying to the east of other places, actually situated to the west of the others named, and vice versa. The reason (of such errors) are either confusion of the data as to the distance on which the longitude and latitude were estimated or that the population have changed their former places.

Geographical studies among the Muslims included not only the lands of Spain, North Africa, South Europe, and the Asiatic land mass, but also the Indian Ocean and the adjacent seas. The Muslims were able to sail over the high seas, improving the means of navigation and the art of cartography.

XVII

Cartography

Cartography has been practiced in the Middle East since ancient times, but with the advent of Islam, it received a new impetus due to the political and administrative requirements of the expanding Islamic world. It is not, however, until the early decades of III/IX century that we come across the first detailed world maps drawn in Arabic. This become possible through the introduction to the Islamic world of the Greek, Indian, and Iranian astronomical and geographical works in the AD eighth and the early ninth centuries. Thus, from the period until the AD seventeenth, cartography was practiced as a science in the Muslim world and passed through several stages of development. Muslim astronomers and geographers drew world maps and regional maps, as well as sea charts, following various traditions until their medieval techniques of cartography were replaced by the modern ones.

The first world map, the original form of which is not extent, was constructed by the scholars of Baghdad who worked in the Bayt al-Hikma under the patronage of the caliph al-Mamun. This map was named after the caliph as al-Surat al-Mamuniyya. According to al-Masudi (d. 345/956), who had seen this map, it depicted "the universe with spheres, the stars, land and the seas, in habited and barren [regions of the world], settlements of people, cities, etc." It was, he says, more exquisite than the world maps of Claudius Ptolemy, Merinos, and others. The maps drawn during III/IX century may be called the Greco-Muslim tradition in cartography. However, the Greek cartographers drew their maps with latitudes and longitudes as straight lines as though on a plane surface and without any regard to the spherical shape of the earth. Al-Biruni, criticizing Marinos for some assumptions in his map of the earth and also al-Battani for his determination of the direction of Qibla, says that "they treated the meridian circles as parallel straight lines. Thus they have fallen into this outrageous error."

During the IV/X century, Abu l'Hasan Ibn Yunus (d. 399/1009) along with al-Hasan bin Ahmed al-Muhallabi prepared a world map for the Fatimid caliph al-Aziz (365-86/975-96). It was drawn on a Tustari silk cloth. On it were shown the climes, mountains, rivers, cities, seas, and the different routes; and Mecca and Madina were prominently depicted on it. It cost 22,000 dinars. Except for some differences in the southeastern coast of Arabia and the northern coast of Africa, it confirmed to the map of al-Khwarazmi. Also, in this century, al-Balkhi initiated a new tradition in Islamic cartography, which exercised a deep influence on later cartographers and became the most popular style of cartography in the Islamic world. This new tradition of cartography differed fundamentally both in approach and content from the Greco-Muslim tradition and could be described as reflecting the Islamic political point of view of the time. The

Greco-Muslim maps placed Iraq in the central clime, whereas the world maps belonging to Balkhi school, Mecca occupied the central position.

It was, however, left to al-Biruni to introduce new concepts in physical geography, which resulted in innovations in the world maps hitherto drawn by the Muslim cartographers. He was first to propound the theory that Indian Ocean must have a connection with the Atlantic through certain channels south of the mountains of the moon, the traditional sources of the Nile. He argued that just as al-Bahr al-Kabir (the Indian Ocean) penetrated into the northern continent (Asia) on the east and entered it in many places, creating many islands there, similarly, the continent to keep up the balance jutted out into al-Bahr al-Junubi (the southern sea) in the west. He continues that in this region, the sea had entered the mountains (of the moon) and the valleys, with a continuous ebb and flow and was stormy, causing shipwrecks and preventing sailing; but inspite of this, it was still connected with the Uqiyanoos (the Atalantic) through these narrow passages. He then says that toward the south and beyond these mountains, signs of the connection of these two seas have been discovered, even though no one has personal experience of the their connection. Thus, al-Biruni conceived of the inhabited continent as being surrounded by the "encircling ocean." Al-Biruni's theory was adopted by many a later geographer and cartographer.

During the V/XI centuries, Mahmud al-Kashghari drew a rather unusual world map with a linguistic basis, giving prominence to the Turkish-speaking regions and placing Kashghar (a town in Chinese Turkestan, Sin Kiang; the same name is still used in Chinese official documents) at the center of the world with other regions receding to the periphery. In Sicily (Italy), the well-known geographer al-Sharif al-Ifirisi (d. 560/1166) who lived at the court of Roger II produced a series of world and sectional maps at the orders of the king. Taking the Ptolimaic maps as the basis, he constructed a large map of silver. He then drew a world map, and by dividing each of the seven slimes into then longitudinal sections, he drew a separate and detailed map of each of these sections into which he incorporated the geographical information collected from Arabic as well as Norman sources. The maps form a part of his monumental geographical work of Kitab Nuzhat al-Mushtak fi khtirak al-afaaq, and except for the silver map, all have fortunately survived the vicissitudes of time.

An interesting world map belonging to the middle of the VI/XII century exists an anonymous work entitled Mukhtasar ibn Hawkal, in which the shape of the inhabited world is drawn elliptically rather than round. The Indian and the Atlantic oceans are separated by a narrow isthmus of land near the sources of the Nile, which is connected with the terra incognita and which is partly visible. To this century also belong the six maps of Ahmad al-Tusi, one of the earliest Muslim cosmographers and author of the Persian work *Kitab Ajaib al-Makhulat* (written ca. 576/1180). They were probably drawn in the Balkhi tradition.

During the VII/XIII century, a number of world maps were produced, some of which belonged to the Greco-Muslim tradition and others to that of the Balkhi school. A peculiar world map belonging to the former tradition and dated 646/1128 is found in a fragment of a Persian geographical treatise. In this map, the Indian Ocean passes south of the mountains of the moon and then turning northward joins the Atlantic and the Mediterranean, thus surrounding what appears to be the continent of Africa.

The maps drawn by the cosmographers of the VII/XIII and VII/XVI centuries present some special and interesting features, and new trends appeared in Islamic cartography. For example, some maps in which the Muslim cartographers used a grid of horizontal and vertical lines representing latitudes and longitudes, which form small squares within which place names are shown to indicate their geographical positions. Another world map of Hamd Allah al-Mustawfi (d. 750/1349) depicts the inhabited world, which is divided into eighteen equal longitudinal division and the longitudes are drawn as straight lines as through on a plane surface without converging at the poles; similarly, the inhabited world is divided into nine parallel divisions beginning from the equator and going northward. Thus, the squares formed are approximately of ten by ten, each degree being equal to 56 2/3 Arabian miles. Yet another example of maps is the world map of Hafiz-i Abru (d. 833/1430) while the three regional maps accompanying his work on geography are drawn after the tradition of the Balkhi school. The world map is superimposed on a grid of squares of five by five with vertical lines representing the latitudes. The longitudes begin at zero (passing through the west coast of Africa) and then go eastward up to 180, which crosses a place called Kankduz, and are drawn as straight lines; the latitudes begin at zero at the equator and go up north up to ninety. The climes indicated along the margins, each of which is divided into two parts arbitrarily, have no relation to the actual astronomical divisions of the climes. The southern quarter of the earth is covered by sea, and the southern coast of Africa is round in shape, which is an advance upon some of the earlier maps depicting it as forked.

During X/XVI century Turkish cartographers made some very significant contributions to Islamic cartography. In fact, they may be said to have formed a bridge between medieval Islamic and modern cartography. In summary, it may be said that Islamic cartography, despite its technical drawbacks, as pointed out by scientists like al-Biruni, did serve the purpose of the conqueror, the traveler, and the scholar alike throughout the Middle Ages. The mistakes initially made persisted, even though in certain aspects like regional maps these were signs of progress. Its influence in the Islamic world lasted until the XI/XVII century when it seems to have been replaced by modern cartography.

*   *   *

The end of the text

REFERENCES, NOTES, AND BRIEF BIOGRAPHIES

1. M. A. Salam, the Muslim Nobel laureate, in Muslims and science, P. A. Hoodbay, Vanguard Books (P) Ltd., Lahore, 1991, P. iv.

2. Islamic science in the present context is more in a cultural theme than religious zest.

3. Sabians: People named in the holy Quran (2:59, 22:17), along with the Jews, Christians, and Magians (the Zoroastrians), as having a religion revealed by God. Many religious groups, including various Christian branches and various groups in India, have at one time or another been identified as Sabians.

   An ethnic group in Harran in northern Mesopotamia (today Altin-basak in Southern Turkey near Urfa), who were more or less Hellenistic pagans with roots in ancient Babylonian religions.

   The word "Sabians" is derived from the Egyptian "sb," which means both "wisdom" and "stars." The Egyptian word may be also the origin of the Greek word "Sophia" ("wisdom") and perhaps rather more dubiously of the Arabic word "sufi"("mystic").

4. Pahlavi: The language of the sacred books of ancient Iran.

5. *Nature Magazine*, no. 282 of November 22, 1979, and no. 3564.

6. Al-Mansur: The second Abhasid caliph who founded Baghdad in 145/762 on the west side of the Tigris river near Mada'in on the site of an ancient Babylonian town. The original Baghdad was called Dar as-Salam ("House of Peace").

7. Harun Ar-Rashid: The fifth Abbasid caliph. Baghdad was his capital; and the Caliphate reached its apogee during his reign, which was, however, marred by the downfall of the Barmecides, a Persian family who had long provided the Abbhasids with trusted and able ministers of state. Harun ar-Rashid had diplomatic relations with Charlemagne and with emperor of China. His sumptuous and celebrated court is associated with the present form of the tales of *The Thousand and One Nights*.

8. Al-Mamun: Abu-1-Abbas Abd Allah al-Mamun (c. 167-218/783-833) is the seventh Abbasid caliph and son of Harun ar-Rashid. He promoted scientific study and the translation of works of Greek learning into Arabic. He also founded an academy in Baghdad called the Bayt al-Hikmah ("House of Wisdom"), which included an observatory, for the advancement of science; Greek manuscripts were sought in Constantinople to enrich its library and to be translated into Arabic. A medical school was also founded in his reign.

9. Ibn Rushd: Abu-1-Walid Muha and ibn Ahmad ibn Muhamed Ibn Rushd (520-595/1126-1198) was born in Cordoba. As a philosopher he had little influence in the East, coming, as he did, at the end of the development of philosophy in Islam and perhaps making its summit. In Europe he is popularly known as Averros or Averroes. He became great authority on Aristotle's philosophy and was so celebrated that he was referred as the commentator. For Ibn Rushd Aristotle was the consummate master of the "way" of the mind.

    In Europe a school arose around his *Commentaries on Aristotle*, which was called Latin Averroism. Into the fifteenth century and beyond, he was still a vital force in European philosophy, although his thinking—abstracted from his own Muslim frame work, and belief—was interpreted as that of sceptic oriented toward nominalism or empiricism rather than of the realist.

    Ibn Rushd was the grandson of a judge. His friend Ibn Tufayl, the philosopher, introduced him to the Almohad court, and he was appointed *qadi* (judge) in Seville. Because all learning was virtually one continuous science without border in that age, he was not only a philosopher and a canon lawyer, he also served as physician to Abu Ya'qub Yusuf, the Aloha prince.

    In Europe he is famous for the theory of the unity of intellect, which corrupted into the theory of the common soul. It was called Pan psychism. However, it is really an expression of the Napoleonic concept that true knowledge consists in the identity of the knower with the known.

    Ibn Rushd is also associated with what has been called the "two truths" theory; this contends that there is one truth for philosophers, which is philosophy, and another for the masses, which is religion. His efforts to harmonize the Quran and revelation with philosophy and logic is highly commendable.

10. Ar-Razi: Abu Bakr Muhammad ibn Zakariyya, Ar-Razi (236-313/850/925) was born in Rai (Iran) where he spent the first part of his life. He is popularly known in Europe as Rhazes, sometimes called the Arabic Galen. He is the greatest clinical physician of Islam, well-known both in the East and the West. His authority in medicine has been

second only to that of Ibn Sina whom he excelled in his observational powers. His most famous books are the *Liber Pestilentiae* (in which he distinguished measles from smallpox), the compendium, Al-Mansor (al-Kitab al-Mansuri), and the *Encyclopedic Liber Continents* (al-Hawi). This first became available as a manuscript translated by a Jewish physician in Sicily and was later one of the first books to be printed. Ar-Razi recognized the role that psychosomatic medicine or self-suggestion plays in healing and wrote a treatise explaining why untrained practitioners, quacks, laymen, and "old wives" remedies often have greater success in healing patients than trained doctors.

In the great tradition of the Middle Ages ar-Razi was a universal thinker and pursued all the sciences including theology, astronomy, and music. It was, however, as an alchemist that his other great contribution to European science was made, and his descriptions of the alchemical processes were put into practice by European alchemists such as Nicholas Flamel and Paracelsus.

11. Ibn Sina: Abu Ali Husayn ibn Abd Allah Ibn Sina (370-429/980-1037), also popularly known in the West as Avicenna, was a contemporary of Al-Biruni. His compatriots have given him the honorific title Shaikh al-Rais (leader among wise men). He is the greatest philosopher-scientist of Islam and most influential figure in the general domain of the arts and sciences.

Ibn Sina was born near Bukhara of a Turkish mother and a Persian father. A precocious student, after learning the Quran by heart at the age of ten, he studied the isagogic of Porphyry and the propositions of Euclid, logic, philosophy, and medicine. He wrote numerous treatises of which the most influential was the *Canon of Medicine*, which remained a basis for teaching medicine in Europe into the seventeenth century, and the *ash-shifa* ("healing"), known in Europe as the *sanatio*.

Medicine in Islam was a prolongation of the science of the Greeks, and thus Ibn Sina's concepts were based on those of the Greek Physician Galen. His lofty reputation in Europe earned him the title of prince of physicians. In the East, however, where many other physicians wrote similar medical treatises, he was more renowned as an expounder of philosophy.

Ibn Sina wrote prolifically, served a number of princes as physician. His influence on both East and West was ir.-er.se. In the Islamic world his spirit has dominated the intellectual activity of all later periods while his philosophy and medicine have continued as a living influence tc the present day. He dominated medical science for centuries while his scientific, philosophical, and theological views left their mark upon many important figures such as Albertus Magnus, Saint Thomas, Duns Scotus, and Roger Bacon.

12. Ibn Tufayl: Abu Bakr Muhammad ibn Abd al-Malik Ibn Tufayl (d. 581/1185) was a famous Arab philosopher, known in the West as Abubacer born near Granada in Spain. He was vizier to the Almohad Prince Abu Yaqub Yusuf and introduced Ibn Rushd (Averroes) to the court. He wrote the famous *Hayy Ibn Yaqzan* (*The Living Son of the Awake*; the "living" is man, and the "awake" is God). This philosophical novel describes how a youth growing up isolated on an island, through his own contemplation, arrives at the truths usually considered to be revealed—that is, through the natural faculties of the mind itself—and liberates himself from his lower soul. In his conduct on the island, the youth exemplifies the religious or ethical teachings of a number of different traditions. The relationship of the characters of the novel also implies that philosophy is necessary for the full understanding of religion.

   The *Hayy Ibn Yaqzan* was translated into Latin by Pococke as *Philosophicus Autodidactus* and inspired Daniel Defoe to write *Robinson Crusoe*.

   Ibn Tufayl, along with Ibn Bajjah and Ibn Rushd, formed the Muslim philosophy, which was destined shortly to become virtually extinct and marked to high point of its development.

13. Claudius Ptolemy was a Greek astronomer of Alexandria. He brought out an encyclopedic work on astronomy in about AD 140.

14. *Almagest*: This is Ptolemy's second-century work on astronomy, which explained the apparent motion of the planets through the theory of epicycles and deferent.

15. J. D. Bernal, *Science in History*, Cambridge, Massachusetts, MIT Press, 1974. Also see volume 1, p. 3.

16. Jundishapur: Also called Gandisapora, Gundishpur, etc. An academy founded in the third century near Ahraz, in the region of modern Sanabad in Khuzistan, when Persia was ruled by the Sassanids. The academy was found by Oriental Christians who became Nestorians after the Council of Micea. It was a center that transmitted the study of Hellenistic learning and philosophy to the Muslims.

   Translations were made from Greek to Syriac and later to Arabic. In Abbasid times it was also an important school of medicine teaching the methods of Hippocrates and Galen.

   A number of famous medical figures were associated with it, notably the Bakhtishishu family and Hunayn ibn Ishaq, all of whom were Nestorians.

17. Hunayn Ibn Ishaq: (194-259/809-873). A Nestorian Christian, physician to the tenth Abbasid caliph al-Mutawakkil (232-247/847-861). He translated many famous works of Galen, Hippocrates, Plato, and others. His son Ishaq and his nephew Hubaysh also assisted him in translations.

18. Al-Hakam II: Al-Mustansir Billah Al-Hakam II, second Umayyad caliph of Spain, son of Abd ar-Rahman III. His reign was one of the most peaceful and fruitful of the Cordoban dynasty. In his time Cordoba, as an intellectual capital, shone even more brilliantly than under his father.

19. Ibn Yunus: Abu'l-Hasan Ali bin Abi Said Abd Al-Rahman bin Ahmad bin Yunus al-Sadafi, one of the most prominent Muslim astronomers, died in 399/1009. Ibn Yunus's chief astronomical work, *al-Zidj al-Kabir al-Hakimi* (not all of which seems to have survived), was begun circa 380/990 and completed shortly before his death. Several long extracts have been published and translated, and it is one of the few zidjes (sets of astronomical tables) that have been treated extensively by modern scholars. He quotes a large number of astronomical observations (eclipses and other phenomena). Some made by his predecessors of the ninth and tenth centuries and others made by himself in Cairo; they constitute the most extensive list of medieval astronomical observations presently known. Ibn Yunus is especially careful in reporting the researches of his predecessors, and his criticisms of errors and discrepancies in their works are distinctly modern in tone.

   The zidj of Ibn Yunus was analyzed by Delambre on the basis of Caussin's publication of chapters 3 to 5 and an unpublished translations of most of the remaining chapters by Sedillot that has since disappeared. The observations reported by Ibn Yunus were discussed b/ S. Newcomb, who was interested in their possible usefulness for determining the value of the secular acceleration of the moon. Ibn Yunus's original contributions to plane and spherical trignometry have been treated by Delambre, Von Braunmuhl, and Schoy.

20. Ibn Al-Haytham: Abu Ali al-Hasan bin al-Hasan bin al-Haytham (354-430/965-1039) popularly known in the West as Alhazen (also Avennathan and Avenetan of mediaeval Latin Texts). He is one of the principal Arab mathematicians and, without any doubt, the best physicist.

   Ibn al-Haytham was born in Basra in about 354/965 during the reign of al-Hakim (386-411/996-1021). He went to Egypt where he tried to regulate the flow of the Nile. He abandoned his task when he realized its impossibility in spite of his fears of the caliph's anger. On the death of the latter, he returned to Cairo where he earned his living by copying scientific and particularly mathematical manuscripts.

   His writings, consisting of more than two hundred titles, have been listed by Ibn Usaybia. Most of these works—some of them very short—are devoted to mathematics and physics, but he also wrote on philosophical and medical subjects. Throughout these latter works can be seen his profound knowledge of the Greek authors, notably Ptolemy, whom he edited, studied, and criticized. The works best known to us are the following:

1. *Makala fi Stikhardj samt al-kibla* in which he established the theorem of the cotangent

$$\text{Cotangent} = \frac{\text{Sin, COS (2-1) - COS}}{\text{Sin (2-}}$$

2. *Makala fi hayat al-alam* on astronomy. This work had a great influence on later writers such as Ibn Rushd, al-Djaghmini, al-Kazwini, and Peurbach. This work became so popular that it had two Hebrew translations, three Latin—one edited by J.M. Millas, Las traducciones Orientales . . . . 285-312—one Persian and one Castillain.

3. Kitab fi l-manazir: The work was translated into Latin and published in Basle in 1572 by F. Risner under the title *Thesaurus Opticus*. In this work Ibn Haytham's mathematical genius attained its highest development when he resolved the problem that today bears his name: two points, *a* and *b*, are fixed on the plane of a circle with centre 0 and radius *r*. Find the circle (idealized in a mirror) the point *m* where the ray of light emitted by *a* must be reflected in order that it may pass through *b*. Ibn Haytham's demonstration, which is very complex, leads to an equation of the fourth degree, which he resolves by the intersection of an equilateral hyperbole with a circle. Leonardo da Vinci later became interested in the problem, which he could only solve mechanically for lack of mathematical means. C. Huygens (d. AD 1696) finally gave the simple solution (cf. *Enclclopedia della matematiche elementari*, 1/2 388-9).

4. Makala fi daw al-kamar, an important work on account of the ideas expounded on light, colors, and the celestial movements.

5. *Fi'l-maraya 1-muhrika bi'1-dawair* on mathematics.

6. *Fi'l-maraya '1-muhrika bi'1-kutu* on parabolic mirrors.

7. *Fi anna 1-kura awsa al-ashkal al-mudjassama allati ihatuha mutasawiya wa-anna 1-daira awsa al-ashkal al-musaltaha allati ihatuha mutasawiya*. In it Ibn al-Haytham demonstrates that "of two regular polygons inscribed in the same circle, that which has the greater number of sides has also the larger surface and the larger perimeter."

8. *Fi surat al-kusuf* in which he expounded for the first time the use of the camera obscura in the observation of solar eclipses.

Besides the contributions already mentioned, it should be noted that Ibn al-Haytham established that the astronomic twilight began or finished when the negative height of the sun reached nineteen, and proceeding from there, he fixed the height of the atmosphere at fifty-two thousand paces; he correctly explained atmospheric refraction and the augmentation of the apparent diameter of the sun and moon when they are near the horizon. Like Ibn Sina and al-Biruni he established that rays of light start from the object to travel toward the eye and not the reverse as Euclid, Ptolemy, and al-Kindi maintained. He discovered spherical aberration, but he did not consider the caustic curve; he determined that the Milky Way was very remote from the earth and that it did not belong to the atmosphere since it had no parallax. In the field of mathematics he neatly resolved the problem of al-Mahanoy and wrote a treatise on magic squares and made some contributions to commercial mathematics.

21. Al-Biruni: Abu'l-Rayhan Muhammad bin Ahmad al-Biruni (362-442/973-1050) was one of the greatest scholars of medieval Islam and certainly the most original and profound. He was equally well versed in the mathematical, astronomical, physical, and natural sciences. He is also a distinguished geographer and historian, chronologist and linguist, and impartial observer of customs and creeds. He was born of Iranian family in the suburb of Kath, capital of Khwarizm. He spent the first twenty-five years of his life in his homeland, where he received his scientific training from masters such as Abu Nasr Mansur and Abu'l-wafa, the great mathematicians.

Al-Biruni journeyed extensively in the northern regions of Persia, and when Mahmud Ghaznavi conquered central Asia, he joined the services of this powerful ruler. He even accompanied him in his conquest of India, which enabled him to observe this land firsthand. After this, al-Biruni returned to Ghazni where he lived the rest of his days writing and studying to the very end of his prolific life.

The total number of works is 180, differing widely from one another in length, from brief treatises on specialized matters to major works embracing vast fields of knowledge. Since lack of space makes it impracticable to provide an exhaustive list of the work done on al-Biruni, of which there is a fair volume, though very inadequate for such an important figure. I enlist a few of his works as follows:

1. *Rasail al-Biruni*: It is a single volume compiling four mathematical and astronomical treatises published in Hyderabad (1948).

2. *Rasail Abi Nasr ila '1-Biruni*: This includes fifteen mathematical and astronomical treatises by Abu Nasr among which are most of these written in the name of al-Biruni.

3. *Kitab Tahdid Nihayat al-Amakin li Tashih Hasafat al-Masakin*: geographical extracts.

Besides, al-Biruni's book *India* is the best account of the Hindu religion and of the sciences and customs of India in medieval times. His *Chronology of Ancient Nations* dealing with the calendar and festivities of different nations is unique. His *Canon of al-Masudi* dedicated to Mahmud Ghazni's son, Masud, holds the same position in Islamic astronomy as the canon of Ibn Sina does in medicine while his *Elements of Astrology* was the standard text for the teaching of the Quadrivium for centuries.

In brief, al-Biruni was a universal genius and polymath who turned his attention to every available field of learning. No wonder, he was popularly known as al-Ustadh1 (the teacher). The scope of his inquiries was vast and profound, and he is a great luminary in the history of world science. No one in Islam combined the qualities of an outstanding scientist with that of a meticulous scholar, compiler, and historian to the same degree as al-Biruni.

22. Ibn Zuhr: Abu Marwan Abd al-Malik Ibn Zuhr al-Iyadi (d. 557/1162) was one of the greatest Arab physicians called Avenzoar in medieval Europe where his work was very influential. His works on medicine, which demonstrated a good knowledge of anatomy, were translated first into Hebrew and then into Latin.

Ibn Abi Usaybia mentions nine works by Ibn Zuhr. Two important works are mudjarrabat devoted to medical observations, and the others are the following:

1. *al-Khawass*: The book of simple medicaments.

2. *al-Adwiya al-mufrada*: The "explanation through witness of the libel."

3. *al-Idah bi-shawahid al-iftidah*: Against Ibn Ridwan (d. 460/1008) and his refutation of the *Book of Introduction to Medicine* of Hunayn bin Ishak.

4. *Shukuk al-Razi ala Kutub Djalinus*: the "solution of the doubts of al-Razi concerning the books of Galen."

5. *Makala fi'l-radd ala Abi Ali Ibn Sina*: A "treatise refuting Ibn Sina" on some passages in his *Book of Simple Medicaments*.

6. *Makala fi bastihi li-risalat al-kindi fi takrib al-adwiya'*: An expansion of the *Risala of Yakub bin Ishak al-kindi* on the compositions of medicaments.

7. *al-Nukat al-tibbiya*: "The book of delicate medical questions."

As a physician Ibn Zuhr owed his fame to the practicing skills. He diagnosed without questioning his patients, by examining the urine, and taking the pulse. Unlike the physicians of his time, whom he accuses of using medicine with insufficient precautions, he counsels prudence (hazm) in treatment.

The other important works, which has made concrete in roads in the field of dialectics and medicine, are as follows:

1. *Taysir fi'l-mudawat wal-tadbir*: "Practical manual of treatments and diets" followed by a formulary, the Djami.
2. *Kitab al-Aghdhi/a*: *Book of Foods*.
3. *Kitab al-Zina*: *Book of Embellishment*, written for his son Abu Bakr on Purgatives.
4. *Makala fi 'Ual al-kula1*: "Treatise on diseases of the kidneys."
5. Risala fi illatay al-baras wa 1-bahak : Letter to a doctor in Seville on white leprosy or vililigo and pityriasis.
6. *Kitab al-Iktisad fi isbah al-anfus wa'1-adjsud*

Finally it should be mentioned that Ibn Zuhr, as an article of faith and perhaps also through conviction to the Ashari doctrine—that secondary causes are not necessary. A good medicine cures if God wills it. He himself was stricken by the malady from which he was to die and urged by his son to try new remedies. He declared, "If God wished to change this my bodily frame, he will not give me power to use remedies other than those which will carry out his decree and his will."

23. Of late the subject is under debate.
24. J. Bronowski, *Science and Human Values*, Harper and Row Publishers, New York, 1965, p. 7.
25. P. A. Hoodbhoy, *Muslims and Science*, Vanguard Publishers, LAhdre, 1991, p. 176.
26. R. Blacheres, Maison neuve et larose, Paris, 1966 p. 115 quoted from M. Bucaille, the Bible, the Quran and Science, Taj Co., India, 1986 p. 122.
27. K. S. Ghaneem, *MAAS Journal of Islamic Science*, 8 (1), (1992), 61-99.
28. During AD seventh century, scientific knowledge was flourishing in China.
29. Briffaults in *Making of Humanity* pp. 190-202 quoted from M. Iqbal *The Reconstruction of Religious Thought in Islam* reprinted by K. Ashraf, Lahore, 1971, pp. 129-130.
30. Ibn Khaldun: Abd ar-Rahman ibn Muhammad ibn Khaldun (732-808/1332-1406) is one of the strongest personalities of Arabo-Muslim culture in the period of its decline. He

is generally regarded as a historian, sociologist, and philosopher. He is often called the father of historiography and father of sociology. His life and work have already formed the subject of innumerable studies and given rise to the most varied and even the most contradictory interpretations.

Ibn Khaldun's life may be divided into three parts, the first of which (twenty years) was occupied by his childhood and education, the second (twenty-three years) by the continuation of his studies and by political adventures, and the third (thirty-one years) by his life as a scholar, teacher, and magistrate. The first two periods were spent in the Muslim west, and the third was divided between the Maghrib and Egypt.

Ibn Khaldun was born in Tunis on I Ramadan 732 (May 27, 1332) in an Arab family, which came originally from the Hadramawt and had been settled at Seville since the beginning of the Muslim conquest. He attended courses given by the most famous teachers of Tunis to whom he devotes lengthy sections in his autobiography. He received classical education, based essentially on the study of the Quran, of hadith, of the Arabic language, and of fiqh.

Ibn Khaldun's great work, the Muqaddimah or Prolegomena, is the introduction to his *Kitab al-Ibar* (book of examples and the collection of origins of the history of the Arabs and Berbers). Muqaddimah is an introduction to the historian's craft. It presents an encyclopedic synthesis of the methodological and cultural knowledge necessary to enable the historian to produce a truly scientific work. Initially, Ibn Khaldun was preoccupied with epistemology. Then gradually, meditating on the method and the matter of history, he was led, in full conciousness of what he was doing, to create what he refers to as his "new science" (ilm mustanbat al-nasha), which itself turned out to contain more or less implicitly the starting points of several avenues of research leading to philosophy of history, sociology, economics, and yet other disciplines.

In his preface to the introduction proper (mukaddimat al-mukaddima) Ibn Khaldun begins by defining history, which he expands to include the study of the whole of the human past, including its social, economic, and cultural aspects defining its interest, denouncing the lack of curiosity and of method in his predecessors, and setting out the rules of good and sound criticism. This criticism is based essentially, apart from the examination of evidence, on the criterion of conformity with reality (Kanun al-mutabaka)—that is, of the probability of the facts reported and their conformity to the nature of things, which is the same as the current of history and of its evolution. Hence, there is the necessity of bringing to light the laws that determine the direction of this current. The science capable of throwing light on the phenomenon is, he says, that of umran as science, which may be described as independent (ilm mustakill bi-nafish), which is defined by its object human civilization Cal-umran al-bashari and social facts as a whole.

Ibn Khaldun in his *Mukaddima* was inclined to concentrate on social phenomena in general. The central point around which his observations are built and to which his researchers are directed is the study of the aetiology of decline—that is to say the symptoms and the nature of the ills from which civilizations die. Hence, the *Mukaddima* is very closely linked with the political experiences of Ibn Khaldun, who had been, in fact, very vividly aware that he was witnessing a tremendous change in the course of history, which is why he thought it necessary to write a summary of the past of humanity and to draw lessons (ibar) from it. He remarks that at certain exceptional moments in history the upheavals are such that one has the impression of being present "at a new creation (Kaannahu khalk diadid), at an actual renaissance (nasha mustahdatha), and at (the emergence of) a new world (wa alam muhdath). It is also at present (li-hadha 1-ahd). Thus, the need is felt for someone to make a record of the situation of humanity and of the world. This "new world," as Ibn Khaldun knew, was coming to birth in other lands; he also realized that the civilization to which he belonged was nearing its end. Although unable to avert the catastrophe, he was anxious at least to understand what was taking place and therefore felt it necessary to analyze the process of history.

Ibn Khaldun's main tool in the work of analysis is observation. He had a thorough knowledge on sources of logic and its use and greatly mistrusts speculative reasoning. He admits that reason is marvelous tool but only within the framework of its natural limits, which are those of investigation and the interpretation of what is real. He was much concerned about the problem of knowledge, and it led him finally, after a radical criticism, to a regulation of philosophy. "In casting doubts on the adequacy of universal rationality and of individual reality, Ibn-Khaldun casts doubts on the whole structure of speculative philosophy as it then existed."

The wealth of the ideas provided in the *Mukaddima* has enabled several specialists to find in it the early beginnings of a number of disciplines, which have become independent sciences only very recently. There is, of course, no argument about Ibn Khaldun's quality as a historian. Y. Lacoste writes: "If Thucydides is the inventor of history, Ibn Khaldun introduces history as a science." But he has been regarded also as a philosopher, and it is surprising in particular to discover in his *Mukaddima* a very elaborate system of sociology. His "new science"—his "ilm al-umran," the discovery of which dazzled even himself—is basically a "system of sociology" as an auxiliary science to history. He considers that the basic causes of historical evolution are, in fact, to be sought in the economic and social structures. He was interested particularly in the influence of the way of life and of methods of production on the evolution of social groups. In a famous sentence, he states, "The differences which are seen between the generation in their behaviour are only the expressions of the differences which separates them in their economic way of life." Furthermore, the explanation he gives is not exclusively a socioeconomic but also psychological. The *Mukaddima* do not contain only a general sociology but also a very detailed and subtle social psychology, which may be divided into political psychology, economic psychology, ethical psychology, and general psychology. The intermingled and closely linked elements of this social psychology and this general sociology form a whole complex, which is difficult to disentangle.

Since the discovery of Ibn Khaldun in Europe, he has unanimously considered as "an authentic genius" whose *Mukkaddima* represents "one of the solemn moments of human thought." Certainly a "solitary genius," he does not belong to any definite thought. His works are, in fact, the product of a multitude of agonizing inquiries, and his thinking represents a radical change. The great tragedy of his works is he had no forerunners nor had successors until the contemporary period. The systematic lack of comprehension and the resolute hostility, which this nonconformist thinker of genius encountered among his own people, forms one of the most moving dramas, one of the saddest and most significant pages in the history an Islamic culture.

31. Al-Khwarizimi: Muhammad ibn Musa al-Khwarazmi (d. 226/840) is the first outstanding Muslim mathematician with whom the history of this subject among Muslims properly begins. He was born in Khwarizm, Persia (in some of the European text al-Khwarazmi is also found). Little is known of his life except that he spent some time in Baghdad, and it is said by some later historians that he journeyed to India to master the Indian sciences. He became a well-known scientist at the court of al-Mamun and participated in measuring the degree of arc in the company of astronomers commissioned by al-Mamun for this task.

The writings of al-khwarazmi, which represent his own works as well as the synthesis of the mathematical works of the generation before him, had an immense influence, more than that of any other single mathematician. The word "algebra" is derived from his use of the word "al-Jabr" ("coercion," "restoration"), which first appeared in his book on mathematics *al-maqalah fi hisab al-Jabr wa-1-muqabilah*. It was the Latin translation of this work that introduced the algebraic concept into Europe.

Al-khwarazmi's works on mathematics established the use of the Indian system of counting, which became known as Arabic numerals, and the use of zero. He wrote the first extensive Muslim work on geography revising much of Ptolemy's work and drawing new geographical and celestial maps. His astronomical tables are among the best in Islamic astronomy. His influence is attested to by the fact that algorism, the latinization of his name, al-Khwarazmi for a long time meant arithmetic in most European languages and is used today for any recurring method of calculation which has become an established rule. It has even entered into the technical vocabulary (algorithm) of modern computation techniques.

32. Al-Kardji: Abu Bakr Muhammad bin al-Hasan, mathematician and engineer, is a native of al-Karadj (in the Djibal, Iran). He went to Baghdad where he held high positions in the administration and composed his works al-Fakhri, al-Kafi and al-Badi, in which he attempted to free algebra from the tutelage of geometry. He returned to his native land and might have died after 410/1019, the probable date of the composition of his inbat al-miyah al-khafiyya. Adil Anbuba in the introduction of his edition of Badi (Beirut, 1964) lists twelve works of his author, most of which are lost. The following are of interest in the present context:

1. *Al-Fakhri fi'l-dJabr wa'l-mukabala.* This work demonstrates the revision of Diphonates's work *Arithmetica.* Also, it attempts to study the successive powers of a binominal and the discovery of the generation of the coefficients of (a-b) by means of the triangle, which is now named after Pascal or Tartaglia.

2. Al-Badi fi 1-hisab, in which are developed the fixed points treated by Eulid and Nicomachus and in which an important place is accorded to algebraic operations.

   Al-Karadji expounds for the first time the theory of the extraction of the square root of a polynomial-with an unknown and resolves the systems $X2 + 5$ and $X2 — 5$. In these problems, he often utilizes the expedient of changing the variable, the auxiliary variables, or the process through substitution.

3. Al-Kafi fi'l hisab: This work is mainly devoted to the use of functions and as such a summary of arithmetic, algebra, geometry and the register based on the processes of mental calculus (called hawai "aerial") as opposed to "Indian calculus."

4. Inbat al-miyah al-khafiyya: It is an excellent manual of hydraulic water supplies. It contains some autobigraphical notes, as well as a discussion of a series of conceptions relative to the geography of the globe. He describes a certain number of surveying instruments, the geometrical bases of which he demonstrates, and end with very concrete details on the construction and servicing subterranean tunnels (he makes an express allusion to those of Isfahan) for providing water in arid places. He likewise discusses the basic of the sharia, the legality of the construction of wells, and hydraulic conducts and in what circumstances these might be prejudicial to the people.

33. Abu Kamil Shudja: In the Islamic world Abu Kamil Shudja bin Aslam bin Muhammad al-Misri exercised a considerable influence on the development of Western algebra and made valuable contribution to the theory, which he turned into a powerful instrument for geometrical research building upon the foundations laid by al-Khwarizmi. He solved systems of equations involving up to five unknown quantities, represented by different kinds of coins. He discussed problems of a higher degree but only those that could be reduced to quadratic equations (irrational quantities here are admitted as solutions). His work contains first steps leading to a theory of algebraical identities. He also dealt with problems of intermediate analysis (integral solutions), which indicate close connection with analogous problems studied in India. No details of his life are known. All that is available in literature is that he lived after al-Khawarizmi (died about AD 850) and before Ali bin Ahmad al Imrani (d. 344/955-6) who wrote a commentary on his algebra.

The *Fihrist*, 281, lists a number of books on astrological and mathematical subjects as well as on other topics such as the flight of birds. Two of these titles—*Kitab fi 'l-Djam Wa 1-Tafrik* (on augmenting and diminishing71) and *Kitab al-Khata a/n* (on the two errors)—have been the objects of elaborate discussions. None of the works mentioned in the *Fihrist* have survived in Arabic. A work preserved in Arabic is al-Taraif. It deals with the integral solutions of indeterminate equations.

In the definition of diazr (radix, root), mal (census, capital) and added mufrad (numerus, absolute number). Abu Kamil closely follows al-Khwarizmi, but in many respects he goes far beyond his predecessor. Thus, he effects the addition and subtraction of square roots involving irrationalities only by means of relations corresponding to our modern formula.

$a + b = a + b + 2ab$

For example, to subtract the square root of 8 from the square root of 18, he gives the rule "subtract 24 from 26 and 2 remains. The root of this is the root of 8 subtracted from the root of 18." The same example is found in al-Karadji's treatise on algebra al-Fakhri.

The problems occurring in the treatise "on the pentagon decagon" are solved in a clear and simple mode by applying algebraic methods to geometry. Throughout his treatise, Abu Kamil chooses special values—in most cases the value ten—for the given quantity instead of denoting it by a letter or even equaling to one. In this respect, he has not freed himself from the method of al-Khwarizmi; but in his way of handling the problem, he is far superior to his predecessor, and his work definitely marks an important progress.

34. Abu L-Wafa: Muhammad Abu l'Wafa al-Buzadjani bin Muhammad bin Yahya, probably of Persian origin, was born in Buzadjan in Kuhistan, I Ramadan 328/June 10, 940, and died in Iraq in Radjab 388/July 998.

The chief merit of Abu l'vafa is in the development of trigonometry. It is to him we owe, in spherical trigonometry, for the right-angled triangle, the substitution, for the perfect quadrilateral with the proposition of menelaus, of the so-called rule of the four magnitudes.

(Sine a : Sin c = Sin A : 1), and the tangent theorem (tan a : tan A = Sine b : 1) ;

From these formulae, he further infers cos.c = cos.a. cos.b.

For the oblique angled spherical triangle, he probably first established the sine proposition. The world of science is also indebted to him for the method of calculation of sine of thirty, the result of which agrees up to eight decimals with its real value. His geometrical constructions, which are partly based on Indian models, are also of great interest.

Of his other mathematical and astronomical works, the following is the list:

1. Fima Yahtadj ilayh al-Kuttah wa '1-Ummal min Ilm al-Hisah: This is an arithmetic book, identical with the al-Manazil fi' 1-Hisab mentioned by Ibn al-Kifti.

2. Al-Kamil: This is also identical with Almadjist mentioned by Ibn al-Kifti.

3. Al-Handasa: Same as Persian book of the geometrical constructions. This book is the compilation of his lectures.

Nothing unfortunately has remained of his commentaries to Euclid, Diophantus, and al-Khwarizmi or of his astronomical tables called al-Wadih; but the tables called al-Zidj al-Shamil—in Florence, Paris, and London of an unknown author—are very likely an adaptation from Abu '1-wafa's tables.

35. Umar Khayyam: Abu '1-Faph, Umar ibn Ibrahim al-Khayyami is a great mathematician astronomer and a great poet of the medieval period. Practically nothing is known of his life except he was born near Naishapur where he spent most of his days and died in that city. Even his date of birth and death are contested by scholars more so, the date of death varying by as much as twenty years (b. 429-440/1038-1048, d. 517-525/1123-1132). His collection of the poetry in four-line stanzas called *rubaivyat* ("quatrains") has been translated in many languages. Khayyam's fame in the West is due to a powerful nineteenth-century English translation by Edward Fitzgerald. Unfortunately, he has depicted him as chief propagator of the philosophy of "live, drink,

and be merry," whereas in reality he was a Sufi and a gnostic of high standing. What appears to be lack of concern or agnosticism in his poetry is merely an accepted form of expression, within which he incorporated both the drastic remedy that the gnostic applies to religious hypocrisy and also the reestablishment of contact with reality.

Behind the apparent skepticism of Khayyam lies the absolute certainty of intellectual intuition. In 467/1074-75 he was already a famous mathematician and was called in by Malikshah to reform the calendar. This calendar, known as the Jalali calendar, is still in use in Persia and is more accurate than the Georgian. Khayyam was highly respected by his contemporaries as a master of the sciences, although he wrote little and accepted few students. In one of his treatises, he calls himself a student of Ibn Sina; but since he lived much later, this could only mean that he considered himself as belonging to the school of Ibn Sina. In fact, he translated one of the Ibn Sina's works from Arabic into Persian.

Umar Khayyam's classification of knowledge seekers into four categories has remained famous both in the Islamic world and the West:

1. The theologians, who become content with disputation and "satisfying" proofs and consider this much knowledge of the creator (excellent is his name) as sufficient.

2. The philosophers and learned men (of Greek inspiration) who use rational arguments and seek to know the laws of logic and are never content merely with "satisfying" arguments. But they too cannot remain faithful to the conditions of logic and become helpless with it.

3. A few who say that the way of knowledge is none other than receiving information from a learned and credible informant; for in reasoning about the knowledge of the Creator, his essence and attributes, there is much difficulty. The reasoning power of the opponents and the intelligent (of those who strangle against the final authority of the revelation and of those who fully accept it) is stupefied and helpless before it.

   Therefore, they say it is better to seek knowledge from his works of a sincere person.

4. The Sufis who do not seek knowledge by meditation or discursive by meditation or discursive thinking but by purgation of their inner being and the purification of their dispositions. They cleanse the rational soul of the impurities of nature and bodily form until it becomes pure substance. It then comes face-to-face with the spiritual world so that the forms of that world become truly reflected in it without doubt or ambiguity. This is the best of all ways because none of the perfection of God are kept away from it, and there are no obstacles or veils put before it. Therefore, whatever (ignorance)

comes to man is due to the impurity of his nature; if the veil is to be lifted and the screen and obstacle removed, the truth of things as they are will manifest. Prophet Muhammad (peace be upon him) said, "Truly during the days of your existence, inspiration come from God. Do you not want to follow them? Tell unto reasoners that for the lovers of God [gnostics], intuition is guide, not discursive thought."

In the Islamic world the influence of Khayyam was foremost in the domain of mathematics and his philosophical treatise. These show him to be a true hakim as do his quatrains, which contain spontaneous reflections upon different aspects of human existence and, if seen in the correct light, confirm rather than deny the gnostic background of his thought. Khayyam is perhaps the only figure in history who was both a great poet and an outstanding mathematician. Islam has produced a few other figures who have been accomplished in both domains but none with the brilliance of Khayyam.

36. Al-Balkhi: Abu Zayd Ahmad bin Sahl al-alkhi (236-322/850-934) is a famous scholar known today principally for his geographical work. He was born at Shamistiyan, a village near Balkh in Khurasan, about 236/850. He died upward of eighty years old in Dhu'l-Kada 322/October 934.

Al-Balkhi traveled to Iraq by foot with the pilgrim caravan. He remained there for eight years and studied philosophy, astrology, astronomy, medicine, and natural science. Besides, he pursued the study of the religious sciences along with philosophy. He is cited as an almost-unique example of one who was equally expert in both, and he is named by Shahrastani among the philosophers of Islam. The works of al-Balkhi on religious subjects were much praised by competent judges, especially his Nazm al-Kuran, evident!/ a work of tafsir. Yakut gives the titles of d6 out of about sixty works of al-Balkhi, i.e., he adds thirteen titles to the forty-three listed in the *Fihrist*. Of these Hadjdji Khalifa mentions less than half a dozen in our own time apart from a *Kitab Masalih al-Abdan Wa'1-Anfus* for which al-Balkhi is widely cited.

Al-Balkhi's work *Suwar al-Akalim* is the basis of the geographical works of al-Istakhuri and Ibn Hawkal and thus to mark the beginning of what has been called the classical school of Arabic geography. It seems to have been a world map divided into twenty parts, with short explanatory texts. His interest in geography may have been due to his teacher al-Kindi, for whom a translation of Ptolemy's treatise on the subject was specially made and another of whose pupils, Ahmed bin al-Tayyib al-Sarakshi, wrote a Kitab al-Masalik Wa 1'-Mamalik, apparently the first of several geographical works in Islam with that title.

37. Al-Farabi: Abu Nasr Muhammad bin Muhammad bin Tarkhan al-Farabi—referred to as Al-Farabius, Alfarabius, or Avennasr in medieval Latin texts (258-339/870-950)—was one of the most outstanding and renowned Muslim philosophers. Among the Muslims he was called al-muallim ath-thani, "the second teacher," after Aristotle, whose works had become available in Arabic, thanks to translations made at the Academy of the Caliph al-Mamun in Baghdad.

Very little is known of al-Farabi's life. He was born in Turkestan at Wasidj in the district of the city of Farab and is said to have died at the age eighty or more in 339/950 in Damuscus. His father was a general and afforded him the opportunity to study with the best teachers. His early training was in religious sciences and languages in which he was very proficient.

Al-Farabi was convinced that philosophy had come to an end everywhere else and that it had found a new home and a new life within the world of Islam. He believed human reason is superior to religious faith and hence assigned only a secondary place to the different revealed religions, which provide, in his view, an approach to truth for nonphilosophers through symbols. Philosophical truth is universally valid whereas these symbols vary from nation to nation; they are the work of philosopher prophets of whom Muhammad (peace by upon him) was one. Al-Farabi thus went beyond al-Kindi, who naturalized philosophy as a kind of appropriate handmaiden of revealed truth; on the other hand, he differs from al-Razi and gives an important and indispensable function to organized religion.

Al-Farabi, like al-Kindi and virtually all Muslim philosophers, also drew upon neo-Platonism for his metaphysics; and he developed al-Kindi's ideas further. Al-Farabi made several distinction regarding the intellect (the extension of being into the center of man). He divided the intellect into the following:

1. The "active intellect" (al-aql al-fail, "intellectus agens"), which is the nous of plotinus and the logos of philosophy, or the "world of ideas" of Plato.
2. The "potential intellect" (al-aql al hayulani, "intellectus in potentia"), the latent capacity to acquire eternal truths, which subsist in the "active intellect."
3. The "acquired intellect" (al-aal al-mustafad; "intellectus acquisitus"), learned knowledge.

Al Farabi developed the terminology of Arab scholasticism by drawing upon the Quran, a terminology that was to be adopted into Latin and later adopted by Saint Thomas Aquinas. Al-Farabi devised terms for necessary and contingent being, act and potency, substance and accident, essence and existence, matter and form.

More than one hundred works of varying size on different subject matters—logic, physics, metaphysics, ethics, and politics—attributed by the Arab bibliographers. Nevertheless, much of his work is directed toward philosophical research. They all are concerned with the sovereign position to be given to philosophy within the realm of thinking and with the organization of the perfect society and the philosopher-king.

Al-Farabi also adopted the theories of Plato's republic in his Rislah fi Ara Ahl al-Madinah al-fadilah and his al-siyyasah al-Madaniyya (*Statecraft*) but naturally, as a Muslim, saw the ideal state in the past; and in al-madinah al-fadilah ("the virtuous city"), he assigned the perfect rule was that of the prophet himself. He was himself a musician, a flute player, and wrote an influential work on music, Kitab al-musiqa, in which he drew analogies between music and mathematics.

Al-Farabi was the first person in Islam to classify completely the sciences to delineate the limit of each and to establish firmly the foundation of each branch of learning. He was for this reason called the second teacher, the first being Aristotle who accomplished the same task in ancient times and set the precedent for the Muslim philosophers. Besides philosophy, logic occupies a major portion of his work. In fact, he was the real founder of logic in Islamic history, including the commentary or paraphrasing of the whole of the *Organon* of Aristotle. His works on mathematics, physics, ethics, and political philosophy have left a concrete impression on his successors notably Ibn Sina and Ibn Rushd.

38. Ibn Bajjah: Abu Bakr Muhammad bin yahya (c. 500-533/1106-1138) is a philosopher, poet, musician, and composer of popular songs. He was known in Europe as Avempace. His thoughts greatly influenced Ibn Rushd (Averroes). Ibn Bajjah was born in Zaragoza, Spain, and died in Fez, having served as minister to the emir of Murcia. He wrote a commentary on Aristotle and treatises on the physical sciences notably on astronomy. In addition, he studied astronomy and mathematics.

Ibn Bajjah's most celebrated work is *Tadbir al-Mutawahhid* (*Regime of the Solitary*), which he left unfinished. Although externally it seems to deal with political philosophy, it is actually a metaphysical work based on the central theme of union with the active intellect. Ibn Bajjah developed an elaborate theory of spiritual forms. He distinguished between intelligible forms abstracted from matter and intelligible forms independent of matter and believed the process of philosophical realization to go from the first to the second. This doctrine is of utmost importance in physics where he applies to the force of gravity with results that had a far-reaching historic effect.

It is, in fact, in the domain of the philosophical aspect of physics that Ibn Bajjah is best known in the West. None of his works were translated into Latin, but through quotations by Ibn Rushd and others, he exercised an influence, which is to be seen even in the writings of Galileo. In the early *Pisan Dialogue*, there are two important elements—the impetus theory and the Avempacean dynamics—both of which have their basis in Islamic sources as elaborated by the late medieval Latin philosophers and scientists. Ibn Bajjah's attempt to quantify projectile motion by considering the velocity as proportional to the difference between the force and the resistance rather than to their ratio is of much significance in the light of the later attempt of Bradwardine and the Mertonian school to describe motion quantitatively. Ibn Bajjah under the influence of Aristotelion cosmology criticized Ptolemaic planetary system and proposed a system based solely on eccentric circles.

Ibn Bajjah's work survive in their original Arabic in a few manuscripts and in Hebrew translations. The most important arable manuscripts are the following :

1. Risalat al-Wada (letter of farewell)
2. Risalat Ittisal al-akl bi '1-insan (treatise on the union of the intellect with man)
3. Tadbir al-Mutawahhid (regime of the solitary)

Besides, there are many other manuscripts that are lost since Second World War or the commentaries by Ibn Bajja on the logical works of al-Farabi.

39. Al-Khazini: Abu'1-Fath Abd al-Rahman al-Khazini lived in Persia in the beginning of VI/XII century. Originally a Greek slave who flourished in Merv who studied mechanics and hydrostatics in the tradition of al-Biruni and the earlier scientists. He also wrote works on astronomy and physics, which are as follows:

1. Al-Zidj al-mutabar al-sandjari al-sultani: Astronomical tables based on his personal observations, of which he made a résumé in 525/1130. These were utilized, either directly or indirectly, by the Byzantine scholars George Chrysococces (in Trebizond, ca. 1335-46) and Theodore Meliteniotes (in Constantinople, ca. 1360-88). In the contents of these works one always finds the ephmerides of the Pseudoplanet Kayd.
2. *Risala fi'1-alat* (or al-alat al-adjiba al-rasadiyya on astronomical instruments; *Book of the Balance of Wisdom*).
3. *Kitab al-Mizan al-hikma* written in 515/1121. This is a basic work on the hydrostatic balance. It comprises eight discourses (*makalas*) divided into chapters (*babs*) and subdivided into sections (*fasls*) and contains a series of theorems deriving from the classic works of Archimedes, Euclid, and Menelaus.

In brief, the works describe above are outstanding and in particular in the science of the balance in which al-Khazini is the undisputed master. His *Book of the Balance of Wisdom* is the outstanding work in this science in which he also discussed the view of earlier scholars including Rhazes, Khayyam, and al-Biruni. It is particularly of interest that al-Khazini describes an instrument that, according to him, al-Biruni used in his famous measurements of specific weights of different substances, for al-Biruni himself never revealed the method by which he arrived at his results.

A. Mieli, the Italian historian of science, has compared the determination of specific weights by al-Biruni and al-Khazini with modern results as follows:

Substance	According to al-Biruni based on the fixed value for		According to Al Khizni	Modern values
	Gold	Mercury		
Gold	(19.25)	19.05	19.05	19.26
Mercury	13.74	(13.59)	13.56	13.59
Copper	8.92	8.83	8.56	8.85
Brass	8.57	8.58	8.57	8.40
Iron	7.82	7.74	7.74	7.79
Tin	7.22	7.15	7.32	7.29
Lead	11.40	11.29	11.32	11.35
	Emerald	Quartz		
Sapphire	3.91	3.76	3.96	3.90
Ruby	3.75	3.50	3.58	3.52
Emerald	(2.73)	2.52	2.60	2.73
Pearl	2.73	2.62	2.60	2.75
Quartz	2.53	(2.58)*	—	2.58

* The method of al-Biruni is based on measuring the values of different substances by taking a particular substance with a fixed value. The values for gold, mercury, emerald, and quartz fixed in each column are given in parentheses, and in each case the other values are given based on these fixed values.

40. Al-Battani: Abu Abd-Allah Muhammad bin Djabir (c. 244-317/858-929) was a great astronomer and mathematician. Al-Battani was from Harran (today Attinbasak in Turkey, near Urfa) and belonged to Hellenist pagan religion (Sabian religion) of that city but became a Muslim. He studied in Raqqa in Syria on the Euphrates and died

in Samarra. In medieval and Renaissance Europe (where he was known as Albategni or Albatenius), he was accounted one of the most important authorities on astronomy; indeed, his calculation (az-zij as-sabi) of planetary motion was remarkably accurate, and he also made original contributions to mathematics, notably in spherical trigonometry.

He wrote:

1. *Kitab marifat matali al-burudj fi ma bayna arba al-falak*: The book of the science of the ascensions of the signs of the zodiac in the spaces between the quadrants of the celestial sphere. It deals with the mathematical solution of the astrological problem of the "direction" of the significator.
2. "Risala fi tahkik akdar al-ittisalat": A letter on the exact determination of the qualities of the astrological applications. It is a rigrous trignometrical solution of the astrological problem when the stars in question have latitude (i.e., lie outside the ecliptic).
3. Sharh al-makalat al-arba li Batlamiyus. Commentary on Ptolemy's TetrabilonJ
4. Al-Zidj : Astronomical treatise ad tables—This is the most outstanding work and the only one that has survived to us. It contains the results of his observations and had a considerable influence not only on Arab astronomy but also on the development of astronomy and spherical trigonometry in Europe in the Middle Ages and the beginning of the Renaissance.

Al-Battani determined with great accuracy the obliquity of the ecliptic, the length of the tropic year and of the seasons, and the true and mean orbit of the sun. He definitely exploded the Ptolemaic dogma of the immobility of the solar apogee by demonstrating that it is subject to the precession of the equinoxes and that in consequence the equation of time is subject to a slow secular variation. He proved, contrary to Ptolemaic, the variation of the apparent angular diameter of the sun and the possibility of annular eclipses. He rectified several orbits of the moon and the planets. He propounded a new very ingenious theory to determine the conditions of visibility of the new moon—amended the Ptolemaic value of the precession of the equinoxes. His excellent observations of lunar and solar eclipses were used by Dunthrone in 1749 to determine the secular acceleration of the moon. Finally, he gave very neat solutions by means of orthographic projection for some problems of spherical trigonometry.

*   *   *

The End